Growing up in Amarillo, Texas, I remember hearing The Bellamy Brothers for the first time around the age of eleven. I was so intrigued by their sound and lyrics that I would record their songs from live radio broadcasts onto a cassette then spend the rest of the week learning how to play every note in the song! I still play The Bellamy Brothers on my bus before I hit the stage, and I feel they are two of the most impactful artists that ever made country music. Their music is timeless! **—JOHN RICH**

I have great respect for Howard and David Bellamy as they've been working in the music business for more than forty years, proving themselves time and time again as great singers, songwriters, and musicians. I don't know anyone who has pushed country music to the world quite as much as The Bellamy Brothers. They've covered Europe many times and have toured in India, Sri Lanka, New Caledonia, and Qatar, just to name a few. They're great people, as well as great country legends, and it's always a pleasure when we get the chance to work together. **—GENE WATSON**

"Let Your Love Flow" quickly become my favorite go-to feel-good record shortly after it was released, and then we did a tour together of the West Coast starting in the Bay Area and going to San Diego. On the tour, I really got to know Howard and David and quickly admired them as people. They have always been very talented, witty, bright, and funny—truly my kind of people. Over the years we've toured Europe and done this and that, I've sung on their records. They are one of my favorite duos, along with The Everly Brothers. I love Howard and David with all my heart and I feel guilty being in the Country Music Hall of Fame without them, but their day is coming. **—BOBBY BARE**

By the time I got to Nashville, the Bellamys were already off and running with monster hits. At Fan Fair, I met and knew their precious mom, Frances, several years before I finally got to meet Howard and David. With a mom like that, I knew they had to be great guys; and, indeed, they are! Mom must have told them to be nice to their "little brother" because they treated me with kindness and respect from the start. I was fortunate to get to do several shows with them over the years—fun times I'll treasure always. Howard and David are masters at putting great music together and delivering it with ease and believability. They somehow knew how to make music fun, and I learned a lot from them. I am forever grateful to them for being a special part of my Heroes and Friends Tribute at the Bridgestone in 2017— they are certainly both to me! —**RANDY TRAVIS**

I often use the term "road warriors" to describe the likes of musical entities such as ourselves, like Charlie Daniels, Willie Nelson, and others who defy age—and possibly human logic—to keep plugging away, singing, playing, and touring at a high level. The Bellamy Brothers have always topped that list! The brothers are indeed The Knights Templar of the music business, and The Oak Ridge Boys have a ton of love and respect for their incredibly enduring career. With countless, timeless hits in their quiver, they've not only made their mark in the Good Ole U.S. of A. but around the world. And I mean AROUND the world. We often sit on the bus in, say Fargo, North Dakota, and marvel that Howard and David are doing a show in Bahrain or Zambia or the Faroe Islands that night. I'm not even sure where the Faroe Islands are, but I know the Bellamys have played there several times to a packed house and an appreciative crowd that knows every word to every song. The Bellamys's cultivation of foreign markets is downright amazing. And yet they are just as popular in Texas as they are in Egypt. We have been friends for many years, and we are honored by that friendship. Howard and David, The Bellamy Brothers, we love them dearly, and we are proud to be a small part of their lives, their career, and, yes, this amazing book! —**JOE BONSALL on behalf of Duane Allen, William Lee Golden, and Richard Sterban of THE OAK RIDGE BOYS**

Let Your Love Flow

The Life and Times of the

BELLAMY BROTHERS

DAVID BELLAMY & HOWARD BELLAMY
WITH MICHAEL KOSSER

DarBella Publishing, LLC

Cover and Interior Design by
GKS CREATIVE, NASHVILLE

Front Cover Photo: Jason Lee Denton
Back Cover Photo: Jarrett Gaza

FIRST EDITION

ISBN 978-0-9995062-0-2
eISBN 978-0-9995062-1-9

This book is dedicated to the memory of Homer and Frances Bellamy

SPECIAL THANKS

Michael Kosser

Susan Bond Bellamy

Judy Seale

Rob Battle

Jesse Bellamy

Noah Bellamy

Cole Bellamy

Dustin Bellamy

Aaron Bellamy

Cheyenne Bellamy

Ginger (Bellamy) Clements

Lindsey Seale Chance

Penny Phillips

Bobby Braddock

Roger Ramsey Corkill

Charlie Waller

Cindy Waller

Tanner McKendree

Chris Shaheen

Rachelle and Lexi Jackson

Ronnie Campbell

Al and Kathy Cooper

Andy Cobb

H.C. Young Jr.

Sylvia Young

Melanie & Courtney Owston

Jim Riscky

Ray Schneider

Vivian Bond

Jason and Chrissie Massey

John and Donna Tracy and Family

Ralph and Sharon Wegis

Russell & Dawn Stubbs

Wally Dentz

Randy Hiebert

Jim Heep

Rocky Marvel

Tim Thomas

Galen Butler

Mike Bradley

Sherry Floyd

Gary Pena

Ron Taylor

Lori Sandman

Bruce Smarr

Bob Saporiti

Jan Woods

Teri Leas

Jimmy Bowen

Emory Gordy

Reggie Young

Richard Bennett

Dennis St John

Alan Lindgren

Neil Diamond

King Ericson

Bob Thompson (Norton)

Blake Shelton

Larry E. Williams

Blair Mooney

Jim Stafford

Gallagher

Gola

Sandro Diener

Greg Roach

Lukas Moser

Terry Cologne

Lisa Fults

Dr. Michael Gerber

Inge Gerber

Joe Lichtie Broyles

Darlene & Ricky Budd

Stephanie Davis

Stephanie McKennon

Dr. Douglas Nelson

Joe DiStephano

Laura Ritchie and family

Mariah, Lillith and Brenn

Waylon & Willie Bellamy

Scott Adkins

Kim Bookless

Derrek Kupish

Gwyn Moores

Thanks to all the loyal promoters, buyers, and believers (U.S. and around the world). Not only have they kept the wheels rolling but many have become lifelong friends. Also thanks to all the great musicians (studio and touring) we have worked with over the years; we couldn't have done it without you.

CONTENTS

INTRODUCTION

This book is about two Florida cowboys who journeyed from country poverty to worldwide musical stardom because they had the talent and because it never occurred to them they couldn't make it happen. It is written in their own words.

Charming troublemakers, these two cowboys, but they had three things going for them that almost guaranteed their success in life, if not in music:

1. They came from a hard-working, close-knit family that believed in them and never failed them.

2. The two brothers, for brothers they are, had contrasting personalities and talents that complemented each other. Unlike many other show-business duos, these boys were close when they were young, stayed close throughout their rise to stardom, and remain close today.

3. They had the toughness and stamina to fight for their career in a music industry that is programmed to grind up artists like so much street garbage. The constant succession of defeats and victories they experienced were not exceptional for recording artists. It was the way these brothers fought and outlasted their tormentors that made them different.

The Bellamy Brothers have been delivering great music for a long time, and they continue to project the joy, energy, harmonies, and lyrical insights that have gained them an international following spanning six continents and numerous islands. That is not an exaggeration. In addition to their nationwide popularity at home, they have performed in more than seventy countries, usually repeatedly. Forty years after they made the whole world smile with "Let Your Love Flow," fans anxiously await their next appearances in Germany, the U.K., Switzerland, Ireland, the Netherlands, Denmark, Dubai, Singapore, Australia, New Zealand, and so many more places where they have left great memories of their music. They typically play 135–150 dates a year, foreign and domestic, to satisfy the demands of their fans.

Homer Howard Bellamy Jr. is the older of the two, and it would be easy to call him the steadying influence were it not for the fact that when he got into trouble, which happened often enough in his earlier years, there was usually the devil to pay. Let's just say that Howard, as everybody calls him, is a mellow fellow (until you stir him up) who never felt he had a calling to fame and fortune and spent much of his youth in a low-key search for a future he could take or leave. The younger brother, David Milton Bellamy, is a different sort. While still in high school, he made up his mind that his future would be music. He says it's because he couldn't do anything else.

This story is a great story to tell. It's told mostly through the voices of Howard and David, and that's not easy, because two voices can confuse a reader. When one of them says, "I woke up one morning with a chicken snake sharing my sleeping bag," which one is "I"? So each chapter will begin with the name of whoever is speaking at the time. Anytime someone new speaks, I will insert his or her name. There are only four voices in this book: David Bellamy, Howard Bellamy, David's wife, Susan Bond Bellamy, and The Bellamy Brothers's overseas booking agent, Judy Seale. Turn the page. They're ready to meet you.

Michael Kosser
Nashville, Tennessee
5 January, 2018

1

Humble Beginnings

Homer's Bull, Running Moonshine, and Singing in the Orange Grove

DAVID BELLAMY: Our dad, Homer, walked into the kitchen and said, "Boys, what kind of tomato plant did you say that was growing in the hog pen?"

After almost choking on his corn flakes, Howard quickly recovered and said, "It's a hybrid tomato plant."

Homer scratched his head and walked out the back door toward the barn.

We weren't sure that he believed us, and our dad was no fool when it came to plants and gardening. He kept our family of five fed from his garden and if a plant didn't grow something to eat on it, to him it was a weed and needed grubbing up. A few weeks later, he asked, "When are we gonna have some tomatoes off that plant?" By now, of course, the plant was about eight feet tall and would have taken three people holding hands to circle it. We knew we were gonna have to harvest it soon or come up with another story he wasn't going to buy.

Then it happened. On a routine check of the plant's progress, to prune a few buds and cure them in the hot Florida sun then smoke them to check the potency, we found that one whole side of the plant had been stripped off clean. Across the barbwire fence that separated the cow pasture from the abandoned hog pen, our dad's prize Charolais bull was rolling around on his back like a little puppy. "Oh, shit, we've killed Homer's bull," was all I could come up with to say to Howard. We watched the bull all afternoon, knowing he had eaten more of the leafy homegrown in a few minutes than we would have smoked in a month. He continued to roll and play for half an hour, then he got up and tried to breed every cow in the pasture, following one and then another. After a conquest or two, he took a long nap.

It was years before we told Homer about his bull eating our pot plant and he didn't ask anymore about our hybrid tomatoes, because he had had a good idea all along what was growing in the hog pen. Homer had run moonshine on horseback across the sloughs and hammocks of West Central Florida before there were fences and he often told the story of finding hogs passed out drunk from drinking the runoff of a still, their eyes picked out of their sockets by the buzzards.

Homer wasn't the first one to have to deal with one of our little pot patches. Our Uncle Dick's chickens had gotten out of their coop and scattered into the woods. He went into the woods looking for his chickens. Maybe he had been drinking a bit. And maybe he needed to take a leak. So he did, right on a live wire that was part of an electric fence concealed in the brush to protect a patch of cannabis that we had cleared and planted on his property in an opening in the woods. The voltage ran up the pee stream and shocked the shit out of him too. Once he'd recovered, he took one look at the patch, put two and two together, and called the fire department. We were in L.A. at the time and Mom called us to tell us that Uncle Dick had found a pot patch. Somehow, nobody ever connected it to us.

HOWARD BELLAMY: I have found that in life, playing dumb and innocent can get you a long way.

DAVID: Our dad's profession was he was a rancher. He did day work for other ranchers. He used to break people's horses for them; that was his main gig. His cowboy work was endless because our Uncle Doug was the wealthy one in the family. He had a bigger ranch, so we worked for him a lot, but Dad was the real cowboy in the family. We were raised in a ranching community, so nearly every day, Dad would saddle up the old horse and work cattle for *everybody* in the area. Florida's got some big, open, wild cattle country. You have to pen the cattle using horses, dogs, and bullwhips. The story is, the reason they called Florida cowboys crackers was because of the sound of the bullwhips. In fact, they didn't call 'em cowboys, they called 'em cow hunters, because you literally had to hunt them. You had to get out there among the palmettos and swamps and rattlesnakes and moccasins.

When people say ranching, it usually depends on what part of the country you're in. Ranching's completely different in Florida than it is in Wyoming. Before you can herd them, you gotta find 'em first because the Florida growth is so thick, you've got to have dogs to locate them. I remember our dad coming in from a day job on a ranch one time when he got off the horse to open the gate and I saw him limping. I asked him what was wrong. It was really wet, and as he was chasing the cattle, the horse turned a curve on a muddy, slick place and fell on Homer's leg. And his leg was all swelled up huge, and he didn't even go to the doctor. It was awful. Broke his nose, too, working cattle. It's dangerous work!

It was not out of the ordinary for him to ride a half-broke horse home for lunch. We'd see him coming down our dirt road with a bucking horse snorting and galloping sideways. He'd tie him up to an orange tree, get something to eat, climb back into the saddle, and buck him all the way back to the neighboring ranch.

When Homer wasn't breaking horses or running moonshine, he played music at dances—or frolics, as he liked to call them—and he'd have his buddies over at our house jamming the night away. He played mostly with the Vadosky Brothers, two siblings from Masaryktown, a nearby Czech settlement, who played accordion and fiddle. Homer liked to tell the story about him and the two Czech boys playing a frolic at a neighbor's house one night that got so wild that the back porch they were playing and dancing on fell off the house.

HOWARD: On another occasion, on the way back from a frolic, part of the band was in a Model T that hit an alligator so large it flipped the car. When the car rolled over, the guitars, fiddles, and a loaf of bread washed away down a creek. According to Homer's accounting, they had to jump in the gator-infested creek and retrieve the instruments, and they never did sound the same.

DAVID: It became second nature during our formative years for me, Howard, and our sister, Ginger, to stay up on Saturday night listening to Homer and his buddies play honky-tonk and western swing music while they sipped moonshine.

The rowdy frolics were not our only early influence. After the music and the moonshine wore off, our mother, Frances, would wake us all up early Sunday morning and we'd head to church to sing hymns and listen to the preacher hold forth on sin. Homer never complained about observing the Sabbath; he was a godly man, even though I'm sure he went to church more than one Sunday still tipsy from Saturday night.

In the fall and winter months, we worked in the orange groves with the Jamaican migrant workers who came to Florida for the picking season. With long wooden ladders that reached to the tops of the tall, old orange trees in the grove behind our house, the pickers would ascend the thorn-studded trees and fill their pickin' sacks, then climb down and empty them into crates that were scattered around the bottom of the trees. We always looked forward to the Jamaicans's picking each year; they'd sing while they worked, with one of them starting a song or chant and all the others answering from the treetops. Sometimes one of their kids would sit on the ground beating out rhythms on an orange crate.

They'd sing songs about working, fishing, Jesus, songs in broken English, and love songs in romantic-sounding Caribbean languages we'd never heard. The island migrants were joined by local laborers who picked up work in the groves during harvest time, and we were always thrown into the mix to help fill the boxes full of oranges and get them off to the packinghouse. This made for a very lively, colorful event each year, and it helped us earn a little extra Christmas money.

One warm Florida winter's day, while Howard and I were filling orange crates on the ground, we heard a great rumbling noise coming from the tree above us. We looked up in time to see a very large object falling rapidly from the sky. A Jamaican woman had broken one of the rungs of her ladder and on the way to the ground her weight took out most of the other rungs. She hit the dirt with an incredible thud right between the two of us. We stood there too startled to speak, but as she started to stir and we figured out that the impact hadn't killed her, the whole incident struck us funny, like a Roadrunner cartoon, and we began laughing uncontrollably. Homer ran over and chased us to the house with threats of a good ass beatin', then turned and went back to help the other migrant workers get her up and see if she needed a doctor. The woman took a few minutes, caught her breath, drank some water Homer brought her from our well, then climbed back on another ladder and began filling her pickin' sack with sweet Florida oranges.

Living Poor on Rich Land

There was always a lot of laughter in our house. Food, music, and our family's sense of humor are what got us through the hard times and kept us from realizing how poor we were.

Homer, Frances, and Ginger, along with Howard and me, were the labor force on ninety humble acres of land where we grew up in Darby, Florida. I realize that ninety acres sounds like a lot of land to city folks who live in an 800-square-foot apartment or suburban folks in their house on a quarter acre, but ninety acres meant a lot of hard living for a family of five in those humble times. On any given day, the whole family would be digging sweet potatoes by hand or pulling a breeched calf from a momma cow. Frances cleared palmettos by hand from the loamy land, using only a grubbing hoe, to make space for planting crops to sell to the farmers market. She would stop only occasionally to get a drink of water or to chop the head off a rattlesnake that got in the way of her work. Homer called us land poor, which meant we had land but not much else, and it took the whole family working that land, as well as Homer and Frances holding down other jobs, to make ends meet. In addition to working our crops, orange groves, and cattle, Howard and I worked the ranches of neighbors and relatives.

HOWARD: I don't think people realize how country we were or are. We were raised here on this old home place, and we literally did not have hot water. We did not have any indoor toilets. We did not have a telephone. None of that happened until I was around fifteen, sixteen years old and David was eleven or twelve. It was wild, like Marjorie Kinnan Rawlings wrote about in her novel *The Yearling* about Florida, just wild palmettos and wiregrasses, rattlesnakes, moccasins, and gators. Even our cattle were wild. We were rural, like, forty miles from Tampa, and the people in Dade City where we went to high school, about twelve miles away, even they considered us, really, hicks.

A couple of times in our early lives, we were so poor that our dad actually considered selling the farm. The one time I remember most was when a guy made a bid on the land by writing a letter to him. Homer and Frances sat around the kitchen table and discussed it all evening, and in the morning Homer put the letter back in our mailbox, accepting the offer.

What they didn't know was I had listened to their whole conversation and after Homer went to work, I walked to the mailbox and took out the letter before the mailman came. Homer scratched his head a few times over the next few weeks wondering why the guy might have changed his mind, since he never got a reply.

DAVID: Our Uncle Doug (Homer's brother) had twelve hundred acres just down the road from our place and we worked his land and cattle as well as our own. The chores included marking and branding calves, picking watermelons, stretching barbwire, and a hundred other things that always needed tending to. We did a lot more than just work on that ranch; we lived off the bounty of its

8

land. Uncle Doug's place had large fishponds with every variety of fresh water fish imaginable. Sometimes we'd catch a largemouth bass big enough to feed the whole family.

During droughts the ponds and sloughs would dry up into small bodies of water and leave the fish in small pools. Homer and Doug would make seine nets by attaching a wooden pole at each end of a net; then, with a man on each end, they would drag the net through the shallow water till it was full of fish. Then they'd drag it onto the bank of the pond where we'd have tubs and buckets waiting to be filled with whatever was in the net—bass, perch, bluegill, stumpknockers, catfish, and occasionally a water moccasin or an alligator.

Frances and Aunt Mae (Uncle Doug's wife) would have a fire going on the bank and as soon as the fish were clean, they'd salt and pepper 'em, dip 'em in some corn meal, and fry 'em up in a big cast iron skillet with hush puppies, a pot of cheese grits, and a jug of sweet tea. This idyllic setting was a common backdrop for us as we grew up in Darby. We may not have always been living in perfect harmony with the earth, but we were singing in the same key. Sitting on the banks of those fishponds with names like "Burnt Island" and "Dog Hole," we never imagined that our lives would change much.

Abraham, the Yankee Bullet, and a Little Background

Our family had a history.

Our great-grandfather Abraham Bellamy joined the Confederate cause, along with most of his male relatives. They signed up in Conway, South Carolina, to fight the Yankees when the American Civil War broke out in Charleston. He received a leg wound in the Battle of Chickamauga, Georgia, south of Chattanooga, Tennessee, then he was captured and held as a Yankee POW in the infamous Douglas Prison Camp in Illinois. Douglas was often referred to as Eighty Acres of Hell because of the horrible living conditions and death rate among prisoners. Abraham was among the small percentage of prisoners who lived through the Camp Douglas experience.

Toward war's end, he escaped and found his way back home to Horry County, South Carolina, to reunite with the girl he had married just prior to his enlistment, Susan Vareen. The Vareens ran a good-sized plantation growing sugarcane, cotton, and peanuts, as well as livestock. Abraham had married well, but soon after his escape and homecoming, the couple decided to move to Florida. Some of our relatives have suggested that he moved south for his health, since the rifle ball in his leg was never successfully removed after his injury. I've often wondered how much better the climate could have been for him, since Florida was mostly swamp and hammock land at that time and the mosquitoes and gators would have been as bad as a Yankee flesh wound.

Whatever their motive was, they braved the elements in a horse-drawn wagon and after a couple of relocations in their new state, in 1870 they finally settled on the piece of land that we call home to this day. According to rumors and old deeds, there were about ninety acres of land bought for about fifty cents an acre, probably with the wife's money.

Abraham Bellamy didn't live a long time after he settled in Florida, but he and Susan had children, and the Bellamys were an established family by the time he died. One other notable fact, Abraham and Susan, or Susanna, as she is sometimes referred to in the historical records, donated two acres near Hudson, Florida, to be used as a cemetery. It is still known as the Vareen Cemetery. You can find it by driving west from I-75 on State Road 52 and north on U.S. 19. From there, it's 0.1 miles. Both Abraham and Susan are buried there.

About forty-five years earlier, in 1824, long before Abraham and Susan drove their horse and buggy to Florida, one John Bellamy (Bellamys say that all Bellamys are related) built the first road in the state. It's still called the old Bellamy Trail, and it ran from Pensacola to Jacksonville. The road was built, reportedly by slave labor, five years after Florida became a state. The road followed the Old Spanish Trail and it is said that there were stumps that jutted out in the middle of the road that tore up many wagon axles. It's also reported that construction was delayed by heavy flooding and Indian attacks.

Homer, Frances, and World War II

Our dad, Homer, was twenty-seven years old when he was drafted to serve in the army during World War II. At the time, he and Mom had one child, our sister, Jewel Virginia, who we've always called Ginger. The army sent him from Florida to El Paso, Texas, for basic training, and then he was transported with hundreds of other soldiers to the Aleutian Islands off the Kenai Peninsula of Alaska to fight the Japanese.

He spent most of the war in a foxhole loading ammunition into antiaircraft guns to fire at enemy planes that flew over U.S. territory. When he returned home, he suffered from severely frostbitten ears and toes. After that experience, he never did like cold weather, nor did he ever acquire a taste for Japanese food like many other veterans from that generation, nor did he care to discuss the war.

Homer was a quiet man and unless you were close to him, you'd think he was downright shy. He loved his family, his cattle, his land, and music, and hated company dropping by. Homer hiding under the bed or slipping out the back door and waiting in the cowpens until the visitors left was a common occurrence in our house. But of our parents, he was the talented one. We got our musical ability from our dad, and from our early childhood we hung around him and his buddies. They'd come to our home over the weekend and play music always, and all that rubbed off on us. Our dad was very dependable, but he wasn't ambitious. He was leery of people who he considered overambitious. His focus was having food on the table and taking care of his family.

He probably would have been more skeptical of the music business than Frances, even though he played music. He never imagined that you could make a living at it. For Homer, music was strictly a passion, never a vocation.

Frances and Homer were polar opposites. Frances was the kind of person who never took no for an answer. She wasn't really a pushy person, but she was very persistent.

HOWARD: If you told her she *couldn't* do it, that meant she was *going to* do it. It was like a bet to her.

DAVID: That's something both of us probably inherited from her.

Homer married Frances in 1941. Frances's maiden name was Cooper. She grew up in Turkey Creek, Florida, near Plant City. She was the daughter of Johnny and Katie Cooper. Grandpa Cooper was a carpenter and a truck farmer, and Grandma, with six kids, was mostly a homemaker, but she picked strawberries during the season and worked in the fields during harvest time.

At the time Homer and Frances were married, they were working in the Hav-A-Tampa Cigar Factory. Here's our mother's brief account of their wedding day:

"Homer had to work the second shift at the Hav-A-Tampa cigar factory, and me and my sister (Doris) sat on a street bench in Ybor City and ate devil crabs and smoked a cigar waiting for Homer to get off work and take us dancing."

Hurricanes and Cracker Horses

When Homer returned from fighting the Japanese in the Aleutian Islands, he went back to hiring himself out as a ranch hand, breaking horses, marking and branding cattle, and working in the orange groves. He drew a small government check for his military service and when that was combined with ranch work, truck farming, growing crops, raising cattle, and running a little moonshine, it made up the family's income.

On Groundhog Day, February 2, 1946, Howard was born at Jackson Memorial Hospital in Dade City.

HOWARD: Actually, *I'm* Homer too. I'm a junior. It's Homer Howard Bellamy. So, oh yeah, Homer's always the dumbest name in the world.

DAVID: Until you go to Greece. Then it's like, *The Iliad*, you're poetry. Ginger had come along four years earlier. I showed up on September 16, 1950, four and a half years after Howard was born and right in the middle of a hurricane. It was a storm of considerable size, and one my family would often make reference to when I caused turmoil in their lives.

Frances planned to go to the same hospital where she had given birth to Howard, but the dirt roads were flooded and the bridge over the Bee Tree Branch was washed out on Darby Road about a half mile from the farm. The doctor drove his car as far as he could, parked it, and waded across to meet Homer, who was on the other side of the branch, waiting atop a horse named Cracker. Homer reached down to the soaking wet doctor and pulled him up in the saddle behind him, and they rode double back to our house in the wind and the rain of Hurricane King.

The doctor's name was Wardell Stanfield. He had recently moved to Dade City from Missouri after finishing med school. He spent all night with my family on the eve of my birth, and around 5:30 the next morning, I arrived. Dr. Stanfield would become a lifelong friend to us and over the next fifty years would share many emotional moments with our family, including life, death, and near-death experiences.

The night I was born, Howard and Ginger spent the night with our cousins Sylvia and Helen Miller, and when they showed me to Howard the next day, all he said was, "He ain't gonna ride ol' Cracker." Turns out he was right. The ol' horse that Howard laid claim to, the same one that Homer rode to bring the doctor through the storm to deliver me, died before I was big enough to ride him. Howard claims that's when he decided to quit being selfish and start sharing things with me.

When We Were Boys

Howard mentioned earlier that as kids, our world was slightly akin to the Marjorie Kinnan Rawlings novel *The Yearling*. All work, play, and entertainment revolved around our family and home life. We were a close-knit group; our parents never left us with babysitters except our grandparents when they had to work the same shifts. Most of the time they tried to work different shifts so one of them could be home with us while the other one was at work.

One of the earliest memories I have of growing up on the farm was being rocked to sleep on the back of our plow horse, Tony. Homer used the big draft horse to plow his gardens before he had a tractor. In his own very unique way, he combined farming and babysitting while Frances worked and Howard and Ginger were at school. He'd sit me on Tony's back and I'd ride up and down the rows of crops while he gripped the worn wooden handles that were bolted to the steel plow that Tony pulled through the loamy soil and sandspurs. I held on to the big leather collar that circled Tony's neck. The reins ran though brass hoops attached to the collar, then onto the harness until it reached the bit in his mouth.

Homer could rein Tony through the garden without either of them stepping on a single vegetable, and the rocking rhythm of the big horse's steps put me sound asleep after riding up and down a few garden rows. Homer would then gently lift me down off Tony's back and lay me in the shade of a live oak tree to nap. Then, with the verbal command of a "gee" or a "haw," he'd continue to plow the long rows.

Growing up in a very rural area, we had to learn to make our own fun and games when we weren't doing chores. That included rotten orange fights, riding wild calves, fishing, hunting, making bows and arrows, swimming in a waterhole, and learning to play Homer's old Dobro guitar.

It was a big deal when we finally got a tractor. Old Tony was probably the happiest about it because after we got the tractor, we used him almost exclusively for a diving board. We'd wade him out into the water hole with us and a few neighbor kids on his back, dive off his back into the water, climb back up, and dive back in. That horse would stand there all day if we wanted him to; I guess he figured it beat the hell out of pulling a plow.

When Homer wasn't using the tractor for work, one of our favorite pastimes became something we called "tractor skiing." We got the idea to shape two fence boards into skis, tie a rope to the tractor, then strap the boards to our feet with some hay string or tire rubber and take turns skiing behind it. This game went through several evolutions before we remembered the old galvanized bathtub that we had hauled to the cow pasture to make a watering trough after we got a new tub in our house. We discovered that it would slip and slide a lot better than the wooden fence boards if we chained it to the drawbar of the Massey Ferguson tractor; that way one of us could drive while the other one got the ride of his life.

I was pulling Howard through the pasture one day when I noticed a cow with a new calf not more than a day or two old. Knowing how protective she'd be of her baby, I carefully steered the tractor until I lined up the bathtub exactly between the momma cow and the newborn, then I came to a dead stop and turned around to watch the action from the safety of the tractor seat, in time to see Howard peeking over the rim of the tub. A split second later he dove to the bottom of the tub, just as the momma cow started hooking the tub with all the fury her horns possessed. She commenced to slobber all over Howard, then rolled him over in the tub a couple of times, then she kicked it a few times in rapid succession trying to get to her calf on the other side.

By then, Howard was covered in cow shit and snot and was yelling every cuss word he knew at me. I was laughing so hard I could hardly get the tractor in gear to pull him out of harm's way. I only had one big problem—the incident was still fresh on his mind the next time it was my turn to ride in the tub.

We were both capable of making trouble, not because we were particularly nasty, but because we were active. And when little boys are active, they're just naturally gonna push the envelope, especially with a bit of encouragement from the adults around them.

HOWARD: When something goes bad for one or the other of us, we have a saying: "Our turtle died." Or David's turtle died or Howard's turtle died. Comes from when David was about ten and I was in my mid-teens. If you're old enough, you might remember those dime store turtles; they'd sit on a rock in a glass bowl. I don't know who bought 'em, maybe our mother, but we had these two identical, I mean *identical* turtles— size, color, everything. So one day we came in—and we'd really gotten into these turtles—David comes running over to the bowl to check on the turtles and one of them is laying upside down, dead as a doornail. And David yells out, "Howard's turtle died!"

15

How in hell did he know it was mine? So now if something bad happens to one of us, the other one might say, "Your turtle died."

This is a kind of sad story in a way. Homer's ma, Nora, could be really mean. I mean, mean beyond reason and years later they suspected she had Alzheimer's, but in those days they'd just say she went crazy. They'd put me in the back seat of the car with her and she'd do mean things. My grandfather, whose name was Frank, he just told me one day, "If she gets out of line, just nail her to the porch," and I took him at his word, as kids are bound to do. One day I was sittin' on the porch with her and her long dress was spread across the porch and I saw my opportunity so I grabbed some eight-penny nails and nailed her with one. It doesn't sound good that I nailed my grandmother, does it? You know, she got that look they get. I remember it so vividly – I just remember her being so out there, so unpredictable. Kids think funny things. To me it was like what he told me could cure her, even. And as a kid, you'll do anything your grandfather tells you. And it worked, as long as that nail held.

Cow-pasture Christians

DAVID: Church was a big part of our lives growing up in rural Darby. It was an important spiritual and social event for our family, each Sunday service and Wednesday night prayer meeting at the Amelia Baptist Church where the whole community gathered. The original church was situated on the north end of State Road 581, now known as Bellamy Brothers Boulevard. It was a small, traditional country church with a steeple and rows of windows down the side with shutters but no screens. On more Sundays than not, a horse would wander up from the pasture during preaching and stick his head in the window to see what was going on.

Many summer Sundays would bring a classic Central Florida thunder and lightning storm the area is famous for. The rain would pound the tin roof so hard it would put extra emphasis on the hellfire and brimstone message the preacher was preaching from the pulpit.

The music from our church was one of the most important parts of our upbringing. Every hymn was magical, and even before we could read the words in the hymnal, Howard and I would stand on the old wooden benches alongside Homer, Frances, and Ginger, belting out the melodies. Every few months after church we'd have baptizing for the people who had joined the church and we'd go down to a pond in one of the pastures just off State Road 52, where the preacher and the deacons would do the baptizing. Howard, Ginger, and I were baptized there and from that day forward, whenever we did something bad, Frances would say one of our toes must have been sticking out of the water when the preacher baptized us.

After baptizing, the whole congregation would go back to the church to have dinner on the ground and sing hymns. Some of the best food we ever ate was fried chicken, pole beans, and banana pudding sitting at those long wooden tables under the live oak trees in that church yard singing a chorus of "Love Lifted Me."

Sister's Eyes, Johnny Cash, and Wrestling Alligators

If you read any of our official biographies, they usually say our first public performance was with our dad at the Rattlesnake Roundup in San Antonio, Florida. The truth is we played music all over the place so I'm not sure either one of us remembers the very first time we played together in front of people. It was probably in church, at a family reunion, or at a get-together at our house when Frances would say, "Homer, get Ginger and the boys and y'all play something."

Homer showed us a few chords at a time on his guitar. Pretty soon we knew enough of them to play a few songs. Meanwhile, Ginger was learning to play the accordion. She'd suffered through five eye surgeries by the time she was seventeen, and one of the doctors told our parents the accordion might help improve her hand-eye coordination, so our parents did what they did every time one of us kids needed something they didn't have the money for: they sold a cow.

Ginger was already playing the accordion real good when I started playing it. With what I learned from her accordion teacher, the guitar chords Homer and Howard taught me, and the hymns we sang in church, that's kind of how our whole music journey started.

We spent most Sunday afternoons after church looking through the newspapers for used guitars and orphaned calves to raise on our milk cows. We also collected banjos, ukuleles, drums, puppies, chickens, rabbits, horses, pigs, or anything anybody was giving away or selling cheap. Most of the time, our house looked like a combination feed store, ranch house, music store, and pawnshop.

While gospel music was a major influence on us, there were other musical influences in our lives. Our parents listened to a little AM country radio station in North Tampa called WHBO. Frances sang "It Wasn't God Who Made Honky Tonk Angels" with Kitty Wells while she cooked dinner. Homer picked out chords and licks from songs like Ernest Tubb's "I'm Walkin' The Floor Over You" after he came in from working in the fields. We didn't give it much thought at the time, but music was obviously important to our folks because they managed to save a little out of their meager earnings and take us to a concert at Fort Homer Hesterly National Guard Armory in Tampa to see Johnny Cash, Faron Young, and Webb Pierce. It must have been quite a splurge for them and, other than an all-night gospel sing and Homer's moonshine-induced jams with his drinking buddies, it was the first public live music event we'd ever been to.

It burned such a lasting impression in our brains that to this day when we're giving interviews we mention the rhinestone spider-web suit Webb Pierce wore and the stark, rugged sound of the Man in Black. Thirty years later, when we played a show with him in Frankfurt, Germany, we got the chance to tell Johnny about the time we saw him in Tampa in the '50s.

HOWARD: We had walked into his dressing room and found him relaxing on a couch while he was waiting to go on. His face lit up and he boomed out, "The Bellamy boys!" Turned out he'd been waiting to meet us.

DAVID: We didn't take a lot of vacations due to our permanent lack of funds, but our family always looked forward to one annual pilgrimage. One of Homer's best and oldest friends since childhood lived in Daytona Beach. Every summer as soon as school let out, Frances made a big sack of bologna sandwiches and peeled and fried up potatoes and we were off. The beaches from Daytona and across the panhandle of Florida near Panama City have long been referred to as the "Redneck Riviera," but it could have been the South of France as far as we were concerned. Never mind that we were sleeping on the floor on pallets of extra quilts Frances packed in the "cooter hull" of the car (that's the trunk, in case you're wondering). We couldn't have been happier if we were bedded down in the finest hotel on the beach. We spent every day swimming and catching waves in the Atlantic. At night, we'd go to the Boardwalk to ride bumper cars and eat saltwater taffy.

Vacations usually lasted just a few days at the beginning of summer because there were cows to feed and Homer never got many days off working at the citrus plant, but coming home at the end of the trip was as much fun as going. Depending on what route we took, there were some of the greatest attractions that three farm kids had ever seen. We could stop and see the world's oldest cypress tree, a 3,500-year-old granddaddy of them all that they called "The Cypress Methuselah," or visit the alligator farm and watch a Seminole Indian wrestle a gator, or go by Ross Allen's snake farm in Ocala to see him milk rattlesnakes to gather their venom for snake bite victims. These were tourist traps even a poor Florida cracker family couldn't afford to pass up.

We lived about thirty-five to forty miles from Tampa and we didn't go there that often, but when we did it was a big adventure.

HOWARD: There was no Interstate 75. It was all winding backroads. And our dad, being a guitar player and singer as well, we knew every country song and we'd sing all the way back home at night, at the top of our lungs all along those winding roads—fond memories that never go away. Between those journey sing-alongs and the church singing, and the singing at home with Homer and his friends, I'd say that singing was as natural to us as breathing.

Sometimes after our shows, people will ask me, "Why don't you sing more?" Well, harmony is singing and I'm singing all night. I always loved singing harmony. I challenged myself to find a way to harmonize to any song, and I still do. I can't help myself. And later when I was in the FFA Barbershop Quartet, we won the state championship with our barbershop harmonies, and still I love barbershop.

All that singing then affects the way we sing today. I didn't know it, but from the beginning I was experimenting, trying different things, jumping from this harmony note way up there to a closer harmony note.

DAVID: We're always jumping around. One of the newer songs in our show is one called "The Dying Breed." I start off singing lead and Howard sings harmony then he switches to lead and I sing harmony. We switch back and forth between the lead and harmony the whole song.

HOWARD: And old gospel groups know there's a term called "lead harmony." Even country record producers, they don't know what that means. It's when the voices are equal, and the harmony is not like a second part. It's like when the two parts make the melody.

So many times, when we're in the studio working with a different engineer, when we put a second part on the song, there's a "ghost harmony" thing that happens in our blend sometimes, and the engineer starts looking for the track where the third harmony is. There is no third harmony, but you can hear it nevertheless. It's the strangest thing; we've had so many engineers, just drives them crazy, and we tell them, there's no other part. We *like* to call it ghost harmony. It seems so appropriate. Siblings often have such similar tones in their voices that it's easier for *them* to create that sound than for other duos.

DAVID: And it all started when we were so young that singing was just something we did whenever the family got together. Like when families sit down at the table to eat together, a night in the living room together, or the drive back from Tampa, or any one of a dozen other activities would lead to the start of a song, and hitting the note brought satisfaction, then hitting the perfect harmony note—and you could tell, you could about feel it vibrating in your body when the two notes were perfect. Harmony.

It was a physical thing. Like when our dad's fried chicken or our mom's potato salad tasted just right. There was my A and Howard's C, together, and we knew it was perfect before we knew there was an A-note or a C-note. Because we started so young, we never had to practice making a good blend. Because as kids, without knowing it we'd gotten our practice in the dark of night on those winding roads between Tampa and Darby.

Uncle Doug's TV and the Fire Arrow Story

Howard was born at the beginning of the baby boom and I was born in the middle of it and even though those few years don't seem like a long time, where we lived there were a lot of cultural changes in the four and a half years between us. For one thing, television had made its way into people's homes. Our Uncle Doug was the first person in Darby to have a state-of-the-art black and white set at his house, so a couple of times a week we'd get to lay around his living room in front of this magic box that transported moving pictures through space. We watched *Lassie* and *I Love Lucy* and the variety shows that were popular. We liked them all but it was the westerns that captured our imaginations. *Gunsmoke, Gene Autry, Roy Rogers, Zorro, The Rifleman, Have Gun Will Travel, The Lone Ranger, The Cisco Kid, Wagon Train, My Friend Flicka*, and pretty much all the serial westerns that Hollywood started producing in the '50s.

Our Grandma Cooper was a good seamstress, so I got her to sew me a mask and cape like Zorro. When Grandpa Cooper bought me a coonskin cap, Grandma went through some old clothes and found some hand-me-downs to finish out my Davy Crockett outfit. Then Grandpa loaned me his twelve-gauge shotgun to round out my ensemble.

We saw so many cowboys and Indians shows that our main toys became cap pistols, BB guns, bows and arrows, and homemade swords. This was, of course, the era before some smart TV network lawyer came up with the phrase, "Don't try this at home." So when I saw Zorro jump from a rooftop, I borrowed Frances's umbrella to help break my fall and jumped from the rooftop, turning the umbrella inside out and bringing on a severe reprimand. Howard showed a little more restraint than I did in acting out a lot of the television characters. He says it's because he was older and always had to do most of the work while I played.

There was this one incident, however, that did slow me down a bit and convinced me to stop copying everything I saw on TV westerns. The scene was a family get-together at Aunt Hattie's house. Most of Homer's brothers and sisters were attending with their spouses and kids. I had decided earlier in the week to take my bow and some fire arrows I'd made so I could impress our big city cousins from Tampa. I soaked small strips of cloth torn from bed sheets in kerosene and carefully tied them to the arrow tips because being the genius I was, I had figured out how they did it on the television westerns.

Aunt Hattie's house was only a short walk across the cow pasture. Frances, Homer, and Ginger drove the car around the dirt road to take all the food they had cooked to Aunt Hattie's. Howard and I walked through the field and climbed under the barbwire fence on a beautiful, warm, dry, fall Sunday afternoon. Ginger, Howard, and I loved those family get-togethers. The food was legendary. In addition to Frances bringing a pot of chicken and dumplings, Aunt Hattie made lemon meringue pie for dessert from lemons she had picked off the tree and eggs she had pulled from under hens that morning. Our uncles and aunts from Tampa brought devil crabs from Ybor City, the Cuban area of Tampa. We lived for these breaded, fried, stuffed-with-blue-crab delicacies.

Our Uncle Harold always brought along a few of the biggest, loudest firecrackers that money could buy and he thought nothing of lighting one and dropping it under the table right in the middle of dinner. That was one of the highlights of the party that we always looked forward to.

Right after dinner began to wind down, most of the women started gossiping and cleaning up the table. The men moved to a corner of the yard where they smoked cigars and a couple of them pulled pint whiskey bottles from their back pockets. I convinced a small group of kin to watch my archery skills while Howard stood there looking like he already thought that this might not be the best idea I'd ever hatched in my fevered brain.

Without the slightest hesitation I struck a kitchen match and lit the tip of an arrow with the kerosene-soaked cloth tied to it, then laid it across the bow, fitted the arrow into the string, pulled it back behind my ear, and fired it high into the open field just across the fence from Aunt Hattie's yard.

At first it looked as if the fire might go out as the arrow sailed into the air, reached an impressive height, then started to descend, but there was one thing I hadn't thought of in my haste to impress our kin: I had shot the arrow into a field of grass that had been cut several days earlier and was lying there drying out before being bailed into hay. I had intended to fire a couple more arrows after the first one just for show, but that never happened because as soon as the arrow hit the ground, one of the kids hollered, "*The field's on fire!*"

I saw Howard dive under the barbwire fence and I threw down my bow and followed him, knowing exactly what he was gonna do. We helped our dad burn off fields every year, so stomping out a pasture fire came second nature to us. Most of the cousins climbed under the fence with us and headed toward the fire that was now growing bigger by the minute. Howard started stomping. I started stomping. A couple of the cousins were stomping, too, but it seemed the more we stomped, the more the flames spread. It took no time for word of the fire to make its way around Aunt Hattie's yard. The menfolk started coming through the fence; some of them broke limbs from the big live oak tree with the picnic tables of covered food still sitting under it.

By now I had swallowed so much smoke that I was ready to quit and just let the grownups put it out, but then I looked over and saw Howard still stomping. It seemed like every time he'd get one little spot put out, three more would spring up. I thought surely Homer and our uncles would get it put out, but alas, I was wrong. You've heard of the perfect storm; this was the perfect fire. The arrow I shot came down perfectly in a row of cut hay that had dried and would have been ready to bale in the next couple of days; then a perfect breeze had sprung up just in time to take hold of the fire and make it impossible for me, Howard, my cousins, and my uncles to stomp it out. The breeze then sprung into the perfect wind that started carrying the flames higher and farther and burned thirty acres of hay that would have been used to feed the cattle in the coming winter.

I thought about running as fast as I could back through the cow pasture to our house and hiding out, but it seemed like no matter where I turned there was fire. Howard and I finally made it back to the yard to find our cousins already there. Most of them looked like they were terrified to get anywhere near me. Our mother came running over with various aunts and young'uns. She looked like she was relieved to see I wasn't burned or hurt. She also looked like she was gonna give me a good ass beatin' when we got home.

I felt like things couldn't get any worse, but of course I was wrong, because just at that moment a smart aleck cousin yelled, "The barn's burning!" Sure enough, the hay already stacked in the barn was ignited by the prevailing winds carrying sparks from the burning field and landing on the bales. That alone would have been bad enough, but then the last thing I expected to happen happened. Out of the corner of my eye, I saw Homer suddenly run into the smoking barn and jump up into the driver's seat of Aunt Hattie's tractor. The entire congregated family turned to watch as we heard the tractor motor start up then saw it slowly pulling out from the burning barn with both of the big back rubber tires in flames. The fire was shooting off the tires as Homer drove it out in the open near a water spigot. An uncle grabbed the water hose and started spraying down the tires. Others were picking up hands full of dirt and throwing it on the burning rubber. I stood there speechless, watching the smoke rings rise from the hot spots while the men put out the last of the fire. Thanks to Homer, the tractor was saved, except for the back tires. Sorry to say, the barn didn't fare as well.

Growin' Our Own, the Old South, and Whiskey in the Mailbox

It took a while for the flaming arrow incident to blow over. It was also a while before I could sit down and a while before the relatives warmed up to me again. We didn't attend as many get-togethers for a while, and of course I wasn't allowed to make any more fire arrows, but other than those little details, life went on. Homer and Howard helped repair the barn and we shared our hay with our aunt and uncle that winter.

We still walked to Aunt Hattie's for breakfast because we loved eating what she cooked on that old wood stove of hers. Nothing tasted as good as her scratch buttermilk biscuits made with ham and bacon from the hogs our families butchered and cured in the smokehouse. Eating took priority over almost everything in our family. Whatever season it happened to be, we had food for it. We slaughtered a yearling in the spring and a young hog (a shoat) in the fall. Homer, Howard, and I would do the butchering, then Frances and Homer would saw the meats into the desired cuts with a meat saw on the back porch.

We hung most of it in the smokehouse, until we could afford a deep freezer. After we got the freezer, we'd cut and wrap it and as soon as it was stacked in the freezer we'd start eatin' the steaks on top and eat our way to the hamburger in the middle of the pile, and down to the stew meat and soup bones on the bottom. Our parents would make something out of every part of whatever animal we'd slaughtered, including hog head cheese that consisted of all the meat from the hog's head mixed with herbs and a vinegar solution and hung up in cheese cloth to let the blood and vinegar drip through it. We also used to clean chitlins, which are hog intestines washed and slung clean.

That's right, "slung clean," then the casing is cut or deep-fried or you can use it to stuff and make sausage. One of our favorites was "cracklins," which are homemade pork rinds; the pig's skin was dropped into a big black wash pot with an open hot fire under it in the backyard with boiling lard inside. No one worried much about their cholesterol. Everybody worked so hard that being overweight wasn't an issue.

Nowadays they would call the animals we butchered free range. That term hadn't come along yet when we were growing up; they were just yard run chickens and if Frances was gonna make dumplins, she'd send me and Howard out to wring a chicken neck or two, boil some water, pluck it, gut it, and get it ready for the pot while she rolled out dough for the dumplings.

HOWARD: One time when David was about five or six, I decided to kill a chicken for dinner by chopping off its head instead of wringing its neck. David stood beside me, out of the range of the hatchet, his mouth agape, fully attentive. I brought the hatchet down and caught just enough of the chicken's right eye to send it flying into David's open mouth. Before he could think to spit it out, he swallowed it. Remember?

DAVID: I remember gagging the rest of the afternoon.

Meat was only part of the menu. Homer grew amazing gardens of tomatoes, watermelons, corn, squash, eggplant, and black-eyed peas in the spring and summer, and strawberries, collard and turnip greens, and sweet potatoes in the fall and winter. We had oranges, grapefruit, tangerines, tangelos, lemons, limes, and every other citrus fruit imaginable, even kumquats. We preserved the surplus of summer foods in Mason jars for the winter. We were poor people who never went hungry, and our bounty, however humble, was always open to friends and neighbors, as theirs was to us—and that included people of other races and colors.

Many myths exist about racism in the Old South. As kids in the '50s, we grew up exposed to the stereotypes and saw the "colored" drinking fountains and doctors' offices with separate entrances for "white" and "colored." But in our immediate family, discrimination didn't exist; in fact, our parents were anything but prejudiced. It might have been because we were as poor as the people we were supposed to be better than, but whatever the reason, we knew people and had friends who were Indian, black, Polish, Czech, and Cuban, and some who weren't sure what they were.

There were two old black brothers who lived in shacks on a neighboring ranch. We thought their names were "Ole John" and "Ole

Les." That's what everybody in the community knew them by and the only names we ever heard them called. They were friends of our parents and everybody in the community their whole lives, and Homer and Uncle Doug watched after them like they were part of the family. During hurricanes or any kind of inclement weather that flooded the roads or washed out the bridges, as was the case quite often where we lived, they'd saddle their horses and swim creeks to carry supplies to the two old brothers. Every year at Christmas, as soon as the turkey came out of the oven, we'd pack a couple of boxes of the tasty bird with all the trimmings, and Homer and Uncle Doug would take them dinner before we ate. Until they had performed that ritual, Christmas was never Christmas.

Both brothers would walk about fifteen miles into town to get supplies, carrying an empty croaker sack over their shoulder. Homer would pick them up on the way and squeeze them into our '51 Ford with us, then he'd drop them off in town to fill up their croaker sacks, then he'd time his trip so he could pick 'em up when we left town and give them a lift home.

There was a very old black Indian woman named Flossie who lived a few miles from us. I'm not sure in this day and time what would be ethnically or politically correct to call her. Whatever it might be made no difference in those days; Homer and Frances made regular stops by her little shanty and dropped off some of whatever they picked from the garden or cooked that day. Us kids were mostly scared of her because she looked really old and we thought she was a witch because she had all kinds of herbs and trinkets hanging from the ceiling beams of her shack.

When she talked she had kind of a slow quivery voice that scared the hell out of us. Nobody was exactly sure how old she lived to be, but our cousin Sylvia Young, who was county commissioner for twenty years and a pretty good local historian, claims she lived to be well over a hundred. People who knew her say it was all those herbs and tonics she brewed. However, there could have been one other reason for her longevity: the mailman left a shot of whiskey in her mailbox every day when he delivered her mail.

Try and get that kind of service from the post office these days!

Ginger's Parties and Having Ninety Duck Fits

Ginger was the first of us kids to become a teenager. She was also the first to start bringing home the influences that came with being a teenager by having dance parties in our carport.

Homer would back the car into the yard, then run an extension cord out the kitchen door so Ginger and her friend Lucille McKendree could set up their record player on the carport and invite friends over to dance and play games on summer weekend evenings. This was a revolutionary concept to me, being eight and a half years younger than Ginger, and watching them play spin the bottle while listening to Elvis Presley, the Everly Brothers, Roy Orbison, and Buddy Holly coming out of those little speakers was completely mind blowing.

The other thing that was apparent at these parties was that the girls seemed to like the boys, which was a lot different than it was at my school, where the girls spent most of their time screaming and slapping at you just because you tried to show them your pet hog-nosed snake. It took me a while to figure out the girl-boy thing at those parties, but it took me no time at all to be mesmerized by the sounds of those little records, called 45s, that played the most wonderful songs—songs that were so powerful that you would remember where you were and who you were with when you first heard them. It took a while before we realized just how much influence the country, rock and roll, and R&B records, along with the hymns at the Baptist church, the Jamaican fruit pickers singing in the orange groves, the old timey country radio that Frances did her housework to, or the Jimmie Rodgers songs that Homer got drunk on and sang every Christmas would have on us.

I started playing trombone in the school band in the third grade. Trombone was not my first choice of instruments, but all the trumpets and saxophones had been handed out and the band director suggested that I try the trombone. My skills on the horn were limited, but I did fill the very important spot of third chair trombonist in the Pasco Elementary School band and playing any instrument beat doing pretty much anything else in school.

The band director would give me whatever instrument was left over or nobody else would play, so I learned enough tuba for the marching band and enough bell lyre to play at the pep rallies.

Howard and I both played sports. I played Little League baseball in San Antonio, Florida, for the Blue Team known as the Colts. Howard played football and basketball in junior high and high school, but his career with the Pasco Pirates was cut short when he received a concussion during a game. This was the second concussion of his young life, the first one coming a few years earlier when he was thrown from a runaway horse riding back from Grandpa's house.

Howard was in the Future Farmers of America, where he excelled in judging cattle and singing in the FFA Quartet. The group competed all over the state and won the state championship one year for best high school barbershop quartet. Howard made a lot better grades in high school than I did. The schools we attended were geared toward agriculture, which was Howard's strong suit, not mine.

By the time all three of us kids were in school, Homer and Frances were both working at Pasco Packing. In its heyday, it was probably the largest citrus plant of its kind in the world that produced orange juice and byproducts of oranges. Their income at the plant, combined with that of our cattle, orange groves, and crops, made all our lives a little better. They worked different shifts, which made work on the farm harder, but hard work was pretty much a way of life for them. When I started first grade, Frances left Pasco and took a job driving our school bus after our Aunt Mae retired from driving it.

Homer would come home at the crack of dawn from the third shift at the plant and would wake us up with the fireplace burning on cold school mornings and the radio playing "Wings Of A Dove" by Ferlin Husky, "He'll Have To Go" by Jim Reeves, or "North To Alaska" by Johnny

Horton. Homer quoted songs like an actor quotes Shakespeare and made them into mysterious references in his conversation. For example, he'd say, "I'm gonna make like Hank Snow." That meant he was leaving, headin' out, or "Movin' On," which was the title of one of Hank Snow's hits.

Frances also had a language of her own—not lines from country songs but expressions she'd used all her life. Most of them were understood only by those of us who grew up around her. For instance, she would say that somebody had "ninety duck fits," which would mean that that person had got overly excited about a certain thing, in a positive, negative, or hysterical way. Or she'd say, "I've got a rinktum," meaning she had an idea, or a possible way to solve a problem, or something to pour over it or rub on it to fix it or make it feel better. When she had doubts about certain things, she would say, "I'm juberous" about that situation, meaning it spooked her.

Between them were probably enough quotations or sayings to write some kind of family dictionary or book of wisdom. Homer had other great lines he used all the time that weren't from songs. One of them he'd use every time Frances asked him to take her shopping. He'd say, "I'd rather put on a wooden beak and pick shit with a blind rooster." When you grow up hearing all these phrases and expressions they sound normal, but when an outsider would come along and say, "What's your mother talking about?" that's when we finally figured out that not every family said "ninety duck fits" in casual conversation.

2

Baptism By Fire

The Outhouse Roof, The Accidents, and Pop Culture

DAVID: As the '60s rolled in, we were still a couple of naïve country boys, curious about life and the future but never imagining the changes we would see personally and our whole generation would experience.

We should have had a clue that change was in the air on May 5, 1961, the day our teachers marched us out onto the playground of Pasco Elementary School to watch a rocket climb into the horizon just across the state at Cape Canaveral, carrying Alan Shepard, officially starting the space race with the Russians.

We had TV in our house now and the plumbing had been moved indoors, although we were kind of fond of the old outhouse. For one thing, instead of a roof, it had a RC Cola sign nailed to the top of the shed. That sign was reportedly stolen from Club Iola by a renegade uncle of ours who rode his horse into the bar and onto the dance floor. He was the only family member with a bad reputation, so we thought that was pretty cool—nothing major, you understand, but he was notorious enough that when we met somebody and mentioned that our last name was Bellamy, they'd say, "You must be kin to that crazy son of a bitch who rode the horse into Club Iola."

This new decade with its modern technology had a different energy. Somehow things moved faster than before. Our small community of Darby seemed a lot more isolated when we were growing up, but as we approached our teenage years, school functions, social gatherings, sports events, band concerts, singing at church, family get-togethers, and eventually our playing in clubs all contributed to speeding up the pace of our simple country lives.

In most of the interviews we've done over the last forty years, someone always asks how we made it in the music business and what kind of plan did we follow. Howard and I usually say almost the exact same words at the same time: "We've never really planned anything in our lives." That's not entirely true, of course. I did make a plan to bring those fire arrows to the family get-together, but that didn't work out so well, so after that disaster I guess we really decided to let the chips fall where they were destined to fall.

Case in point: I was daydreaming in my ninth-grade English class one day when a couple of guys came to the door and asked my teacher if they could talk to me. I walked out into the hallowed halls of Pasco High School and said, "Hi, what's up?" and they said they'd heard I owned a set of drums and wanted to know if they could borrow them. I asked, "What for?" They said they were putting together a band for the talent show at our high school. We talked a little more and I soon learned that they not only needed drums, they also needed a singer, so in a matter of minutes I loaned the drummer my drums and became the lead singer for my first band, The Accidents.

The talent show was called The Limelight. It was the biggest event of the year at Pasco High, except maybe for the homecoming football game. Howard was already signed up to sing with the FFA Quartet in the show. I was playing an accordion duet with a girl from the senior class, and Howard and I were both part of a folk group singing some

Woody Guthrie songs. There were usually baton twirlers, piano solos, comedy skits, and even the faculty and school staff got into the act with the janitor singing a brutal rendition of "Sixteen Tons."

In the mid-'60s, becoming a rock-and-roll country R&B folk band, which is about the only way I could describe the sound of The Accidents, elevated our meager status to "hip," even though we didn't know what that meant yet. Oh, but we were gonna learn real fast what it meant, and what "cool" and groovy" and a lot of other words would mean in the new context of the '60s.

In November of '63, just a couple of months after I turned thirteen, President John F. Kennedy was assassinated in Dallas, Texas. Our school got the news just as we were being dismissed for the Thanksgiving holiday. Howard remembers getting out of school early that day to help our Aunt Hattie butcher turkeys for Thanksgiving and hearing the news on the little transistor radio that I had won in a raffle at the Kash and Karry Grocery Store. That day became one of those universal moments in time that people remember their whole lives, like the bombing of Pearl Harbor and the September 11 attacks on the World Trade Center.

Speaking of remembering, three short months after the Kennedy assassination, on February 9, 1964, The Beatles made their first appearance on *The Ed Sullivan Show*. This among certain other notable events of the time, such as Marilyn Monroe posing nude on the cover of *Playboy*, Elvis Presley's first television appearance, birth control, TV in every living room, Woodstock '69, and Andy Warhol's tomato soup cans would someday mark the birth of our modern pop culture. Even if you were one of those people who thought that events like these meant the beginning of the decline of civilization, you still couldn't ignore them. You might as well have stood on the railroad tracks with your hands up trying to stop a freight train.

Our sister saw Elvis a few years before The Beatles, also on *The Ed Sullivan Show*, and went weak in the knees. I loved Elvis but his image was bigger than life, a superstar before there *were* superstars. I mostly remember just being a little kid dancin' around the living room to his music and wondering what was making Ginger so hysterical, or as Frances described it, "She had ninety duck fits when she saw that Elvis Presley on TV."

Johnny Cash's voice echoing through the old National Guard auditorium was also very magical to us, but his success seemed unattainable to a couple of farm boys in the cheap seats.

And yet seeing John, Paul, George, and Ringo generate that much raw musical energy through a little black and white TV screen was completely relatable. For one thing, they looked to be closer to our age, and the girls were mobbing them, and that's pretty much all a boy going on fourteen needed to know.

A year later, I was singing with The Accidents on the stage of the Pasco High School auditorium. The song was called "The Little Black Egg," and we instantly became known locally as a *band*. Most of the kids at school didn't care that we knew only a couple of songs. To them we were a bona fide music group, and it worked wonders for our egos. We started to dress like a band, wear our hair like a band, cop attitudes like a band, and of course we would soon start picking up other habits, mostly bad ones, that came with being a band.

After the talent show, the band started hanging out at the farm. We set up what equipment we had in a little house that Homer and Frances built for Grandma to live in after Grandpa died. When she remarried a few years later and moved to town, Homer started using it as a hay barn. The little wood frame house became known as "the shack" and would become the site of many jams, rehearsals, and recording sessions over the years. Our current recording studio is built on the spot where the original shack stood, and we've recorded most of our albums there since the early 1980s.

It still amazes me how accepting our parents were when the entire band came over and started to rehearse, hang out, and pretty much live in the shack. Maybe all the nights Homer and his buddies drank moonshine and played music at our house prepared them for this, or maybe they just figured since my grades weren't that good and I wasn't the greatest of farmhands, they might as well let me play music.

Our family still played at gospel sings, rattlesnake roundups, and family reunions after I joined The Accidents. At local events, you could find Homer sitting on a chair with his Dobro in the back of our pickup, with me and my accordion on one side of the truck bed and Howard on the other side with a banjo, ukulele, or whatever instrument he'd grown fond of that week. We'd play songs like "Waitin' For The Robert E. Lee" and "I'm Goin' Back To Alabam," then we'd do a hymn like "The Old Rugged Cross." I also played accordion occasionally for local department store fashion shows. They usually wanted me to play "The Girl From Ipanema" while the models walked around a swimming pool showing off the latest styles. They paid me twenty-five bucks for an hour of squeezing that bellows, but I got ribbed pretty bad by the band, who loved to make bad accordion jokes.

The Revival at the Clay Sink Baptist Church

There's one gig from this era that I don't think Howard and I could ever forget. It happened while we were playing a revival meeting at the Clay Sink Baptist Church.

Our mother's good friend Vera Boyette called and requested that we play a "special" for the revival, so Howard and I decided to work up "I'll Fly Away," with me on accordion and Howard accompanying me on guitar. The only problem was I'd been practicing "Downtown," a lush '60s Petula Clark pop hit, all week from sheet music I was trying to learn to read, so you might say that song was stuck in my brain.

Our big moment came at the revival, standing in front of the pulpit right after the congregation had finished singing hymns and right before the preacher was scheduled to start his sermon. I kicked off "I'll Fly Away," and Howard joined in. We could do that old church standard in our sleep so we were pure perfection at first but then, somehow, some way, right in the middle of the song, the melody switched in my head and I started playing "Downtown." No matter how hard I tried, I couldn't seem to get my brain or my fingers to go back to "I'll Fly Away." I looked up from my accordion keyboard just long enough to catch the look of terror on Howard's face as I searched the keyboard for a clue to where my fingers should be. It seemed like an eternity before I found it, but finally I managed to get back on the right note sequence, just in time to end the old hymn in the usual way.

Beads of sweat were rolling down my face. I heard Howard draw a huge sigh of relief when we hit the final chord. The preacher was kind. He complimented us and said, "Thank you, Brother Howard and Brother David," so I started thinking, maybe everybody just thought we'd done a swingin' gospel version of the old favorite and didn't notice how far we'd strayed into a completely different song. But then, as we packed our instruments in their cases and made our way from the pulpit down the aisle to take a seat on the long wooden church bench, Howard and I made eye contact with one another, then we saw Ginger sitting on the bench by our parents. We could tell by the puzzled look on her face that she had noticed our blunder. She had way too good an ear to miss a sin like that.

That was all it took. Howard and I started laughing uncontrollably and no matter how hard we tried, we couldn't stop. The preacher was trying to start the sermon, but everyone in the little wooden church was looking at us and by then we were laughing so hard that tears were streaming down our faces. In just a few short minutes we'd gone from being praised, complimented, and blessed to dashing outside in the middle of the sermon to sit in the car till the preaching was over and pray for mercy.

Somehow we were able to salvage our reputation and make amends to the preacher. He even invited us to return for the next revival and play another special. Luckily for us, the preacher took seriously the parts of the Bible that talked about forgiveness.

While we never again mixed up "I'll Fly Away" with "Downtown," we continued to play a rare mixture of musical styles for our audiences. We sang Jimmie Rodgers songs like "T For Texas" with Homer, I played

"Lady Of Spain" with Ginger on the accordion, The Accidents worked up "Satisfaction," and Howard continued to compete in barbershop competitions, singing "Jesus Is The Waymaker" with the FFA Quartet.

Playing for Beer and Homer's Crooked Fence

The original Accidents had five guys in the lineup. I started out as lead singer and then switched to playing organ (and singing) because we needed keyboards and nobody else had experience in that department (those accordion lessons were finally paying off).

It didn't seem to make any difference at that point in time that the musical backgrounds of the players in the band were so diverse that it's a wonder we were ever able to decide on a song to play together. In the early days, The Accidents's main motivation was girls. For some reason I don't understand to this day, take almost any goofy kid, put a guitar in his hand and place him in front of a band on the stage, and at least a few of the girls in the audience will get wet and excited. We all wanted some of that.

We soon figured out that we could make enough money for gas, beer, and girls, and maybe have a couple of bucks left for band members to split. We discovered that the best way to get gigs was to learn songs people liked, so we started learning the current hit songs off the radio. We learned rock songs for the rocker girls and country songs for the country girls and, well, you get the idea.

In our very first band lineup, we had a Gibson Trini Lopez model guitar, a Sears Silvertone guitar, and a Fender precision bass all plugged into one old Gibson amp while the drummer played my blue sparkle Silvertone drum kit that I ordered from the Sears catalog after our parents sold a cow in order to buy the kit for me. There was an electronics shop in Dade City that had a couple of speaker columns and a Bogen amplifier with an RCA microphone. We rented the whole P.A. system for fifteen bucks a day and we'd all crowd around and sing on that one mic.

We mostly played local parties and dives in the beginning. Soon we were getting invitations to play a lot of beer parties. Our normal rate for these gigs was gas money and all the beer we could drink. One of the wealthier families in Dade City had a lake house they used mostly for parties on Lake Jovita in San Antonio just a few miles from our farm. On Friday nights, you could find us there crankin' out tunes, drinkin', and taking notes on which girls drank the most beer.

The lake house was surrounded by orange groves on three sides and the big lawn opened up to a dock going down to the lake. We set up on the porch facing the lake and everybody danced in the yard. People brought us beer while we played and it wasn't unheard of for a band member to pass out mid-song. Our drummer fell off his stool one evening while we were playing during a thunderstorm. We carried him into the yard and laid him under an oak tree where the rain could hit him in the face and sober him up. Meanwhile a party guest got behind the drums and we continued to bash out songs.

As you can imagine, The Accidents was a very loose organization, but eventually we had a full set list of songs that allowed us to play a variety of gigs. We played songs by Hank Williams, Bob Dylan, and the Temptations. We played recreation centers, bowling alleys, and dances after football games. Then we graduated to beer joints and strip clubs. Most of these fine establishments ran the spectrum as far as musical taste and clientele. Our decision to play a wide variety of music worked well with most of the club owners, but since we were underage, we had to talk our parents into signing for us to get police identification so we could play clubs with liquor and dancers. I think the only reason all the parents finally consented to sign was because we had to keep our nose clean in order to keep our police IDs.

We still played the teen clubs and homecoming dances and we were practically the house band at Louie's Bowling Alley in Brooksville. The owner, Louie Bacalini, had dances every Thursday and Friday night during summer vacation. He charged fifty cents a head on the nights we played. We did four forty-five-minute sets and at the end of the night Louie would hand us a half a dozen cigar boxes full of quarters to split among the band. We loved the teen clubs because we knew a lot of the girls in Brooksville and Dade City, but it was the night clubs that got us playing fulltime and allowed us to earn and learn.

We played the Shan-Gri-La Club on the infamous Dale Mabry strip in Tampa for seventeen months straight, six nights a week, five sets a night. It was a grueling schedule but our instrumental and vocal skills became more polished and we got to where we could sing almost every song a customer could request.

Our police IDs meant we could only be on the stage and not hang out in the bar since we were underage, so we spent most nights taking our breaks between our sets in liquor storerooms or in alleys behind the bar until it was time to go back on the stage. The owners and managers of these upscale venues were usually wise guys who gave you advice and orders in broad terms like "Don't try any funny business," and "Play stuff that makes guys buy drinks for the broads." They didn't bother telling us that the alleys and storerooms were where all the deals went down.

So while the underage band was supposed to be safely tucked away from the sins of the nightclub in a liquor closet, one of the dancers would come in there between dances to conduct business with some guy from the club while we were "hanging out."

No doubt there was a certain amount of moral conflict with playing all week in a strip club and then doing a Sunday special in church, but I'm sure I came up with brilliant ways to rationalize it. My parents knew where I was working but they didn't really know what went on there. Howard came by now and then to check on us and hang out during our breaks, but Homer and Frances, who were the hardest working people I've ever known, did not go out much. Their lives were dedicated to taking care of and supporting the family. Their outings consisted mostly of church and school functions or visiting kinfolks and going to town to get groceries. They were such devout parents that their first rule about going out was that they wouldn't go anywhere that they couldn't take us kids.

I guess that's what gave me this sudden flash of brilliance: we'd been playing the Shan-Gri-La for a few months when I decided to invite them for an evening out at the club for their upcoming wedding anniversary. We'd been going over pretty good with the club owner and the patrons and we now had a song list that was impressive by anybody's standards. I guess I was just so proud that I was earning a living playing music, however meager it was, that I wanted them to see me plying my profession. It never occurred to me what a shock it might be to their systems to walk in and see two topless, almost nude, girls, one of them dancing in a cage on the far side of the stage, and the other dancing on a wooden pedestal that was connected to the Farfisa organ I was playing.

My parents came in while we were on stage. I had already made arrangements with the waiters to seat them and get them something to drink. Homer had a couple of shots of Old Crow and Coke while Frances drank her Coke straight. The dancers kept grinding away, but Homer and Frances stayed and listened to three whole sets until Frances said they'd better head back because Homer had to get up early and build fence.

The next afternoon I woke up late, as had become my routine since I started playing clubs. I wandered into the kitchen to see what Frances was cooking. I was, of course, waiting to see if there was going to be any discussion of the night before.

For a while Frances cooked, silently, then she commented on how good the band looked and sounded. Homer came in from the pasture about that time and sat down to eat, also in silence. After lunch he pushed his plate back, looked at me, and said, "I watched them girls twirl them tassels so much last night I got a crick in my neck and my eyes went crossed and I believe that's the crookedest damned fence I ever built."

Cows, Integration, and the Frat Boys

Everything we learned, it was kind of a baptism by fire. We didn't know it, but that way of life prepared us for a lot of what would come later. It certainly prepared Howard for his first profession.

HOWARD: The way we learned how to swim, they throw you in a pond.

DAVID: Our dad was just: throw you in . . . and . . . you'd swim out. We

40

learned pretty much everything like that. Now, riding horses, we'd been riding horses since we were babies, so we didn't know how *not* to ride a horse. A lot of stuff was second nature because you just did it all the time. You saw them doing it, and you did it.

We'd ride around in a pickup truck on a wooden bench behind the glass, no seat belts, no nothin', we'd just sit on that bench.

HOWARD: Our dad bought a '56 pale blue Ford pickup. I would love to have that thing today; it's my favorite automobile ever. Only one cab, there wasn't dual cabs then so my sister, my mother, and my father sat in that front seat and he put a bench across the front of the bed of that pickup and put David and me right up against the cab on that bench. It's where we sat everywhere we went. We got slingshots and—if you knew some of the things we did in the back of that truck. We shot a schoolhouse window out one time, I remember that. Not to mention the night I gave up my innocence to the preacher's daughter with barely a struggle.

DAVID: I'll tell you the wildest thing that happened in that blue truck—I think it was the old blue truck, though it could have been the old one after that. An old cow died and we were draggin' her as far away from the house as you could get. You didn't go out and bury a dead cow 'cause the thing was huge. You left her for the buzzards, but you didn't want that going on right by the house, so you dragged her as far away as you could and still be on your property. We drug her way down in the woods, just Homer drivin' and me and Howard in the seat by him. We had on brand new straw hats we had just got. We come back across that front pasture and we had beds of watermelons out there. We hit a big hole, bigger than we anticipated, and my and Howard's heads went through the windshield, and took those new hats and pulled them down over our heads. Those hats kept that busted windshield from cutting our heads and faces and whatever. Just minor concussions, and back then you didn't make a fuss over that.

HOWARD: We come home to our mom and listened to her rail our dad out for puttin' us through the windshield. You know, the safety features that are in everything today they just weren't around in those days. He'd been in a war and something that was totally dangerous to most people he kinda saw it all humorous.

DAVID: We could be working cattle in a pen and one of them put a horn in your britches and tear your britches to shreds and everybody would *laugh*!

HOWARD: *It was entertainment!*

DAVID: It was high entertainment.

HOWARD: It's just the way we grew up and all the other rural kids— especially ranchers' kids—working the cattle in the pens with our dad was an experience that you had to see it to believe it.

DAVID: He was a mild-mannered guy, but he turned into another human being in the cow pens. Because it was very intense work, you know, they'd break out and get loose and you gotta get 'em back, you gotta get all the bulls cut, and if you do one wrong thing you can screw up everything so boy, you better do what he said in the pen, or it was like a war in those times. Our uncle and our great uncle both had ranches out here and—

HOWARD: We were the only two boys in the family—

DAVID: We'd go from one ranch to another cuttin' bulls.

HOWARD: All day.

DAVID: We got no cooperation from the bulls.

HOWARD: You'd have to catch every one of them and they're weighin' at least three hundred pounds.

DAVID: We'd pick out a young bull. Howard would get on his head and I'd get on his legs.

HOWARD: And he'd be tryin' to kick while you're cuttin' his nuts out. You don't think that'll wear you out? And there's a certain way to hold them while you're . . . if you pull their legs too far the wrong way, their nuts'll suck up into their belly—you can imagine—and you can't find them. There's a whole art form to it.

DAVID: Like Howard says, nothing *seemed* that dangerous to us at the time. I remember drivin' to the cattle auction, just me and Homer and Howard, and the old cow that was in the back put her horn right through the window between our heads. That was like just *normal*. Dad would say, "*Look at that ol' son of a bitch!*"

I guess Howard took it a little different than I did. I still feel close to that way of life, but I didn't want to earn my living doing it. It's a tough life. I mean, it's one thing if you own the ranch and you've got boys doing the grunt work. It's another thing if you're one of the boys having to cut those calves. And I've actually seen Howard—wasn't it over at Uncle Doug's where you got your pants kicked off?

HOWARD: They kicked my britches off.

DAVID: A calf actually kicked his pants off.

HOWARD: He kicked me and hit that seam where the pocket—those old Levi's that had that button there, and it literally ripped that seam to my foot and the pants just busted wide open! And I've been kicked in the chest so hard it's knocked the breath out of me. You get injured easy, but what's crazy is nobody ever wanted to discuss those things and there were no doctors to go to out here. I mean, we'd have to be *dying* for someone to go for the doctor. All those things that would happen to us in that cowpen, they were just normal, in our way of life and all the other ranch kids we grew up with.

DAVID: And it was normal to *continue* that way of life. So Howard got involved in buying cattle because as he grew up with them he got to know a lot about them. It was a decent living when he got into doing it and when you grow up poor, earning a decent living is a pretty big deal. We still played music together, but around the time he started his cattle-buying career, I was in a band playing in strip clubs—I was still in high school and I had a police ID. It was a much safer way to make a living than cuttin' calves all day long—at least until the old mobsters came in and a fight broke out and they started throwing whiskey glasses at the band. That's why clubs like that started stringin' chicken wire in front of the stage.

Also about that time, Howard almost found himself a career a bit more glamorous than buying cattle.

HOWARD: I didn't find school that hard. I made pretty good grades,

I was president of my class, and my last year I only went to school half a day because I had all my credits and stuff and I worked the rest of the time as a vet's assistant and various things. I had just graduated, you know, been to the prom and the whole bit, and one day I was all by myself at home when I heard someone knock on the door. I opened the door and I see these two guys with badges on and they flashed their FBI cards at me and I'm thinking, *Holy shit!* So I said, "Well, come on in," so they came in and started talking to me. Turns out my high school principal had recommended me to the FBI and what they offered me was basically a scholarship that could have ended up with me becoming an agent. We sat and talked and, of course, it excited me. I basically said, "Yeah," and got very interested and actually ended up going ahead and got fingerprinted at our local city hall here and the whole bit, and was gonna do that; that was gonna be my future.

But in the meantime, I had taken some cattle to an old Jewish feller in Bartow, Al Kaplan, who had a company called Midstate Packing. Mr. Al and I hit it off big and he was in need of a cattle buyer and I knew a lot about it so he offered me the job. A car, expense account. I was basically nineteen years old. An offer like that was unheard of. I had to call the FBI and tell them I wasn't coming to Virginia to go to school. Those were big turning points in my life, being recruited by the FBI and getting a really good job that I knew how to do right out of high school. That guardian angel thing, you know, that thing just falls on your lap.

DAVID: He'd worked cattle in some capacity for all his life, either judging them, as a veterinarian's assistant, or managing the family's cattle with Homer. Howard also got married right after high school and married men, if they're lucky, find a job like this. *But*—and there *is* a but—his new job required him to spend a lot of time on the road between Florida and South Georgia at cattle auctions and sale barns. Many of the buyers and clients he worked with were good ol' boys who drank heavy and Howard got to joining them on a pretty regular basis. It wasn't unusual to see Howard slide his company car into the oyster shell parking lot of a club where we were playing. He'd have a few drinks and check to see what we were up to. Once he'd gotten a couple of steady paychecks from his new job, he also helped us buy some much-needed band equipment. But Howard didn't join the band. He was content to be a cattle buyer. Or was he?

HOWARD: I was never really content with anything. Everything was a step toward something else. You know if I saw a bigger door open, I was—I guess you'd say an opportunist. Aren't we all? That door had opened and it was something I loved to do; I knew a lot about it, and the money was good, and the booze was good. Al Kaplan took me under his wing and treated me like a son, and that went on for five or six years until one night I was driving with the booze in me and ran under a semi—more about that later.

Music didn't mean any less to me than it did to David; I just knew I had to make a living. I had to make some money doing something. I've done so many jobs it's unbelievable. I've always had an income. Now, David was always pointing in the direction of music, but he never really made any money out of it until his time came.

DAVID: I couldn't do anything else much. Although in high school and college we had a band that did support itself, we seemed to always be dead broke, but as I look back on it now, our peers and stuff, we made more money playing in the band than they did working at the gas station or wherever they were working. So we actually did kind of support ourselves doing it; it's just that nobody got rich, you know. I mean, we didn't know you *could* get rich. I just knew that there was not really much else I could do. I either had to stay home and get into the family business, which was poverty farming and cattle, or find a way to make a living making music.

Howard and his first wife, Pam, moved into a mobile home community on the Old Lakeland Road just north of Dade City because it was close to the Midstate Packing home office and to the cattle auctions he worked. The crowded little mobile home community was a far cry from the open spaces he was used to on the farm in Darby. Most of his neighbors were elderly, retired, and went to bed early, and they were not real fond of hearing Howard driving around the subdivision late at night, half lit from a night of drinking with the cattle buyers, burning rubber, trying to figure out which mobile home he lived in. When he was drunk, he told us, "All them house trailers looked the same."

With Howard being married with a steady job and me playing late nights almost every night in clubs, for the first time we weren't playing music together on a steady basis, but when we did get a chance to play with Homer and Ginger, it was as if we'd never stopped. There was one major cloud that hung heavy over the family during these years. Ginger had gone through serious hard times, losing her daughter Carla Sue at just eighteen months. We'd never experienced the death of someone so young in our immediate family and it was made even harder by the fact that she died in Howard's arms one afternoon from what the doctor diagnosed as nothing more than a mild case of the flu. We'd never imagined a tragedy like this. She was just there one day and gone the next.

Needless to say Ginger suffered deeply from the loss, but somehow family and friends helped pull her through it, although it was surely something much greater than us that kept her from completely losing it. Later Ginger and her husband had a son named Terry but their marriage then fell apart. Ginger had a breakdown and had to be hospitalized. Terry came to live with us and eventually Homer and Frances adopted him because they were worried his father might come back someday and try to take him. Ginger was very sick for a long time and we worried if she would ever recover, but she has the strongest faith of anybody I've ever known. While her faith may have been unflappable, ours was not, so we watched anxiously as she endured repeated surgeries and other setbacks. In the meantime, Howard and I were out there blowin' in the wind, if you know what I mean.

Those of you who were around in the '60s understand that suddenly— or not so suddenly—there was this huge cultural swing in America, and much of it was related to a particular weed that grew wild all over the South but grew better when it had a little human help. Understand that we didn't get involved because we smoked a couple of joints or thought we were cool musicians now. It's just . . . somewhere between my sophomore and junior year in high school (1966–67), almost everyone I knew started turning on. No matter what you called it—ganja, herb, weed, hooch, a doobie, or plain old joint—almost overnight the stuff was everywhere. Marijuana had been around forever and we'd seen jazz and R&B musicians in the clubs smoking it during their breaks, but it mostly remained in underground circles, something that *avant-garde* musicians and poets did.

Not anymore. Suddenly it burst out of the small circle of beatniks and beelined straight into Middle American youth culture. Some say it happened after the British music invasion; others argue it started from America's West Coast hippie movement. There was even a rumor that smoking pot became popular after Bob Dylan got The Beatles stoned. I don't personally know if any of those stories are correct, although the time line does correlate pretty closely to those events. All I know is one day a friend of ours had a matchbox full of grass that he rolled into a couple of joints. We smoked them in the old cemetery in San Antonio, Florida, and got high for the first time and spent the rest of the day laughing.

The next day it seemed that everybody I had known to be a straitlaced, conservatively dressed, shy, non-opinionated kid became a philosopher, let his hair grow long, and started wearing clothes that were casual, hip, unisex, and undefined by our school dress code. Needless to say, some of these cultural changes clashed head on with our little rural high school in Pasco County, Florida. The girls I knew that never uncrossed their legs stopped wearing bras and started discussing the sexual revolution. It was hard to tell if pot was the cause of all this or the excuse everybody had been looking for to let their hair down.

And then, I actually integrated our county, long before it was cool.

HOWARD: He didn't really realize what he was doin', but he caused a stir in the local hometown.

DAVID: They integrated our schools; I think it was '66. They sent five black kids over to our high school during the busing era. I became friends with about four of them 'cause I was in band with a couple of them.

We had these two friends who started dating: this one white girl that was a friend of mine already and one of the black guys that came over. That was a little too much for the town. Integrating was one thing, but dating was a bit excessive for those who thought they were the morality police. We used to go to the rec center because The Accidents used to play there for Friday night dances every two or three months. Well, they wouldn't let the white girl and the black guy in the rec center. So our bass player and myself went over to the black rec center, which was literally across the tracks, maybe three hundred yards away; we went across to the black rec center because we played there, as well. We got a couple of girls from there and brought 'em back to our rec center and danced with them. I guess we were looking for a response.

Little did we know how *big* a response we would get. The whole police force came out. And the NAACP got involved. And it became a much bigger deal than we had anticipated. It got settled, and I think that white and black kids could probably dance together after that. It was not anticipated to be like a civil rights movement—just a few teenagers determined to have it their way—but it kind of ended up being one. Funny because just about all the kids involved were just friends; it was a small circle.

Our family's reaction was interesting. They weren't mad at us for doing it because at heart they weren't prejudiced. I think it was more the heat they were taking from outside. One of my friends, his father was a college professor, kind of a liberal, he was defending the deal, saying, you know, you can't arrest people for dancing together, and I think my friend ended up getting his little hippie house burned down over that deal.

HOWARD: You can see we had a normal childhood life. Of course, the ultimate is to get your book turned into a movie. There's something about growing up in the rural South that makes for good movies, so a lot of the old great movies were done about the South. Because it's so different from the way that most people grow up.

DAVID: There's a lot of atmosphere involved. Me and my wife, Susan, were in New Orleans at The Court of the Three Sisters, old courtyard restaurant, really great old place, good New Orleans food. We were sittin' out in the courtyard and the lady at the table next to us says a bird came and shit on the table. She called this ol' waitress over to the table and said, "Lady, this bird just came and pooped on my tablecloth." The waitress looked at her and said, "Honey, *that's ambience.*" I think that's the thing about the South: you have a lot of ambience.

We were once asked to do a favor by our friend Ronnie Campbell.

Later on in this book, Ronnie blessed us with a load of buffalo hides. He's always been politically wired, and we owed him a favor so he wanted us to come down and play for a New Orleans mayoral candidate. So we went down and played on the *Natchez*, that old riverboat? What they didn't tell us was that it was an all-black audience, including the candidate. They might have known "Let Your Love Flow," but that was about all they knew of our song list. So we pulled out every R&B song we ever knew, going way back to our roots, trying to play some old school stuff, and we ended up being great friends with the candidate after he became mayor. It was kind of like *The Buddy Holly Story*, when he came out and played at The Apollo and everybody looking at him and his band and wondering, "Who are these hillbillies?" And the food was worth doing the whole gig.

One of those black students who first integrated our high school, a kid named David Burgess, joined the glee club. He sounded like Otis Redding to us, and within a week of integrating the school, we had him in The Accidents singing highly requested songs like "My Girl," "I Can't Help Myself," and "I Feel Good." There were still plenty of rock, pop, and country songs for the rest of us to sing, but we felt we had really extended our range of requests by bringing in David.

Then we made a huge mistake. We'd been wanting to change the name of the band for a while but if there was one name in the world worse than The Accidents, we chose it when we decided to call ourselves The

Heterogeneous Grouping (varied, diverse, made up of different elements). We may have known what it meant but I don't think anybody else did and anyway they couldn't pronounce it—I mean, who'd wanna even try? Wouldn't you know it, when they finally did find out what it meant, they said stuff like, "Oh, I get it, it's because you have that black guy singin' in the band now!"

Everything went downhill from there. Musically, we considered ourselves to be ahead of our time, kind of a rockin', redneck, psychedelic soul band. But our musical integrity didn't really matter. The black clubs didn't like us because the band was all white except for our singer. Most of the white clubs, dances, and rec centers didn't like our black front man because they resented integration.

The Heterogeneous Grouping seemed doomed from the start and probably wouldn't have lasted as long as it did except we stumbled on one wild and crazy group of guys who loved us. Remember *Animal House* with John Belushi? Well, thanks to the frat boys, we got to live that lifestyle almost every weekend. The fact that we had a black front man who came up during the show to sing Wilson Pickett songs right after we'd delivered a soul-stirring rendition of "Born On The Bayou" followed by the occasional psychedelic jam made us perfect for the Greeks. We played fraternities every weekend at The University of Florida, Florida State, University of South Florida, St. Pete Jr. College, Saint Leo, and even schools in Miami. From formal attire to toga parties, these soirees always had kegs of beer, bags of weed, and people shedding their clothes. There were lots of drunk girls, and the frat boys were always eager to get us high. Every act of perversity you could think of went on at these parties, soaked in beer and hazed in reefer smoke.

One late evening during one of these thinly disguised orgies, near the University of South Florida, I was pounding the keys on my Farfisa organ and singing "Louie Louie" when suddenly the organ started gaining in volume, then began winding itself down like a slow-dying cow bellowing its last breath. The rest of the band was looking in my direction like I knew what was going on. Almost the entire audience was already up on the lower bandstand with us, which meant they were having a good time. The frat crowd usually ended up on stage grabbing loose drumsticks to beat on the skins, playing the keyboards and singing along on the mic or just strumming drunk air guitar.

As the organ sound wound down to nothing, we were forced into taking a break. After we explained the problem to the group of drunk frat boys whose main interest was getting their dates completely hammered and getting their togas off, we found the DJ and got him to play a few slow songs to dance to while we checked out the problem. It was fairly obvious after we unscrewed the top of the organ and found a rat's nest built on the electric wires that ran along the length of the keyboard to the power supply. The mama rat had laid old straw from our hay barn along with shredded pieces of newspaper up against the wire. Apparently the volume of the organ had got too loud or the wires had heated up or maybe she just got hungry. At any rate, she started chewing into the live wire, and once she got through the insulation, the electricity ran through her and the entire litter of baby rats, and barbecued them all. The decline in volume and a big puff of smoke that billowed out from under the organ were the only warnings we had that something was not right.

We were in a hurry to get back to playing, so we unplugged the organ, removed the rat family, cut the burned wires away, reconnected them, and wound some electric tape over the bare joints. When we turned the organ back on, it worked, somewhat, but we couldn't turn down the volume so I turned my amplifier down as much as I could and the rest of the band turned their volume up. The drummer kicked back into "Louie Louie," and the toga crowd went back to humping the dance floor, doing the "dog" or the "gator" or one of those frat dances that resembled a pagan mating ritual.

Away from the frat parties, the band still encountered discrimination when we stopped at restaurants or gas stations going to and from gigs. People would look at us like they were gonna string us up, especially if we were in really rural areas. The irony was that we were probably more redneck than they were, we just happened to have long hair a few years before they started growin' their hair long and, of course, we had a black guy hanging out with us.

The musicians and performers we met (and the frat boys) were the only people who accepted and appreciated what we were doing musically. Ray Charles has always been a favorite of ours, and knowing that he was influenced by country singers like Eddy Arnold made him all the more special to us. When I first heard Ray singing country songs like Don Gibson's "I Can't Stop Loving You," and "You Don't Know Me," written by Eddy Arnold and Cindy Walker, I figured that would break down all racial barriers, musically, socially, and otherwise. Of course, I was an idealist and wrong about a good many things in those tender years.

Aside from the black and white issues, we had another major problem. We'd hired a professional sign painter to paint "The Heterogeneous Grouping" in big, purple, psychedelic letters on the side of the used Ford Econoline van we'd recently acquired and when we decided to give up on the name, we found we didn't have the money to paint over it. Of course nobody knew what it meant or how to say it, and every now and then someone would pull up beside us at a red light and ask if they could buy a bottle of milk off the truck.

Higher Education and Band Evolution

Like most kids graduating high school, I had some decisions to make about my future. Most of the guys in the band were graduating at about the same time, so one of us geniuses figured out we could go to St. Petersburg Junior College (the Beach Campus, of course). When you translate that into band language, it meant babes in bikinis, clubs to play, and happy parents because we were going to college. We knew we weren't going to get into Ivy League schools with our grades. In fact, we'd missed so many school days since we'd started playing clubs, it was amazing that we could graduate.

I would have probably flunked out if it hadn't been for Frances, who was still driving the school bus. She also worked in the high school cafeteria as the assistant manager, and between the two jobs she was able to keep an eye on me. She saved my butt so many times from getting expelled or flunking out that I lost count. The teachers, superintendent, and all the school board were friends of hers, which didn't hurt but that didn't mean I got special treatment. Our band had to make a deal with Mr. Malone, our principal. If we stayed out of trouble in school, we could keep our long hair. If not, he'd send us straight to the barbershop.

My grades were at least good enough to get me into junior college so we enrolled, found a house for rent across the street from the campus, and settled into college life in Clearwater, Florida. One of the guitar players in the original Accidents (Mark) switched to playing bass guitar. Our original bass player (Jerry) joined the army after high school. We still had our original drummer (Paul), and by now he'd even managed to borrow a little money and buy himself a new drum kit. The old blue sparkle set he borrowed from me in the ninth grade had to be retired after the wear and tear of too many beer parties.

Rodney, The Accidents's original guitar player, had a girl friend who didn't want him out late at night in strip clubs, a recurring problem that caused quite a few band members to lose more than one high school sweetheart. So we found a guitar player (Tom) who was already in his first year of college at the University of South Florida. Tom was from up north but what the heck, we already had problems because we had a black guy in the band. Surely they wouldn't complain about one little Yankee guitar player.

Tom was pretty versatile and more progressive than our first guitar player, so we started to rebuild the band with just drums, bass, guitar, and organ. Mark and I did most of the singing. My keyboard playing was improving, but since I had learned to play the accordion instead of the piano, my left hand was always a bit of a handicap.

We couldn't decide what to do about Dave. He was a good friend and a great singer. We used to introduce him on stage as Soul Brother Number One and he'd come running out like James Brown and launch into something like Sam Cooke's "A Change Is Gonna Come." He was a handsome guy with stage presence, so we wanted to keep him in the new band lineup and use him in the clubs that weren't prejudiced. As fate would have it, we never got the chance to play with him again.

A friend of his called me from Orlando, where he'd been living with his mother since graduation, and told us that David had been an eyewitness to the murder of his sister by his brother-in-law. He had suffered a major breakdown and had to be sedated and hospitalized in a psychiatric ward. We found out later that he had also been treated with electroshock therapy. We went to see him in the hospital, but he was so medicated that he didn't recognize us. It was ironic, this talented singer that never did any drugs and always jokingly criticized us for smoking pot was now completely doped up as we all stood there scared straight by the circumstances we'd encountered.

The decision was finally made for us. There were just too many disasters The Heterogeneous Grouping couldn't overcome. While we were still trying to recover from the shock of recent events, we got a call from a guy who ran an R&B club about backing up some soul acts he had touring in Florida. The first show we played was with Eddie Floyd. Eddie had written a song for Otis Redding called "Knock On Wood," but his record label decided to release his original version instead of cutting it on Otis. In 1967 it became a monster hit for Eddie, and a few months later at a club called The Plantation in Sarasota we were his backup band for three shows. All three of those shows were packed to the rafters with crazy, adoring fans, and that was the first time we experienced what it was like to be onstage with a recording artist who had a big hit record. Women were throwing underwear, shoes, jewelry, phone numbers, hell, they would have thrown their husbands if they thought it would have gotten Eddie Floyd's attention.

We also backed up Little Anthony and the Imperials and Percy Sledge, but as much fun as it was, we lost money doing it. Most of the agents and managers figured they were doing you a favor by letting you on stage to back up a nationally famous recording artist. You had to look at it more as an ego boost than a moneymaker. We came to the realization that we weren't going to make much of a living as a backing band.

The frat parties were fun and paid pretty good, but they only happened while school was in session; we'd lost our soul singer and weren't even "heterogeneous" anymore. Right about this time we should have put our heads together, pulled in the reins a little, and started working on a game plan to reinvent the band, but instead we started partying more, trying to forget our misfortunes.

We were still at college but we weren't attending classes. We got up, looked for gigs, got stoned, went to eat, checked out the beach—I'm sure you get the picture. One of the problems was that we lived really close to the campus. The street in front of our house also ran past the administration office, the theater department, and the psychology building. The girls that majored in psychology loved stopping by our little house to catch a buzz after a hard day in the classroom trying to figure out what was on Freud's mind. Of course we did our best to show them. Another group who found us interesting was those aspiring young actresses from the theater group. They loved to hang out with real musicians.

Our whole setup was trouble with a capital T, and we were on our way to flunking out or getting busted or both, probably sooner than later. But there was something else stirring in the cosmos just up the road a ways that was fixing to change the course of the band and blow the cover we'd been trying to keep as career college boys.

Howard Takes a Crash Course

After a hard day's work, Howard was driving home from Gainesville, heading south on I-75, almost a hundred mile stretch down the middle of Florida. Truth be known, he was driving about ninety miles per hour, coming back from one of those cattle buyer meetings at Dub's Steer Room, an infamous good ol' boy watering hole.

He'd already had a couple of close shaves with the Florida Highway Patrol over the past year, with one car chase ending when he drove his company's Chevy Impala into an orange grove at high speed and brought it to a stop in the top of an orange tree. On his regular visits to our band house in Clearwater, we'd usually hang out, get buzzed, jam, and go to the beach. On one of those sunny afternoon occasions he was driving me, the band, and a couple of school friends home after swimming in the Gulf of Mexico when he decided to get our attention by cutting doughnuts at a red light in the middle of Gulf to Bay Boulevard, the main drag connecting Clearwater to Clearwater Beach.

Most of these college kids hadn't been subjected to this style of redneck driving, so naturally they all started screaming for their lives and begging him to stop. Howard was just having a good time, laughing as hard as he could at his car full of stoned, terrified hippies. I figured he was still trying to get even with me for pulling him between that cow and her calf behind the tractor in the old bathtub. By the time Howard stopped the car by spinning it into the driveway of the campus house, his passengers had finally realized that they were going to live and were falling out of the car laughing about Howard's thrill ride back from the beach.

But leaving Gainesville on this particular night ride home, Howard wasn't nearly as lucky. He wasn't being chased by the highway patrol, but he was flat haulin' ass down the interstate when he passed out and ran his car under the back of a semi trailer that was carrying thousands of live, white leghorn chickens. Howard didn't even hit the brakes when he went under the eighteen-wheeler, which was doing half the speed that he was. He later told me that the only thing he remembered when he woke up was white feathers flying everywhere. He thought he had died and was seeing angels. There were dead chickens scattered all over the road; his car engine was sitting on the ground-up seat next to him. He later observed that he could have reached over and changed the spark plugs.

The trucker he hit flagged someone down and they called an ambulance to carry him to Shands Hospital in Gainesville. When I got the call in Clearwater from Frances, she and Homer had just arrived at the hospital and were still unsure about what condition Howard was in.

Hippie Rehab, Hot-Ianta, and the Broken Tractor

If I told you that Howard survived the crash, stopped drinking, and moved into the house in Clearwater with us, you'd probably think David's decided to write a bad novel, but, well, that's kinda how it happened. Howard was bruised and battered but his injuries proved to be relatively minor, though he sports a scar in the middle of his forehead from that day to this. The car looked like a crushed beer can that nobody could have climbed out alive from, and the only place on it that wasn't totally demolished was the driver's seat where he'd been sitting—it was nothing less than a miracle that he was alive.

After he was released from the hospital, he was pretty shaky and he swears that he picked tiny slivers of windshield glass from his forehead for a few years after the accident. Since the doctors told him not to go back to work for a couple of months, he decided to recuperate at our house in Clearwater.

The crash had got him thinking about his drinking and reasons he should try to slow it down. He'd become accustomed to buying cattle all day, having drinks and dinner with the clients, and carousing all night. Then he'd repeat the process the next day. It was the cattle buyers' lifestyle, kind of like the hardcore musician routine we'd started to fall into playing the clubs. I guess you could call them work-related habits.

Howard had smoked marijuana with us before, but mostly he drank. Now that he was sober, he gradually started smoking a little more pot with us and found it relieved some of the pain of his car crash. As a matter of fact, Howard sort of takes credit for discovering medical marijuana and since that was years before doctors started recommending it, who's gonna argue with him? He also credits pot with helping him break his addiction to alcohol (not that *we're* recommending anything—we're just telling you how it happened). During this time, he also started thinking about becoming a veterinarian.

While Howard was rehabilitating at our house, we started jammin' on our acoustic guitars, just singing some old songs we knew, then we started driving up to the farm to rehearse in the shack with the whole band. Everything sounded real good to us, and Howard decided to put his adulthood on hold for a while. He even enrolled in some classes at St. Pete Jr. College, but as you can probably imagine from what you've read so far, we all were becoming less and less focused on college and the more music we started to play, the more we started to stray. It seemed like now, after every band meeting (and I use the word "meeting" loosely), we came to the conclusion that we were going to have to move some place where we could get more gigs. We were also beginning to realize that the band was becoming interested in developing its own sound.

We even started playing a few original songs we wrote, but we always ended up going back to learning the hits so we could work. During this period of transition, the hardest thing we had to do was tell our folks we were dropping out of college and moving farther away from home to make a living as professional musicians. Somebody had run across this agency in Atlanta, The Rogers Agency, and we decided to pull up stakes and move up there. I think it's safe to say that nobody from Darby, Florida, had ever made a living playing music. Homer loved the frolics and dances he grew up playing, but he didn't have any illusions that he could do it full time and bring home the groceries.

I dreaded telling them about the move because I didn't want to disappoint them. They were proud that I was going to college, even if it *was* just junior college. I was elated that Howard was singing with us now, but I really dreaded saying to Homer and Frances, "Howard's going, too."

Let's flash back a moment—see, when I was about fourteen, I was messing around driving Homer's tractor, singing Roger Miller songs at the top of my lungs. We always sang on the tractor, and Howard claims it's one of the reasons he was able to sing in public because he had to sing loud to hear himself above the old Massey Ferguson tractor motor. Anyway, I ran it into a wild persimmon tree and broke it in two, and no, I don't mean the tree. I mean I literally broke the tractor half in two, cracked the block right down the middle and left two large hunks of metal just lying there with me still in the seat hanging on to the steering wheel as it fell to the ground. When Homer saw it, all he said was, "Boy, what else are you gonna try?" That's probably what he was thinking when I told him the band's moving to Atlanta.

I'm sure they wanted to ask Howard why he wanted to move with us, when he was married and had a good job he could go back to. They probably wanted to ask me when was I gonna finish college and why we couldn't just keep performing at the strip clubs in Tampa and St. Pete.

But our parents did not yell at us about dropping out or how we were gonna survive in the big city. Frances looked at us and said what she always said in times like these: "Y'all come from good stock. Be careful and remember how you were raised." Most people we tell about moving to Atlanta usually ask us why we didn't move to Nashville, since it was and still is the Mecca for country music. Fact is, musically our band didn't fit in anywhere, something that used to bother us until we learned to stop worrying and just enjoy it.

Nashville would have been great, but even though we were country boys, they would have no doubt considered us a rock and roll band at the time. We had a drummer that smacked the drums hard instead of just keeping time on the rim, and our set list went from Hank to Hendrix and from Buck to The Beatles. This was an era when Creedence Clearwater Revival was considered rock and roll and was never played on country radio.

We had been considering a name change for a while and were nervous about it after our last experience. After some heated brainstorming sessions, we decided to rename the band Jericho. As it turned out, it was a good name. It was short and easy to remember, and I guess anything would have worked better than The Heterogeneous Grouping. Still, we resisted the urge to paint the name in big purple letters on any future vehicles. So we packed up Howard's green Opel Kadett, which he had bought after totaling the Impala under the chicken truck. We dubbed his new car "the Jackal" because of its curious shape that had been altered slightly by another minor wreck he had in Clearwater before we moved.

The Jackal had a small but musically legitimate collection of eight-tracks consisting of Aretha Franklin; Crosby, Stills & Nash; Merle Haggard, and The Beatles. Howard, our bass player, Mark, and I drove to Atlanta to meet with the new booking agency and find a place to live. We found a red brick house in Sandy Springs, Georgia, which was still a small suburb in the late '60s, early '70s. The area had old frame homes with hillbilly residents on one side and a new housing development with more affluent folks just up the road on the other side. We discovered immediately that the hillbillies made their own moonshine and the kids of upper middle class suburbia were dealing pot, acid, THC, mescaline, and all the other popular drugs of the moment.

Howard posed as a cattle buyer to rent the house—not much of a cover, but he was the only one old enough to sign the rental papers, and we knew they wouldn't rent to a band of long hairs. Howard put on his boots and his best cattle buyer clothes and told them his name was Buck Bellamy and for the next six months we were the proud renters of a three-bedroom, red Georgia brick home with a den, a kitchen, and best of all, a basement to set up our band gear and rehearse in. We were far enough away from our neighbors that playing a little music shouldn't have been a problem. Once the paperwork on the house was done, I flew home and rented a U-Haul trailer, hooked it on the back of Frances's baby blue Ford Galaxy, and loaded our band gear, a couple of beds, our drummer, and our guitar player. We headed the car toward the land of Joe South, tall pine trees, and red clay.

3
What Was Going Down
Moonshine in the Washing Machine, Homer and Frances, and The Allman Brothers

DAVID: Atlanta, like so many cities of this era, was in the grip of hippiedom when we arrived. Peachtree Street and 10th Street was the southern answer to San Francisco's Haight-Ashbury. The street undulated with freaks, musicians, Hare Krishnas, bikers, and hookers every hour of every day—or as we would say in today's world of instant vocabulary improvement, 24/7. There were head shops, crash houses, coffeehouses, bars, and juke joints to suit every hippie taste. We started hanging out there frequenting some of the establishments such as The Bottom of the Barrel, where we saw Brewer and Shipley play occasionally before they had their hit song "One Toke Over The Line."

Our house was on a street called Dunwoody Place, a little ways north of downtown Atlanta, and the vibe there was a little different from that of Peachtree and 10th Street. Our hillbilly neighbors in the holler made moonshine in their washing machine and dropped by occasionally just to be neighborly. They'd bring a jar of the clear liquor to enjoy and share

61

while they watched us rehearse. The kids of the wealthier families from the subdivision found out that we were a band and came over to get us high and listen to us jam. Our house soon became a cultural crossroads where people drinking white lightning from a Mason jar could swap a sip for a hit from the joint of a young hippie wannabe. Howard went to the local animal shelter and got us a bulldog. We named him Belew and spent our spare time playing Frisbee with him in the front yard while we waited for the booking agency to find us some work.

We tried to become locals but blending in wasn't that easy; we just didn't look like the hillbillies or the upper middle class neighbors. To be truthful, we stuck out like a handful of sore thumbs. Less than a week after we moved in, our landlady walked into the basement unannounced and caught us rocking out. She figured out real fast that Howard was no longer a cattle buyer when she saw him singing "Travelin' Band" and playing the conga drum.

When she opened the door, our bulldog ran in dragging an animal carcass. Now in addition to our not being cattle buyers, we were in violation of the no pets rule. Nevertheless, the landlady turned out to be pretty cool. She had a friend who was in show business (if you consider a chimp act show business). She actually kind of fancied the fact that we were a band and made dinner for us at her house. Her friend came over and we got to see his chimp do his whole act in her living room.

The first gig we did in Atlanta didn't come from our booking agency. The kids from the suburbs who hung out at our house convinced their parents to pay us a couple of hundred bucks to play a party by their clubhouse swimming pool. It wasn't the kind of gig we were hoping for, but we figured it would buy gas, grass, and groceries while we waited for the big gigs to come pouring in.

We set our gear up by the pool, commenced to play, and were in the middle of our second set when the police raided the party and hauled all the rich kids away in a paddy wagon right in front of our eyes. One minute there were a couple of hundred kids swimming, dancing, and getting high, and then there was nobody left except the band and one guy sitting on the end of the diving board high as a kite, laughing his fool head off. Needless to say, we packed up and got the hell outta there.

We'd only been in town a little while when we heard that The Allman Brothers were jamming on Sunday afternoons in Piedmont Park. This was close to the time their first album was released, and seeing them in that setting in that era was something to behold. We'd heard Greg and Duane play at the pier in Daytona when they were still called The Allman Joys, but the band had transformed into a major tour de force that roared like a freight train with the blues. The Allmans played Piedmont Park almost every Sunday afternoon in the summer of 1969. Hippies sat in meditative positions while would-be wood nymphs danced around freeform. The smell of burning grass from passing joints was everywhere. The Hare Krishnas handed out slices of watermelon and portions of brown rice. It was a musical and cultural moment that remains frozen in time for those of us who were there.

We crossed paths with a lot of great singer/songwriters who were part of the Atlanta scene in those days. Mylon LeFevre, related to the great gospel group The LeFevres, was in the middle of recording a gospel rock album when we met him. We also met Tommy Roe and Billy Joe Royal, who became our good friends. Joe South was living in Roswell at the time. Joe's songs hit us harder than anybody's because they had the rock and country roots we could relate to, and Joe's lyrics are as strong today as when he wrote them. We've always considered him one of the greatest songwriters ever.

Billy Joe Royal told us a story once about him and Joe South that I don't think he'd mind me sharing. Billy Joe had a smash hit on a song Joe wrote called "Down In The Boondocks." And while they were driving to Nashville from Atlanta together, Joe kept playing his guitar and singing a new song, saying, "Billy Joe, I think you oughta cut this song. I think it's a hit." After hearing the song about as many times as he cared to, Billy Joe finally turned to Joe, who was sitting in the back seat, and said, "Joe, I just don't like that song. Pitch it to somebody else."

So Billy Joe did not get to record "I Never Promised You A Rose Garden," but Lynn Anderson did, and her version sold millions of records and made the song Billy Joe didn't like song of the year.

Frances and Homer drove to Atlanta to check on us after we'd been living there for a few months. The gigs had not come rolling in like we'd thought they would, but we had been able to pick up a few parties around town and the agency was still promising that they'd get us work. We didn't want our parents to know how flat broke we really were, but it wasn't hard to figure out. In true form, when Frances and Homer arrived, they brought huge cans and boxes of nonperishable foods—rice, biscuit mix, clam chowder, and canned hams, along with extra pots and pans to stock our kitchen. Frances cooked a lot while they were there and Homer fried chicken for us, and the whole band got to eat good for a few days. It was a far cry from the meager nourishment we'd been living on that included swamp rabbits we shot in the woods near our house to make our signature dish, swamp rabbit and rice.

During our parents' visit we heard that The Allman Brothers were playing in the park again the following Sunday, so without a thought we told Homer and Frances, "You gotta hear this band." You're probably thinking, *Didn't you learn from the time before when you invited them to the strip club for their anniversary?* Let me tell you, if the strip club was an eye opener, Piedmont Park was a mind blower.

We parked the car a long way from the park and walked down trails and sidewalks, trying to part the hippie/zombie-like bodies tripping up and down the streets. When we walked into the park, we ran into half-naked girls dancing imaginary ballets with wreaths on their heads made of weeping willow branches they'd cut and woven in the park. There were any number of gyrating acts: jugglers, vendors, and belly dancers performing along a path lined with dealers offering the usual array of street drugs. We finally made it to the pavilion where the Allmans were already in mid-jam—what a relief it was for us to just kick back and listen. Greg's voice sounded like a ninety-year-old black man as he started singing:

Sometimes I feel

Like I've been tied to the whipping post

Duane's slide guitar had this beautiful melodic tone that was honey sweet but at the same time had an edgy squeal like somebody was pulling barbed wire out of a hog's ass. As the music surrounded the massive crowd, we sat on the green summer grass in the middle of this surreal psychedelic scene and of course some hippie kid passed Homer a joint, and without being fazed in the slightest, Homer said, "Son, I don't think I need any of that right now," and passed the joint to someone else. After a few more joints came his way it began to get funny; Homer just kept taking them and passing them on down the line. Howard and I were gettin' kind of nervous since it had been our idea to immerse Frances and Homer in this frantic freak show. We figured that Frances was going to lean over at any moment and say, "We're loading up and heading back to Darby and getting y'all out of this hippie shit!"

But between Homer passing joints and the Allmans jamming, they soon narrowed the generation gap with a lot of laughter and the day became about just hanging out with the parents we loved so dearly and listening to good music. Laughter and music, once again, became our common thread. Later that day as we were riding back to Sandy Springs, Homer, who was always one to understate things, said, "That boy can sure bottleneck that guitar!"

The Alarm Clock, Jimmy Carter, and Quaaludes

We finally got a call from the Rogers Agency saying they had us some club bookings in Savannah, Charleston, and St. Simons Island. The timing couldn't have been better because the Dunwoody Place house in Sandy Springs, Georgia, was getting hotter than the Clearwater beach house had been. Some of the band now had girlfriends who lived with their parents in the new subdivision just up the road from our house, and some of those young ladies started slipping out of their bedrooms when Mom and Dad weren't looking and staying over at our house. This resulted in more than one set of parents beating on our door in the middle of the night looking for their daughters.

Beside the friendly country families living close by, there was a handful of real hard-ass rednecks who didn't like us because we were long hairs. Funny how that works. Just a few years later, the fashions had changed and they were wearing *their* hair long, with mustaches and even beards, but this was *now* so our long hair just made them hate us. A group of these upstanding citizens decided to try and scare us out of the neighborhood one evening, bringing their car to a halt on the street in front of our house. Four or five of them piled out and walked toward our house while the driver stayed in the car and pulled it down the road a ways to wait for them.

We'd been rehearsing all afternoon in the basement and were vegging out, watching TV, and making plans for our upcoming road gigs. Howard was in his bedroom when he heard the car stop and saw the trespassers walking across the lawn toward our front door. As they approached our front steps, one of them yelled out, "This is where them fuckin' hippies live!" That was all they had time to say before Howard reached under his bed and pulled out a snub-nosed .38-caliber pistol he had stuck away for just such emergencies and fired a couple of shots through the window screen, placing the bullets in the ground just a few feet away from where they stood.

It might as well have been a starter pistol at an Olympic race. Them boys commenced to running, yelling, cussing, falling over each other, and generally heading in every direction trying to get out of our front yard. Two of them bumped heads and got their legs tangled as they rolled around on the ground, frantically trying to break free of one another. The moment they separated, both of them broke into a sprint and passed the other runners.

Once they were near the street, they began waving to their buddy in the getaway car to pick them up pronto. The car hooked a U-turn to pick up the rattled rednecks while we all ran into the bedroom to see if Howard was okay. He pulled back the curtains to show us where he'd fired the

.38 through the window screen and found that one of the bullets went right through his alarm clock that was sitting on the window sill. The second hand was still sweeping around and the time was still correct; however, there was a hole the size of a quarter that you could see daylight through. Never again did we hear from the wild bunch who staggered on our lawn drunk that night, but I'd be willing to bet that Howard had forever changed their opinions about peace-loving hippies.

Something was always stirring at the Dunwoody Place house. From the day we moved in, things seemed to happen rapid fire. One of the most bizarre things occurred while we were hitchhiking back from Piedmont Park, where we'd spent the day hanging out. We usually caught a ride home with a carload of stoners heading out of town, but this night a nice-looking sedan pulled over on the shoulder of the road and stopped for us. We jumped in the car, excited that we'd got a cushy ride so easy.

The driver asked us where to and we directed him toward Sandy Springs. He hit the gas and headed in the right direction. The other guy in the car was a nice man with a distinct southern drawl. "Are you boys Georgia residents?" he asked.

"No, sir, we're from Florida; we're in a band called Jericho, living here trying to find some gigs."

He introduced himself, we shook hands, then he said, "I'm running for governor of the great state of Georgia." And he gave us what amounted to a pitch as he asked us how old we were and told us that eighteen-year-olds in Georgia would soon have voting rights. He told us how we could change our resident status after living in Georgia for a while as we rode along, chatting away during the twenty-minute drive. We were impressed with how conservative he was in his speech, dress, and demeanor, yet he still seemed to be totally at ease and enjoying his conversation with a group of scruffy musicians.

His driver left us off by a convenience store near the main road through Sandy Springs. We thanked both of them and got out and assured him we'd check into becoming residents. A short while later, we started seeing campaign billboards with his picture on them and soon we started seeing his political ads on TV. He became governor of Georgia in January of 1971 and a few years after he was governor, he ran for, well, you probably remember President Jimmy Carter.

The pills the doctor prescribed for Howard after his collision with the chicken truck had gone mostly unused. Smoking a little pot was usually all he needed to help ease his pain, but one day he happened to mention that the pills gave him a pretty good buzz. We didn't think too much about that until one night when we discovered we were a little low on weed, so we all decided to try them. We started out innocently enough. We took one Quaalude and one Librium. Then we discovered that two Quaaludes were better than one and so on until someone in the group observed that our living room could be transformed into a wrestling arena.

We moved all the chairs, couches, rugs, lamps—everything—into the den and divided the band into tag team wrestling teams. You know that kid's toy Stretch Armstrong—that's kind of how we felt doing Quaaludes: rubbery, stretchy, like you can bounce off walls. Of course those feelings aren't real, and they can set you up for some nasty outcomes.

The drug can leave your brain and your tongue feeling thick and numb and generally awful when the effects wear off. We must have been really numb because we failed to pull the curtains on the big plate glass window in the living room, where all the action would be taking place. The entire band ended up wrestling in front of the window in their underwear for what seemed like hours. Everybody was so zonked that time felt like it had been suspended, but when the wrestling finally wore us out, I looked out the window and saw three cop cars full of uniforms sitting at the little country church across the street from our house, watching us.

The Methodist Preacher, the U-Haul Van, and the Girl in the Attic

Our plans to get out of town came just in time. It seemed like everybody was on our tails. A Methodist preacher from one of the community churches approached us at a party one night and told us that we were under surveillance by the police. I felt like saying, "No shit, Sherlock," but him being a preacher and all I decided not to. Besides, some of Homer's side of the family were Methodist.

It was just a few days before we were heading down to Savannah, then up to Charleston, South Carolina, and on to St. Simons Island. The trip presented problems because since we'd sold the Heterogeneous Grouping van back in Florida, we had no way to haul our equipment. We had the Jackal (the Opel Kadett) to haul us, but we were about all she could carry, so we rented a U-Haul van from the gas station up the road near Roswell, Georgia. It was an innocent transaction made with a sincere intention to return it as soon as we got back to town.

So there we were, pretty much ready to strike out on our biggest club tour since we'd moved to Georgia to become professional. The Jackal was gassed up, and we'd rehearsed five sets of songs that ran the gamut of popular music. Oh yeah, one little thing I failed to mention: a few days prior to closing down the house and packing up for the club gigs, three girls from the subdivision decided to run away from home and made it as far as our house. None of them were girlfriends of the band, just friends of friends we met, so we put them up and explained to them that we were leaving town soon and they'd have to find someplace else to stay before we left.

You know that old Brook Benton hit, "A Rainy Night In Georgia." Well, we saw it come to life on the evening before we hit the road for our big Southeast tour. While we packed and the three runaways tried to secure another place to crash, it began to rain so hard that the red clay washed down the hills and ran through the streets into streams and then into the rivers. It looked like the whole world was turning burnt orange.

We were loading the van. Everybody was packing suitcases and we'd arranged to leave our bulldog, Belew, with our neighbors the next day before leaving. But of course on this night, while the deluge soaked every inch of earth just a few hours before we planned to be heading out, the police decided to raid our house and look for the girls.

Mark and I had packed early and left the house to hitchhike into Atlanta to catch The Who at the Omni. Meanwhile, Howard and the rest of the band had decided to stay home and finish getting things ready for the trip. A kid from the subdivision got wind of the pending raid and tried to make a warning call to us, but he was too late; there were already three cars pulling into our driveway. One car carried the parents and relatives of a couple of the girls. The other two were police cars. Two of the girls ran down the back steps to the band room basement. There was a door down there out the back, but the rain was pounding so hard that the backyard was washing away into the holler, so there was no way out for the fleeing girls.

The police pushed the door in before anybody could open it and, as always, Belew ran in to greet them, wet, dripping, and shaking water everywhere. In fact, the police, the parents, the bulldog, and everything else in the house were soaking wet.

They asked whose house it was. Howard told them he rented that house. They immediately handcuffed him to the arms of one of the living room chairs then ran off toward the back of the house to see who or what else they could find. What they found in the hallway heading toward the bedrooms did not help things for anybody. Our skinny guitar player was standing under a small square hole in the ceiling that opened up to the attic. A heavyset, underage girl was on his shoulders with her legs wrapped around his neck in a scissor hold, hanging on while his hands were beneath her backside, trying to give her a boost up into the attic so that she could at least try to hide. He was swaying under the weight of the hefty hippie girl. The top half of her was already in the attic but the bottom half was too big to fit through the small opening.

The police grabbed the guitar player, then brought the girl down, slowly, to the floor. Our drummer brought the other two girls up from the basement about that time, realizing their chances of escape had about shrunk to zero. One of the girls' mothers was demanding that the police arrest everybody in the house. Howard, of course, would be in a whole heap of trouble because he was the only one of us who was more than twenty-one years old.

As if there wasn't enough excitement in our little world, Mark and I came stumbling in earlier than expected. We had never quite made it to see The Who because the merry band of pranksters we hitched into town with were too high to find downtown Atlanta. We tried a couple of times to get out and find another ride but the easiest ride we found brought us back home. We walked in to find Howard cuffed to a chair and our drummer and guitar player squashed together on the couch with the three girls, waiting to see what the police were going to do with them.

At that moment, I was pretty sure that life as we knew it was over. The police told us to sit down near the band and the runaways. We obeyed and waited for doom to descend. The only thing I can think of that kept us from being arrested and taken to jail was that Frances and Homer must have spent every day and night praying for us while we were living in Atlanta.

One of the runaways had an older sister who came in with her husband and family members when the police raided our house. While Howard sat there cuffed to the furniture, he started talking to the brother-in-law of the runaway about the situation. The brother-in-law was a level-headed guy and soon figured out that we had just given the girls someplace to stay, and no harm had come to them. He was able to calm down the irate mother, who soon realized how happy she was that her daughter had not been in mortal danger. Then the brother-in-law talked the parents into not pressing charges. As the police, the parents, the children, and our wet bulldog gradually exited the house, it began to occur to us that by some miracle we still had a future in this world. Do you know what a huge, collective sigh of relief sounds like? I do.

None of us got any sleep that night. After retelling the story to each other about fifty times, it was sunrise and then we didn't waste any time leaving. We locked up the house and headed to the U-Haul van, started it up, and began to run it up the slope from our backyard to the street. Only one problem: the previous night's deluge had left the ground under the heavily loaded van so slippery that the van would not climb the hill. The red clay was like oil and the tires found no traction. As young guys, we naturally figured that a little muscle power would solve everything, so we started pushing it up the hill. As the van moved forward, I stepped in the same hole we'd just pushed the van out of. We lost our hold on the van, and the rear right tire rolled backwards over my right knee. It happened so quickly it was over before I could even let out a scream. Fueled by panic, I was able to move out of the way before the front tire followed the rear tire over my knee.

Everybody ran to me to see if I was okay. There wasn't much pain—not yet—so I decided everything would be fine, we should just go ahead and get the van unstuck and head out. We ended up having to unload all the gear from the van, but we finally got it up the hill. We reloaded the equipment, dropped our wet, smelly bulldog off at the neighbors' house and—finally—we were off.

An Unexpected Lap Dance, The Hoof 'n' Horn #3, and the Earth Mothers

My knee started to swell about fifty miles outside of town, and by the time we reached Savannah it had a knot on it the size of a softball. Once we set the equipment up at the club, it had become obvious that I needed to see a doctor.

I was not ready to have the fluid drained off my knee through a six-inch needle, but then nobody asked me, the doctor told me; the pain was intense, and the procedure left me weak as a newborn kitten. Howard took me back to the hotel to rest and gather my strength for the five sets we had to play that night.

Ever since the tag-team wrestling match in front of the big picture window with the police looking on, the band's Quaalude habit had gotten worse and worse. The guys were resourceful and soon discovered that if you took the empty bottle with the prescription label on it to most any drug store, they would refill it for you. There was no computer network at the time, and the pharmacies usually didn't bother to call back to the doctor's office. This gave everybody access to lots of Quaaludes, since all you had to do was drive from one drug store to the next, and in most cases they'd just keep on handing you a new bottle. I guess I don't need to emphasize that this was not a good thing.

The club we were playing that night in Savannah turned out to be an old church that had been converted to a biker bar. The bartender loaned me a stool to sit on to play organ because the shots I had got in my knee to kill the pain had worn off and I felt a whole lot better when I sat down. I took a couple of pain pills and limped onstage. We played two or three sets that felt pretty good. People were dancing and playing pool. A few even applauded for us.

We'd just started one of the later sets in the evening when a girl climbed onto a pool table off to the right side of the stage and unbuttoned the long coat she was wearing.

She had nothing on underneath the long coat.

The whole club immediately turned its attention toward the new attraction. Two bouncers left their posts at the front door and broke into a full run, hoping to catch her and cover her up. She jumped off the pool table before they could get their hands on her and ran up the short staircase that led precisely to where I was sitting on the stool behind the organ. All the guys in the band turned their heads in my direction as she made a little leap and her backside landed, hard, right down on my knee—the sore one, of course. Agony radiated up my leg, but the band played on. The audience was cheering like she and my knee were part of the show as the bouncers made their way onto the stage and pulled her kicking and screaming out of my lap. They wrestled her down the stage stairs and out the back door, still trying to cover her with the coat she stripped off. My knee throbbed in rhythm to the song we were playing as the episode wound to a close and the door slammed shut behind the naked girl and the bouncers. For a few moments, as the pain careened through my body like an angry eighteen-wheeler, I wanted to faint, I really did. I just didn't know how. After the show ended, we found out she was a dancer who was dating the club owner. She had got wind of him cheating on her and decided to get him busted for nudity in his club so he'd lose his liquor license.

We finished the weekend gig in Savannah and threw a pretty wild party back at the hotel. As Frances would have put it, "It was becoming plain as the nose on your face" that the drug use was getting out of hand. You know it's bad when Howard and I are the ones starting to worry that other people are getting too high too often.

The hotel was really happy when we left and took the gang of partying bikers with us. We headed for Charleston, South Carolina, to do a week at the Hoof 'n' Horn #3. We took the stage at 11:30 every night and played sets till 7:00 a.m. The clientele consisted mostly of sailors on leave from their ships in Charleston Harbor and hookers trying to make a buck off them. As always, we were low on money, so when we saw a sign out front of a cheap hotel near the club that read "air conditioning," we pulled in and got a room.

Their definition of air conditioning was a hole cut in the ceiling to let the fresh air in. It also let in the rain and the thick Charleston humidity. The grueling club schedule, plus the five guys crowded into one stuffy little room, made that week the kind of negative experience that makes bands want to break up, but we were made of tougher stuff.

Homer and Frances decided to drive up to Charleston to check on us. After their visits to the strip club and Piedmont Park, we had become a little gun-shy about inviting them to our shows. We wanted to convince them that we were a success as a band, but the venues spoke for themselves—and for us. We were hanging on to our chosen profession by our fingernails.

The first thing they did when they got to Charleston was fill us full of home-style nourishment. Frances brought a basket full of grandmother's cinnamon rolls and we devoured them. They were concerned about our health and wellbeing because everybody was looking kind of frail and thin, but they still didn't try to discourage us from the course we'd taken. They suggested that I come home for a few days to let Dr. Stanfield check out my knee, but we were heading to St. Simons Island after Charleston so I lied and told them it didn't hurt anymore.

By the time they got to the club that evening, the Hoof 'n' Horn #3 was already jumpin' and jivin'. The sailors were in town and their government checks had been cashed. Homer got up during one of our sets and went to the men's room. As he stood in front of the urinal, a "lady" walked in and hiked up her dress and proceeded to pee in the urinal next to him. Of course he'd never seen a transvestite/cross-dresser or whatever he/she was who used the restroom facility beside him, but as we came off the stage for a break, he and Frances were still holding their sides in nervous mirth trying to figure the whole thing out. Homer finally responded with a matter-of-fact "Boys, I think I've seen everything now." At breakfast the next morning, we were all still laughing over Homer's latest new-world discovery. Then the folks headed back to Darby and we moved on to St. Simons, just off the coast a little ways from Brunswick, Georgia.

The rental agreement on our U-Haul was now overdue. They wouldn't rent it to us long term, so we sort of continued on our terms, taking it for as long as they'd let us have it and keeping it as long as we needed it. One other small problem: the van was falling apart. We went down the road with it sputtering and spitting and it ran hot constantly. Howard drove the van and I took over driving the Jackal because we were worried that if we let anyone else drive, our little caravan might dissolve in a Quaalude crash.

The motor for the van sat inside the cab between the driver and passenger seats. You just had to lift a metal cover to get to it. Mark rode with Howard in the van and they stopped about every twenty miles, scooped up some rainwater from the ditches, and poured it into the radiator to cool it down enough to continue the journey. We made it to St. Simons anyway.

The first night of the gig in St. Simons, the guys met a couple of hippie chicks that we called the "earth mothers." They lived in a single wide trailer and invited us to stay with them. In those days, we never turned down an opportunity to save a little money so we agreed, and we all moved in. Their place was decorated in early hippie house trailer motif and after all this time I don't think I'm capable of a more specific description than that. Neither of them worked and they always had weed, but how they got by was none of our business, so we did not inquire. They had a cat that they fed LSD. The poor thing drug his back legs and looked into our eyes like he could read our deepest thoughts—or so we thought.

In a nutshell, this gig was starting to look even crazier than the other two. The club was a "skull orchard," the band was taking more 'ludes than ever, and the van finally broke down completely in the earth mothers' driveway and we'd only been there a day.

Howard and Mark decided that they could probably fix the van but would have to disassemble most of the motor in the process. They ripped parts out and bought parts to put back in, but as they reassembled it, they found that they had cans full of screws, nuts, and bolts left over. When they finished their repair job, the van motor started up but it didn't have much power. Still, we figured it would get us back to Atlanta if we took it slow.

After the van was fixed, we started spending our days down at the beach because the mobile home was obviously a hot spot in town and even if the rent was cheap, it was a little scary when the cops cruised by every couple of hours. Howard and I had been laying out in the sand most of the first morning when I discovered I was hungry and walked a few blocks toward town to get a snack. As I approached a little burger joint, a couple of kids came up to me and asked me if I'd buy them something from the liquor store down the street. I didn't see any harm in trying, they seemed like nice kids, so I took their money and walked into the liquor store and bought a fifth of Jim Beam and a bottle of Smirnoff vodka for them.

The guy in the store didn't say anything to me except thanks when he gave me the change back. I walked out the store and down the block a ways to where the kids waited and gave them their liquor. They told me to keep the change and I smiled all the way to the burger joint. Then as I was walking back to the beach, a police car pulled up beside me; two cops got out and told me I was under arrest. They handcuffed me and put me in the cage in the back of the police car.

I asked them what I did and they said they'd caught some underage kids with liquor and I fit their description of the person who bought it for them. I may have been living the hippie life but at that moment I mustered up all the good ol' boy knowledge I'd ever had to ask them if they would be kind enough to drive down to the beach and let me tell my brother before they took me to jail. They balked at first but I convinced them that he was only a couple of blocks away and I would have to call him anyway to come bail me out.

As the police car turned onto the white sand of St. Simons Beach, I could see Howard lying out sunning just a little ways ahead. As we got closer, I asked them to slow down and pointed him out. The policeman on the passenger side rolled down his window and said, "Are you Howard Bellamy?" Howard sat up and turned around and saw me sitting in the cage of the cop car.

"What did he do?" Howard asked.

"He's under arrest for buying alcohol for minors," said the cop.

Howard came back instantly with the perfect, magical phrase. "He *is* a minor," he answered.

The cops couldn't believe it. They pulled me out of the cage, went though my wallet, and found that I wasn't twenty-one. Now they had a real dilemma. The liquor store owner was a prominent businessman and he was now at fault for not asking for my ID.

We got a good ass chewing from the St. Simons Island Police Department for about the next hour. Finally they asked us how much longer we'd be on the island, and we assured them the gig would be over in a few more days and we'd be outta there. They released me in Howard's custody and they told him I'd better not get into any more trouble, or else. We headed back to the mobile home with the psychedelic cat and the tie-dyed earth mothers to see if we could lay low just long enough to finish the gig, get paid, and leave town without going to jail.

The gig in St. Simons was tough. The band was in bad shape and the clientele was mainly bored guys on vacation who managed to sneak out of the beach resorts and hotels to get away from their wives and kids for a few hours. Pitiful, desperate women sat on stools lining the bar, drinking for free off the liquor tabs paid for by the unhappy husbands. The whole place was pathetic and none of the patrons requested or seemed to care what songs we played. They appeared content to drink and tell lies to the waitresses and the barflies.

On our last day on the island, the earth mothers insisted that we go to the park and have a picnic. One of them had a crush on our guitar player so we accompanied them to the park, which, it turned out, was as good a place as any to chill and stay out of sight from the local police. Back at the mobile home, as we dressed for the gig, earth mother #2 walked out of the bathroom with big red blotches of rash all over her arms, face, and legs. At the park that afternoon, she'd picked some branches and vines to weave into a wreath to adorn her head. Among the indigenous plants she'd picked in the park was poison ivy, and she was now covered everywhere in spots. There was still a little time before we had to leave her for the club, so we jumped in the Jackal and raced down to the drugstore for calamine lotion.

We played the last few sets in this godforsaken club without incident and headed back to the mobile home to work on our exit. The would-be hippie goddess with the poison ivy itch was pacing around moaning, groaning, and complaining that her skin was crawling. I couldn't help but think that maybe it was karma paying her back for the acid trips she sent her poor little cat on.

We wanted to leave St. Simon's like *now*, but we decided we'd better wait till morning. There was no guarantee that the van was gonna make the long run back to Atlanta, and since it may have been reported as a stolen vehicle by now, we figured it would be easier to find gas stations or repair shops during the day without drawing attention from the police. Anyway, now that the gig was over, the band was ready to party. We'd all survived a hell of a week. Relationships were changing within the band because Howard and I had become openly critical of what we considered Quaalude abuse by the others. Hard feelings were beginning to brew and there was no way around it. We were all guilty of getting high but before we'd never let it get in the way of performing. Now we sensed an apathetic attitude about the music, which we resented, and it was obvious that the Quaalude use had taken on an addictive quality because people were getting very annoyed when they didn't get their little pills.

Boys, Don't Ever Come Back to Georgia

So much for trying to lie low for the evening. We got wind that The Allman Brothers were playing at a prom that evening on Jekyll Island, and that was enough to throw a monkey wrench into any good intentions we may have had. Jekyll was just a little north of us and was even smaller than St. Simons. Howard and I decided to drive the Jackal over to Jekyll to check it out, since we weren't leaving till the following morning. Some of the band rode over with the earth mothers. When we arrived, sure enough we found a high school gym full of kids at their prom with The Allman Brothers at the far end of that boomy cavern of a gym, jammin' away.

It wasn't easy for us to blend in with the prom crowd, but there were other gate-crashers and nobody was checking too close. We caught the last hour of the Allmans's prom set. The band's image was a stark contrast in their undershirts and jeans to the kids in their prom dresses and rented tuxes. Half-empty Ripple wine bottles sat on the amplifiers while the whole gymnasium reverberated with slide guitars, drums, percussion, and B3 organ. Some of the band's road crew spotted us and came over to tell us they had some hashish. A minute later, we had it in our hands with no way to smoke it, so we did the only logical thing we could think of: we ate it.

I guess we got caught up in the whole event—the wild deer bouncing across the road as we drove onto Jekyll Island, the sound of the best southern rock band in the world echoing off the walls of a high school gym, the salt air blowing in from the Atlantic Ocean—to tell the truth, we didn't need any excuse, we just ate the hash and now the Allmans were winding down their set just as we were taking off. We talked to the band and the crew for a little while as they loaded up and then we made our way to the Jackal and drove over to the beach and sat on the sand shining white in the moonlight among the sea grapes and driftwood, waiting to level out a little. The trouble was, our idea of leveling out wasn't the same as the police. We got pulled over as we drove off the beach and onto the road to make our way back to St. Simons.

The cop requested that we get out of the car and lean against the hood while he frisked us. We got out okay; it was the leaning on the hood that was hard. I kept sliding off the hood and onto the ground. Howard wasn't doing much better.

"What y'all been drinkin'?" the cop asked.

"Nothin'," Howard answered, which was the stone cold truth. We explained to the cop the best we could about our gig on St. Simons Island and that we were leaving in the morning. The cop listened, then replied, "It *is* morning, boys." He talked a lot like Jackie Gleason's character in *Cannonball Run.*

He held us there while he tried to figure out what we were high on and explained to us that the sheriff in Brunswick and the local police on St. Simons were all friends of his and if he let us go and we didn't leave town, they'd find out all about it. We assured him that we were on our way out of town and got in the Jackal and crept up the road slowly trying to hold the car between the lines. Our slow pace made the short distance back to the mobile home seem a lot longer, which it was. Some of the band was just getting in. Others were still asleep. We finished loading up the van and woke up the sleeping band members, left the earth mothers a thank you note, and headed across the bridge toward Brunswick on a hot, humid morning.

Howard drove the van with Mark riding shotgun. I was creeping behind them in the Jackal, with Tom and Paul both asleep in the back seat. Just before we got across the causeway leading back to the mainland, we saw the red lights flashing; it was the cops who busted me near the beach for buying the booze. We pulled over as carefully as we could and prayed for a miracle. Since Howard had signed for the van, and since the folks we rented it from hadn't seen it since long after the lease expired, he figured he was headed for jail for stealing the van.

"Where y'all from?" was all the cop said when he walked up.

"We're from Florida, but we're headin' for Atlanta," we began, but before we could finish explaining, he said, "I want you boys to head toward Florida and never come back to the state of Georgia again."

4
The Prodigal Sons Return
Don't It Make You Wanna Go Home
(Apologies to Joe South)

DAVID: By the time we got back to Atlanta, we weren't really a band anymore. Everybody was mad at Howard because he'd let his Quaalude prescription expire to keep the band from getting too strung out. Nobody hung together anymore and rehearsals in the basement at Dunwoody Place ground to a halt. I'd seen band members forced to quit back in the days of The Accidents because of jealous girlfriends, but this was the first time I'd seen how drugs could take priority over the music that once bonded us so closely together.

Gradually everybody started drifting apart. We learned that a couple of guys hitched rides back to Florida, and we had no idea whether they went for a visit or to stay for good. Howard and I were left with a rented house, most of the band gear, and the uncertainty of what to do next. We figured that we, too, would have to be heading home soon and the Opel Kadett we lovingly called the Jackal couldn't haul all the stuff we had to move, so we made the decision to trade it in for a new van. The rented

U-Haul van we'd had for months was still a glaring problem sitting in the driveway just waiting to cause more problems, so we asked one of our good ol' boy neighbors to come over and help us run the mileage back so nobody would know exactly how many miles we'd put on it. Only one little problem: our shade tree mechanic neighbor meant well, but he wasn't the sharpest knife in the drawer. He pulled out his screwdriver, took off the faceplate that covered the speedometer, then he slowly clicked the mileage back ten thousand miles by hand one click at a time. Now the van was not only six months overdue on its rental fee, but it had about eight thousand miles less on it than when we first rented it.

He was so proud of what he had accomplished with his screwdriver that we didn't have the heart to tell him he'd missed his calculations by thousands of miles. Later that evening I drove the U-Haul to the gas station we rented it from, parked it in the middle of the other trucks and trailers, and left the keys under the floorboard mat. Howard picked me up in the new van and soon we were southbound down I-75 toward home.

Back in Darby we felt a little like dogs returning with their tails tucked between their legs as we began blending back into farm living. The good thing about coming from a poor family is that our failure didn't stick out so bad. It's not like anybody expected us to go off and conquer the music business. Our parents remained supportive as ever and never rubbed the band breakup in our face or said, "We told you so." Of course, there were several secrets we never revealed, like the band getting strung out on Quaaludes, the underage runaway girls, or the angry stripper landing hard on my hurt knee in Savannah.

They certainly knew that we were not angels. Occasionally Homer would mention that we needed to have a trade to fall back on because it was gonna be hard making a living playing music, but he never tried to force us to do something else.

For a short while after we moved home, Howard went back to living with his wife, Pam, at his in-laws' house, but the two of them were very different people now. Most of my friends and girlfriends were in college or had jobs or new boyfriends, so neither Howard nor I found social situations we could relate to easily. We had ventured out into the world, and home would never be quite the same.

I cleaned up the old shack and moved in with all the guitars and amps. We had no money saved; we had spent it all on the down payment for the new van to move us home. Howard extended his credit and bought a few head of cattle and turned them over for a little profit, then we tried planting a crop of turnip greens to sell at the farmers market, but the turnip greens didn't get the rain they needed and the cow money didn't go far. We weren't going to make it as part-time poverty farmers.

I started going out with a girl who was a cousin of Howard's wife. Actually, it was the girl's mother that I liked. She made the best fried quail, grits, gravy, and biscuits I'd ever tasted. It was probably wrong to date a girl because of her mother's cooking, but the girl didn't seem to mind and her mother loved to cook for me.

We had given our bulldog, Belew, to our Atlanta neighbors before we left because he took up with them while we were on the road. They fed him good and he seemed so contented that we didn't see any sense in ruining his happiness by uprooting him. But we had to have a dog, so Howard acquired a red nose pit bull terrier when we got home from Atlanta. He named the new puppy "Roscoe," and soon we and Roscoe were writing new chapters in our book of adventures.

Back in the Shack and Howard's Bad Back

For a while, the breakup of the band and our retreat to Darby really had me down, but gradually my natural high spirits reasserted themselves and I had a revelation of sorts. I felt a new found freedom in *not* being in a band, *not* having to learn the latest hits off the radio, and *not* having to compromise with a bunch of half-stoned idiots.

Our dad had a profound saying that began to make complete sense to me: "I can't stand a drunk man when I'm sober or a sober man when I'm drunk!" In fact, all of Homer's sayings were making more sense to me every new day that got between me and our Georgia adventure.

I figured out I could be creative right where I was. I borrowed most of the bed sheets our family owned and talked my Grandma Katie into helping me tie-dye them. I draped them from the ceiling of my shack and lined the walls with them to make the room sound better. I set up all the band gear on one end of the shack so we had a place to jam when friends came by, and I pretty much transformed the shack into a full-fledged rehearsal room, recording studio, crash pad, love nest, and all-around redneck hippie hangout.

I learned some acoustic songs by James Taylor and Van Morrison and started dropping by the coffeehouse at Saint Leo College with my guitar, where I set out an empty cup and waited for affluent students to cram it with dollar bills as I sang "Fire and Rain." A lot of rich Catholic girls attended that school from places like Connecticut and Brazil. They loved the whole struggling, scruffy folksinger scene, and it wasn't much of a stretch for me to play that part.

During my coffeehouse gigs, I met this little hippie guitar player from Vermont named Vinny who knew every Grateful Dead song. We started jamming a little and when he found out I knew a lot of country songs, he called up his friend from up north. Chris Cope was a really good bass player with a lifelong dream to be a southern redneck country singer. Then we looked up a local drummer I knew who used to be a drum roadie for Keith Moon of The Who. Cope and I taught him how to play all the Merle Haggard songs we knew.

It was an interesting group, to say the least. We never really rehearsed; we just had a great time playing bars impromptu. We even changed the band's name once a month to keep 'em confused. We were completely counterculture. Vinny had a girlfriend named Cathy who sometimes dropped by our gigs to sing "Me And Bobby McGee" in the style of Janis Joplin. If we didn't have a gig somewhere, we played in the shack and people would come by to drink a beer and listen to us jam or work up a new song I'd written.

Howard jammed with us on occasion, but he had become a sort of outlaw living with his inlaws and that was wearing real thin with him. As if he didn't have enough to deal with on that front, one evening as he was driving home during a heavy rainstorm, he slid off the road and ran our Dodge van into Ray Pond, a local body of water located next to the curve between San Antonio and Dade City on State Road 52. The van sunk to the bottom of the pond with Howard in it. He kicked out the window, swam to the surface, then flagged down someone to call a wrecker to come pull the submerged van out of the pond.

A little while after the accident, he discovered that he had injured his back. The doctor told him he'd have to be put in traction, so with his marriage ending and an injured vertebra, Howard moved into the shack with me. We found a hospital bed with an elaborate pulley device attached to the foot of the bed and a waistband that attached to the pulley with weights tied to the end of a rope to put pressure on it that might relieve his back pain.

We dried out the van the best we could, got it running again, got the window replaced that Howard kicked out, then gave the van back to the finance company. Much as it might have meant to the future of our music career, we were in no shape to make payments on it, not with Howard in traction and me in an experimental freeform country band living on tips people left in coffee cups and the leftovers Frances brought home from the high school lunchroom. No place to go from here but up.

Rattlesnakes in the Garden and a Pig Roast

Almost all the guys we knew from high school who used to get mad at us because we smoked pot were now dealing it and constantly asking us if we wanted to buy some. About now you're probably thinking, *If you boys had really wanted to, you could have stayed away from that stuff.* You may be right; there might have been a monastery somewhere or maybe we could have hung out with the only two kids in the county who didn't get high, but we never ran across them.

For one thing, pot grew everywhere in Central Florida. Wild or cultivated, it flourished like crazy, and the hot, subtropical climate made for perfect growing conditions most of the year. Some of the locals who were in the growing trade developed extremely creative methods of farming the weed. We knew one guy who installed a low, solid metal fence around his patch. He painted the fence camouflage and dropped a few rattlesnakes inside the fence to make people think twice about trying to steal his crop.

In the fall of the year, right about harvest time, we usually had a pig roast. Pigs were easy and cheap to raise, and we'd always had what was affectionately called a "hogkillin'" as soon as the weather got a little cooler. Homer, Frances, our relatives, and neighbors had been butchering hogs since before we were born. They'd fry up chitlins and cracklins, drink beer and moonshine while they played music, and shot the bull with whoever stopped by while the pig was smoking.

Once the pig was done, they'd all gather to eat the pork along with some potluck dishes the neighbors brought to add to the feast in what became a kind of fall harvest festival. When Howard and I started hosting pig roasts, things weren't that much different from our parents' day, except the fall of the year coincided with the harvesting of some pretty potent homegrown, so the party got kicked up a notch. We sat around and shot the bull and drank moonshine and beer, and played music the same as they did, only now we also sampled a lot of the local weed product.

At our most infamous pig roast, the party ran about three days and featured a dozen camping tents pitched under our old live oak tree with an American flag hanging from a massive limb. There were people from foreign countries that some of our friends invited and Homer and Frances couldn't understand a word some of them said, but anytime communications broke down, my parents just offered them more to eat and drink.

We roasted the pig and basted it in sour orange juice and beer all night long and by the end of the next day it was completely devoured, along with heaps of sweet potatoes and mustard greens. We could count the beer kegs that had been emptied but there was no real way to measure what went up in smoke.

The party might have gone on even longer if our dad hadn't spotted smoke oozing from the britches leg of a friend of ours who had rolled over in the campfire after passing out nearby. Homer was just leaving for work around 6:00 a.m. when he saw our buddy's Levi's smoking. He stopped the car, jumped out, and pulled our buddy out of the flames, then turned on a nearby faucet, soaked the kid's pants leg with the water hose, jumped back into the car, and continued on to work.

Roscoe, Shrooms, and the Sleeping Bag Incident, Also Known as the Great Inspiration

When Howard moved back into the shack with me, Roscoe came, too, and by then he had developed quite a reputation. He was far from being a big, intimidating dog; in fact, he had a small frame with a big head and a pure, innocent look about him. He wagged his tail all the time and he always seemed to have a smile on his face. But like many humans, looks can be deceiving. From his puppyhood, he was completely fearless and would tangle with anything from an alligator to a buzz saw.

He couldn't have been over a few months old when he latched on to the nose of a fifteen-hundred-pound bull—the same one that ate the pot plant, but without THC in his system he had the bad nature typical of his breed. Roscoe would not let go until that big Charolais bull slung him so high in the air we lost sight of him. When he finally did come down, he hit the ground looking for the big beast in order to have another go at him. Within a couple of months, he'd done away with the neighbor's duck and our mom's white Persian cat.

I had a game rooster that I kept as a pet because I liked the way he crowed. One day the rooster got out of his pen and decided to strut over to where Roscoe lay sprawled out sunning himself. Having the fighting cock instincts, the rooster spurred Roscoe right where he lay and almost without waking up Roscoe snapped the rooster's head off then went right back to sleep. I was bummed that he had killed my rooster but I can't say the rooster didn't have it coming.

Funny thing is we didn't know about the pit bull personality. We'd mostly grown up with cow dogs, hog dogs, and old bloodhounds around the farm. Roscoe was a new experience for us. He went almost everywhere with Howard, and he'd hang out with us in the shack and listen to us jam. He was really quite mellow most of the time but there was a hair-trigger personality lurking beneath that smile.

To an innocent bystander reading this book, it must seem like we spent a lot of our early years trying to get high, but that was really never our major objective. Our priorities were playing music, chasing girls, keeping Homer's cows from jumping the fence, and trying to eat three squares a day.

It actually seemed like getting high always came looking for us— otherwise, how can you explain the fact that some smartass professor at the University of Florida in Gainesville turned magic mushroom spores loose as an experiment and the wind carried them to every cow pasture in Florida. I know it sounds like I'm making this up, but that's precisely what happened. Hallucinogenic psilocybin mushrooms popped up in every pile of cow manure on our farm. They varied in color from tan to off white, with a little bit of brown in the center of the cap and a purple skirt circling the stem of the mushroom.

Homer would wake us abruptly on weekend mornings and say, "Boys, there's a bunch of kids in the pasture stumblin' around looking like they're huntin' Easter eggs." Sure enough we'd go out and spot a van parked up on the road and hippies wandering around picking mushrooms. We'd ask them to leave because they were trespassing. Most of them had already eaten a couple of "shrooms" and they'd usually just start laughing uncontrollably and head back across the fence.

Now I'm not gonna lie and tell you we never tried 'em, but you'd better believe it didn't take long to develop a healthy respect for the little fungi. Shrooming was not something you could easily disguise. After ingestion, the first thing that would happen would be a wave of nausea akin to swallowing a peyote button, followed by a few hours of holding your ribs to contain your laughter and an occasional chat with our Maker.

I know what you're thinking and I can say that Howard and I agree with you, it's a damn wonder that we didn't kill our fool selves on something in those days. The scary part is, not only hadn't we even made it to the big time yet, at this point there was no sensible reason to believe that we ever would. If we'd thought about it much, it might have gotten downright depressing.

San Antonio (or San Ann, as the locals like to call it) is a beautiful, sleepy little Florida town built around a park with ancient oak trees dripping with Spanish moss. In the early '70s when we moved back from Atlanta, it had two drinking establishments and a Jiffy Mart. There was Ralph's Bar and John and Mary's Grocery Store that actually started out selling groceries then became a bar. The students from Saint Leo's College combined with the locals to make the town interesting, and the street between the two bars usually looked like an open-air, open-container mall with people talking, drinking, dancing, and wandering back and forth from bar to bar. One evening, after a few drinks and an unrehearsed jam, Howard and I wandered back to the shack and I climbed into my bed to sleep off the night's revelry. Howard decided to stretch out in the sleeping bag we kept on a stack of hay bales in the corner instead of the hospital bed with the traction weights on it. I didn't see him when he first crawled into the sleeping bag but I can vouch for the fact that he came out of it like a lightning bolt, screaming and yelling at the top of his lungs. As I jumped up to see what was going on, I caught sight of a huge chicken snake coming out of the bag alongside of Howard. At that moment I laughed as hard as I had ever laughed in my life. Howard almost made a new door in the shack and the snake made his way out through one of the numerous cracks in the wall of the old wooden structure.

At that moment, there would have been no way to realize how important and pivotal that incident would become to our careers in the not too distant future.

Egg Crates, Jingles, and Howard Looks for America

I heard about a recording studio some guy was building in Tampa, so I drove down to check it out. I'd written a few songs that I thought might be good enough to shop to record labels and I wanted to make some demo recordings. Studio 70 was still a work in progress when I popped in unannounced. Blair Mooney was the owner and sound engineer, and we hit it off good enough. I'd seen Blair play bass with his band, Noah's Ark, quite a few times around the area, so we were not complete strangers. We shot the breeze awhile and during the course of our conversation he mentioned that he was looking for some egg crates to glue to the concrete walls of the studio. I told him I lived just down the road from a chicken farm and asked how many of those crates would it take to do the job.

The next thing I know, Blair and I are gluing the stacks of egg crates I got him to the walls and ceilings to achieve a sound that worked well and cost very little. In addition to my resourcefulness, Blair liked some of the songs I had written, so pretty soon we had a deal worked out whereby he'd give me some recording time in return for my part-time labor.

We started off recording a couple of songs with the band I'd been jamming with at the shack but quickly figured out that they were not really studio musicians. After cutting a few tracks that were just passable, Blair suggested that we get some players from around town that had done some studio work. That sounded like a good idea, but how were we gonna get the money to pay them? Blair said he had a few clients doing commercials and asked if I could write a couple of jingles and sing them. Never having written a jingle in my life, I said, "Sure," and spent the next few months recording my demos and writing and singing jingles for Jim Walters Homes, Ford and Chevy dealerships, and Tampa Bay area nightclubs.

Recording was a different approach to music than I had experienced up to now; it didn't have the instantaneous feel of a live performance, but there was a different kind of rewarding feeling when you finished a good recording of a song you wrote and listened to the playback. I was also learning about music production, which is something they didn't have a school for in Darby.

The other thing I loved about the studio was all the different bands and singers that came by. We recorded Hispanic and Jamaican migrant bands straight out of the orange groves, R&B, country bands and soul bands from the country clubs and black clubs in the area, along with reggae bands and rock and roll and glam rock bands. Singer/songwriters, gospel quartets, almost anything you could imagine musically came in and laid down tracks, trying to cut a hit or make an album to sell to the clientele at the clubs and churches where they played and sang.

The guy who made clothes for Jimi Hendrix used to come by with a girl he was producing and cut tracks. He'd lay some tickets on us when Jimi was in town and let us know if Jimi was gonna jam at Dino's, a nightclub in South Tampa, after his concert at Curtis Hixon Hall. The studio also did sound for touring acts like Sonny & Cher, Chet Atkins and Floyd Cramer, and Frankie Laine when they played concerts in Tampa. I'd go along and help roll up cords and load gear at those shows to rack up more studio demo time and try to meet the performers.

I started hanging out at the studio a lot. I liked the atmosphere and meeting the different artists coming in with all their crazy musical ideas and all their hype about their songs and the music business. Most of them were not very well connected to the business but you'd never know it by the bull they were slinging. There were legitimate musicians and artists like Mike Pinera who used to drop by. Mike had a band called Blues Image. They had a big hit called "Ride Captain Ride," and after Blues Image he joined Iron Butterfly. Bertie Higgins used to come in and cut songs he'd written before he had his hit, "Key Largo." Sometimes we'd go to Bertie's place in Tarpon Springs and snorkel for scallops.

I didn't have time to miss having a band because someone was always inviting me to come out to a club to sing. I now had an even better pickup line than "I'm in a band." When girls asked me what I did, I could reply, "I work at a recording studio, write commercials for TV and radio, and I'm recording songs to shop to record labels." Howard used to hang with me some at the studio and sing on demos, but he was not ready to stay in one place. He'd been going through a restless stage and with his divorce behind him and his back injury getting better, he decided he wanted to travel a little.

If we'd only known at the time about reality television, his escapades could have made millions. He bought a used Volkswagen van and with no destination in mind and no estimated time of return, he took his pit bull, Roscoe, his guitar, and his collection of eight-tracks and hit the road. There are rumors that he might have had other things on board as well; I can't confirm that for sure. However, there was one bit of contraband he took on his journey that caused quite a stir when he left, that being the daughter of our local mayor.

Even though I was at the studio more than the farm in the days leading up to his trip, I can tell you the gossip mill was cranked up full tilt around Pasco County. Homer joked that we'd better obey the speed limit when we went into town because it was gonna be hard to get out of a speeding ticket now that Howard had run off with the mayor's daughter. As for me, Howard was a sort of a hero of mine at the time—I mean, we were still just a couple of dirt farmer redneck hippie kids that had failed so far in the music business. If he'd managed to figure out how to hit the road with a beautiful blonde, his dog, and his guitar, more power to him.

I missed him when he left, but I never worried that we wouldn't sing and play music together anymore; every time we met up, that's what we ended up doing, anyway—that's what we were. In a way, it was a relief to me that Howard packed up and went wandering with no worries, no job, and no responsibilities. It was completely the opposite of the way he had always been. I was the one who'd always taken the heat for chasing women, not working, and playing music. Even though I missed him when he left, it took some heat off me and actually improved my reputation.

Southern Rockers and Serious Rejection

During my time at Studio 70, I met a lot of interesting people. There were beautiful women that walked in with sugar daddies who would foot the bill to record them in hopes of getting a hit and becoming a star. There were starving artists who worked all week just to get enough money for a couple of hours to record their demos; the gospel groups always seemed to have the most money and the guys always had little flasks of liquor they'd pull out from inside their silk jackets and share with you. Some people I met at Studio 70 became lifelong friends and associates. Wally Dentz, for instance, was playing bass and harmonica in a band called Raindriver when I met him. A few years later he would join the Henry Paul Band and score a record deal with Atlantic Records. During his time with the band, they toured with The Rolling Stones and recorded several critically acclaimed albums. Wally also played on many of my early demos and would become an important part of The Bellamy Brothers organization, but not just yet, for we were all just trying to get something going.

Wally and I weren't the only local players trying to jump-start our careers in the area. Guys like Huey Thomason and Monty Yoho from the Outlaws also recorded with me during that time. Huey and I even shared a duplex apartment in Tampa for a while. We were so broke we could only pay the light bill on one side of the duplex at a time, and whichever side had the lights turned off that month, we'd run an extension cord through the wall to that side to keep the lights on, then the next month we'd pay the bill on the other side and run the extension cord in the other direction.

Broke was my middle name but I was starting to write and demo songs that were no longer just live jams like we played at the shack. They were starting to take some shape and my lyrics seemed to be coming together and I started working on finding my own voice instead of just trying to sing like my favorite singers.

I was still dependent on my family and still made regular runs up the farm, which was only thirty miles away, where Frances and Homer would load me up with fresh citrus from the orange groves, homegrown beef, and garden vegetables. I never went hungry but in terms of my career, it was like that old Winston Churchill saying: I was going from one failure to another without a loss of enthusiasm. We mailed out demos of my songs to record labels in New York, Los Angeles, Atlanta, Nashville, London, and pretty much anywhere we could find the address of a record label and the name of an A&R guy or a record executive. It seemed like the file cabinet in the studio office was full of nothing but rejection letters written to me. The rejections from the country labels said the song was too rock or pop. The rejection letters from the pop or rock labels said the song was too country. The rejection letters from England said, "We're not looking for any material right now, lovely, thanks and cheerio." Blair and I rationalized all this failure by telling ourselves that all artists get this many rejection letters, as we kept on writing, recording, and sending them more material.

Howard called in from his "trip" to update us on how things were going on the road. Usually he'd call the farm, when he knew I was going to be there, with stories about seeing Van Morrison play a show in Lake Tahoe, which made me really jealous because Van was one artist I'd never seen up to that point and I really wanted to catch him in concert. Howard had lots of other stories too. I really enjoyed the one about him leaving Roscoe to guard his van at a campground while he and the mayor's daughter went grocery shopping. When he returned, Roscoe was gone and there was a note nailed to a tree from the dogcatcher. He went to the pound to retrieve Roscoe and the dogcatcher appeared at the door with a large chunk bitten out of his jaw and growled, "What the hell kind of a dog is that?" It took some doing, but Howard was able to rescue Roscoe from the pound without any harm to him (no harm to the dog, I mean, not the dogcatcher).

Howard also did a little pickin' and singin' on his journey. He ran into a country band in Russellville, Arkansas, while he was picking apples to make a little gas money. They didn't know quite what to think of this long-haired hippie with mutton chops, but when they heard him sing Merle Haggard songs, they hired him on the spot, six nights a week, at the Russellville Holiday Inn. Howard had been playing with the band about a month when a barroom brawl broke out and the steel guitar player unscrewed a leg of his steel guitar and began knocking out customers on the dance floor. Howard took that as a cue that he'd been in town too long.

And speaking of Merle Haggard (which I will, a lot), Merle kinda brought Howard back home from his adventure. It seems Howard played Merle's eight-track so much on his road trip that his girlfriend got sick of it and threw it out the window. Howard was so mad that he drove her back to Florida and didn't speak to her for years. Thirty-five years later, when he and I performed at a cancer benefit in our hometown, that same mayor's daughter apologized for throwing out the tape and conceded that Merle was probably the best country singer who ever wrapped his golden voice around a country song.

"Rainy Day In The South" and the Juke Box Incident

One of the songs I recorded at Studio 70 was called "Rainy Day In The South," and the intro of the recording was nothing less than a huge thunderclap followed by a chuggin' southern rockin' guitar with a thumpin' bass and drums rhythm track. The lyrics were simple but effective:

Rainy day in the South and I wonder
When will it stop raining on me
Can't play my guitar for the thunder
Why in hell won't it stop raining on me

It rocked along pretty good and sounded a little like Creedence meeting up with Joe South. The track had that sound mainly because Mike Pinera came in and played some great edgy guitar on it. At least around the studio we thought it sounded good, and since we were getting all those rejection letters, we decided to press the record ourselves and ship it to radio stations.

Blair called the label Moon Records and we were all pretty excited to see the pressings come in on those little 45 rpm discs they used to have in those days, with the quarter moon logo and my name as the artist and songwriter. Howard, who was fresh back from his Easy Rider escapade, came by the studio to pick me up so we could take a single back to the ranch to play for Frances and Homer. At least that was the original plan, until we got the brilliant idea to stop at a club on the way out of town called the "Losers Lounge" and try to talk the waitresses into putting it on their jukebox.

Our brainstorm didn't go over big with the barmaid, who said the manager wasn't there and they didn't have the key and gave us several more good excuses why she couldn't accommodate us. So we settled down at the bar for a drink or two and the more we drank, the more we schemed, and soon we had a plan. First there was a disturbance at the pool table that got the attention of most of the bar (I might have started it but I'm pleading innocent). Howard grabbed a ring of keys from behind the bar and began trying them one at a time on the jukebox. Finding that none of them fit, he reached behind the bar and grabbed an icepick and shoved it into the jukebox keyhole, which took out the whole lock.

The record that had been playing started skipping as Howard tossed some of the 45s on the floor and slipped my record in a slot. I could see the top of Howard's head bobbing up and down as he crouched down in front of the jukebox. A guy at the pool table was now threatening to kill me for ruining his perfect game but I made sure he didn't get the chance, 'cause just as I saw Howard punch the play buttons on the machine, I bolted for the door.

Howard zipped right past me on the way to the vehicle and we did a Dukes of Hazzard into the front seat of the van at the same time. As he started the car, I heard the thundering intro of "Rainy Day In The South" start to blare from inside the bar. By now there were quite a few people yelling obscenities at us so we couldn't stay and hear the whole song, but as we circled the parking lot the guitar intro ended and we could hear my voice come in, singing the first line:

Rainy day in the South and I wonder . . .

That was it; we'd worn out our welcome, so we hightailed it up Highway 41 toward the safety of the farm.

5
Life Accelerated
My Future Ex-wife and Demos in the Garbage Can

DAVID: I met my first wife while I was working at Studio 70. Her name was Janet Sultenfuss and along with her friend Cathy, she came walking into the studio one day to check it out for some friends who had a band.

Now, if you hear my ex-wife tell the story, she was very young and I robbed the cradle but actually I think she and her friend had fake IDs before they met me and I don't remember her being much younger than most of the girls I dated then, so I don't think I was totally responsible for corrupting them. Given the fact that exes rarely agree on the facts, the fact is that she and Cathy started hangin' out with me and used their fake IDs to go out to clubs where I had friends in bands I sat in with.

I had not had a steady relationship since high school and due to my lifestyle, I didn't really relate that much to the girls I went to school with who were now mostly living "normal" lives. The thought of marriage, children, or any other nesting tendencies completely escaped me at this point in my life. I was still just a redneck hippie boy who had been cast into the fires of pop culture where the sexual revolution was still smoldering, and I guess I figured it was always gonna be that way. Even if our marriage would not be a union that would stand the test of time, Janet and I got along really good in the beginning and began to date exclusively.

Then Blair and I got a chance to meet and play some demos for a record producer from St. Petersburg named Phil Gernhard. I'd heard of Phil from musicians who dropped by the studio but didn't know anyone directly connected to him. As far as I knew, he was just about the only guy in the area who had success breaking acts on a national level. He'd produced the hit song "Stay" for Maurice Williams and the Zodiacs in 1960 and a string of novelty hits for an Ocala band called the Royal Guardsmen. Their first hit, "Snoopy vs. The Red Baron" in 1966, sold a million singles. Gernhard then produced "The Return Of The Red Baron" and several other sequels on the band, including "Snoopy's Christmas." In 1968 he produced a million-selling single for Dion called "Abraham, Martin And John," as well as a string of hits on Lobo (Kent LaVoie), beginning with "Me And You And A Dog Named Boo" in 1971.

Getting a meeting with Gernhard wasn't easy, but somehow we pulled it off. I tucked a reel-to-reel tape of some of my songs under my arm, and we were off to see the wizard. When we first met Gernhard, he seemed a little guarded but nice enough. He didn't say a lot but the gold records, plaques, and awards for songwriting and producing that covered the office walls spoke volumes. Blair explained to Phil that he thought we had some good songs and we'd like to hear his opinion and maybe discuss working together. At that point, Gernhard ceased being the quiet, laid-back music creator and launched into a speech about the huge talent and effort it took to make a hit record, how long the intro of a song had to be, how the hook of a song should come no later than one minute after the record starts and on and on and on. This was the speech that I was destined to hear from Gernhard for many years to come. He continued to explain that he could tell if a song was a hit from the first verse and chorus, all this information pouring out of him as he threaded the reel of my demos on his tape player.

The first song we played for Gernhard was "Rainy Day In The South." This was my first experience playing my music for a "real" record man, and while I sat there a-sweat from the fear of a *live* rejection, he let the song play all the way to the end without any emotion on his face. I can't remember what song we played for him next because at that point every chicken shit thing I'd ever heard about people in the music biz started to come home to roost.

Gernhard stopped the tape recorder then rewound the tape until all of it had returned to its original reel. He then took the tape off the machine and without even turning around, tossed it over his shoulder and rung the garbage can with it.

"Bring me some more songs," he said. No explanation. No critique. I think we responded by saying, "Okay," or "Thanks for the meeting," but most of what I remember about that day was riding across the Howard Franklin Bridge from St. Petersburg to Tampa trying to figure out if he'd just thrown us out of his office or if he really wanted more songs and another meeting with us. One more thing: as I was about to leave Gernhard's office, I waited till he was occupied, then I fished my demo tape out of his trash can.

A Return to the Sleeping Bag Incident

In 1973 Phil Gernhard and Kent LaVoie produced a single on singer/ musician/comedian Jim Stafford. The song was called "Swamp Witch" and it got airplay from a lot of southern radio stations, but it stalled at #39 on the *Billboard* charts because it was played more regionally than nationally.

Stafford was from Eloise, Florida, near Winter Haven, where he was in a band called The Legends with members that included Gram Parsons of Flying Burrito Brothers and Byrds fame. Kent LaVoie met Stafford in Clearwater playing beach clubs and after hearing "Swamp Witch," agreed to help him secure a record deal.

What did all this have to do with our story so far? A lot, actually. Since Gernhard was my only entry to the real music biz world, I'd been going back and forth to his office for a few months, without much luck and without being able to tell if he was serious about my material or if he just liked torturing young singer/songwriters.

Janet and I were doing really good now and while she was in school during the day, I worked on songs or commercials at the studio or drove to the farm to get enough groceries to sustain life. I was writing constantly; sometimes I tried to apply Gernhard's rules of songwriting but mostly I just kept writing like I wanted to. Nothing I did seemed to make too much difference to Gernhard, but somehow he kept me bringing more songs to him.

Then one afternoon Blair and I were hanging out at the studio when out of the blue the phone rang and Blair answered. It was Gernhard saying that Stafford had been in his office that day and spotted a song title of mine on a tape box I had left there. He liked the title, the story, and the song, and wanted to know if he could do some rewriting to work it into his own style of comedic storytelling.

Recall the story about Howard, the chicken snake, and the sleeping bag back at the shack. Turns out I wrote a song based on that incident called "Spiders And Snakes," and that's the song title Stafford spotted on the tape box in Gernhard's office. He opened the box, slapped the tape on the player, and a few days later he and I were on the phone discussing a rewrite.

My whole world was about to change forever.

Sign Here Boy and Go West Young Man

I didn't know it at the time, but Gernhard needed a big hit song fast to follow up "Swamp Witch" so they wouldn't lose the momentum Stafford had going with the regional radio stations that played it.

After my first songwriting telephone call with Stafford, I didn't hear much of anything from him or Gernhard. We didn't even know that they took the rewrite of "Spiders And Snakes" and flew to L.A. to cut it until they were gone. It wasn't like they had to notify me about everything they were doing, but any words of encouragement would have been greatly appreciated. Needless to say, once I found out, I told everybody in Central Florida that Gernhard was cutting a song of mine on Jim Stafford and it was gonna be on the radio. Soon I was wishing I'd waited to spread the good news because it was beginning to look like the whole deal could evaporate.

Weeks went by without updates or calls. We called Gernhard's office in St. Petersburg every now and then to check and see if he was around, but nobody answered. Then just when I had decided that the whole thing was a bad joke, he called and asked me to come to his office to sign contracts.

A crystal ball would have been useful about now. Phil Gernhard was not the most forthcoming person about anything, especially contracts he wanted signed. Blair Mooney may have helped me a lot by letting me write jingles and clean up after recording sessions to earn studio time, but it was obvious he wasn't going to be able to launch a career from his little studio on Florida Avenue in Tampa. Without me pulling up stakes and moving to one of the music capitals, which I didn't have the money to do, it was obvious that for me, Gernhard was the only game in town.

When I got to Gernhard's office he didn't say a word about cutting "Spiders And Snakes," though I found out later that he had already recorded it. At this meeting, he was all business. He bluntly told me that he had prepared the necessary contracts to get things rolling.

That was an understatement. He'd prepared a songwriting contract, a publishing contract, an artist recording contract, and a contract that made him my manager. Oh, and just in case that wasn't enough, the manager's contract also gave him power of attorney and the publishing contract assigned all my publishing rights to him.

To a young singer/songwriter, all that paperwork may sound like the guy really cares about doing right by you. How naïve can you get? I'll be honest with you. I didn't even know what music publishing was. The streams of income from writing, publishing, making records, and so on were completely foreign to me. To make matters worse, I did not have an attorney nor can I remember even knowing an attorney at that time. The only kind of financial transaction I'd ever seen was when a club owner handed us a blue Crown Royal bag with cash in it after playing a strip joint.

As if the contracts were not tough enough to digest, Gernhard decided to put another thought in my head during the meeting. "Jim's got a TV development deal in L.A.," he said. "You should consider coming out to L.A. and writing with him and working on the TV show."

Well, Phil, why don't you just drop a bombshell! I mean, here's a guy that I can't get to even tell me my songs are worth a damn asking me to uproot to the West Coast. This time when I drove back across Tampa Bay from Gernhard's, I didn't even stop at the studio in Tampa; I headed straight up to the farm in Darby to talk things over with Homer, Frances, and Howard.

When I got home we did a lot of talking. On the one hand, my family was excited for me. None of us had ever seen a recording contract or any of the other long, involved legal papers that now lay on our kitchen table. They were hardly prepared to counsel me on what to do. The only time they'd ever used an attorney was when Grandma Bellamy deeded eighty acres to them before she died—oh, and one other time was to survey fence lines on the farm. Those lawyers wouldn't have been anyone to ask about the complex music documents drawn up way out in Hollywood.

If indeed there are times when being naïve and optimistic is a good thing, this was probably one of those times. Over the last thirty-five years, I've pondered this decision and I usually come up with the same opinion: it was a blessing and a curse. I weighed my options but they barely tipped the scale either way, so I rolled the dice, signed Gernhard's agreements with no changes and without any legal counsel, and returned them to him a couple of days later.

In several of the previous conversations I'd had with Gernhard, I'd mentioned that Howard and I had a band called Jericho that toured the southern club circuit, but I was never aware of how much Gernhard heard because he was always so aloof. Apparently he'd heard some of the conversation because after I gave him back the signed contracts, he turned to me and said, "What's your brother up to?" Turns out Stafford was looking for someone to replace his road manager, who was leaving the road to go to work on the TV show that Stafford had going on.

Jim's live act was a one-man show that relied on an assistant who could do lights and sound, check in and out of hotels, rent cars, pick up plane tickets, and generally manage every detail of the tour. I told Gernhard I'd check with Howard about the job. "Just tell him to call Jim," he said.

After I left his office that day, I convinced myself that I had made a good decision signing the contracts. *What the hell*, I told myself nervously, *how many people could say they had signed a recording, publishing, management contract all on the same day?*

I Must Be a Mushroom and Howard's New Gig

Apparently the "Spiders and Snakes" singles were being pressed, shipped, and pre-promoted to radio by MGM Records before I'd even signed the contracts.

I stopped worrying about the details, since I had no control over them. I just kept telling myself that it was all gonna work out. Mainly, I wanted to hear it on the radio. The good news was, I didn't have to wait long. A few days later, I was pulling out of the studio parking lot with a keyboard player who had just played piano on one of my new demos. We were heading down the street for a burger when the DJ said, "Here's a new record from Jim Stafford called 'Spiders And Snakes.'" After I almost wrecked the car, I pulled over and listened to the whole song sitting at the side of the road. You know, even with Gernhard being moody, cagey, underhanded, and not very forthcoming, the record sounded very good on that little car radio. I hurried back to the studio to tell Blair and call the farm. Someone my mom knew had already called her to say they heard Jim Stafford singing my song on the radio and wanted to know if he had stolen it.

Things started hopping now. I took Gernhard demos of some new songs I wrote, and he listened to them without throwing any of them in the trash, but his focus was on talking me into moving to L.A. Howard decided to take the position with Stafford and he was getting ready to meet him in Nashville where Jim was opening a show for The Bee Gees and Roy Orbison. "Spiders And Snakes" was now officially starting to burn up the radio dial.

I figured it was now or never and decided to make the move to California, but first I would ask Gernhard if he thought that I would make enough money from the record to buy a new van to drive out to the West Coast. That may have been the first time I saw him laugh like a normal person. I guess I was pretty ignorant about things, but it was mostly because he kept me that way, probably so I would sign his mushroom contracts—you know, the contracts designed to keep you in the dark and feed you bullshit! Gernhard advanced me $5,000 against my writing royalties from "Spiders And Snakes." The song was in the Top 40 by now, with no signs of slowing down.

I didn't know there was that much money in the world, and Gernhard had suddenly become a great guy in my book. Of course, he never mentioned that the publishing papers he had me sign over to him were going to make him a million bucks. No matter. I took my Volkswagen bug down to Northgate Ford in Tampa and traded it in on a brand new black Ford Econoline van. I put a couple of grand down and my parents cosigned. I was now ready to make the trip to L.A.

Janet was not happy about this new development. Blair wasn't either. Homer and Frances were happy for me and Howard because things were moving for us, but there were so many unknowns in this deal and I knew they were worried about us living in California full time.

Howard left right away with instructions to meet up with Jim and someone named Gallagher on the road and they would run through everything for a few shows until Howard got the hang of it, then Gallagher would head back to L.A. and leave Howard to manage things on the road. Howard's only question was, "Who's Gallagher?"

Comedian, writer, crazy man extraordinaire, Gallagher grew up in South Tampa and began working with Jim after college, writing comedy and handling road manager duties. One of the most fascinating things about him was the props he built, like the little man with a saw that lived in Jim's guitar and sawed his way out right in the middle of the show during a dramatic classical guitar number.

Howard's trip started off with a bang. On his way to Nashville to meet Jim, Roy Orbison, and The Bee Gees, there was a rare blizzard in Music City that grounded all flights, so he had to reach his first road manager destination by train. Homer and Frances took him to the depot in Tampa and got him on board. His train pulled into Nashville's Union Station just before show time. Gallagher picked him up and hauled him over to the convention center just in time for sound check.

Howard called me at the farm the next day and told me that they were staying in Roger Miller's King of the Road Hotel, and that he'd seen a really great artist named Ronnie Milsap in the lounge of the hotel singing and playing piano.

Leaving the Nest

I had everything I thought I might need in my new Ford van: my piano, my guitars, my reel-to-reel tape recorder, even a small couch. I could have lived in the van if I needed to, and with the lack of details Gernhard was giving me about moving, I figured I might have to. I had the trip all planned out. I'd drive a few hundred miles a day, camp out on the land or find a cheap hotel by night, take my time, see a little bit of America, and cruise into California and become the next singer/songwriter sensation. Of course, you know what they say: if you wanna make God laugh, make some plans of your own.

Two days before I'm set to leave, Gernhard calls and says, "We need you to come on out right away. Mike Curb wants you and Jim to start writing songs for Jim's next album immediately!" In my mind I'm thinking, *Okay, Phil, back up a little, this is the first I've heard you mention Mike Curb.* I knew "Spiders And Snakes" was on MGM Records and I remembered Mike Curb's name from one of the source books we had at Studio 70. In fact, I'm pretty sure Blair and I sent him a tape and got one of those form letters of rejection from him or one of his A&R staffers.

Gernhard didn't take any time to explain about Curb. He wrapped up the call by nonchalantly telling me that he'd bought a new home in Coldwater Canyon and his realtor in St. Petersburg was selling his Florida properties and asked me if I would go by his office and bring all his awards to L.A.

By now, the radio airplay on "Spiders And Snakes" was relentless. I didn't know how Gernhard, Curb, and MGM got it played, but someone was making it happen. I couldn't help but feel a warm feeling deep inside. Somebody out there must really care for me because he was getting my song played and making me all sorts of money by doing it. I said, "Of course, Phil, I'll pick up the awards and hit the road ASAP." That evening, Homer and I drove to St. Petersburg and met a guy at Gernhard's office who unlocked the door and gave us complete access to the place. There were boxes of accolades, awards, and gold records just waiting for us to load. We crammed them all in the van with my belongings then drove back to the farm.

Next morning Homer woke me at sunup with a plate of grits, eggs, and bacon waiting on the kitchen table. Frances had a bigger surprise for me at breakfast. "Me and your daddy talked last night and decided if you're gonna drive straight through to L.A., you're gonna need help," she said. "So I'm going with you." Now, rolling into Hollywood with my mom behind the wheel was probably not the coolest way to stake my claim on the big time, but at that particular moment I felt very relieved that she had decided to accompany me. Frances was fearless behind the wheel. She could drive anything and she had a perfect safety record on the school bus she'd driven since I was in the first grade.

By now, Howard had become firmly established in his road manager position. He and Jim first did shows with The Bee Gees, whose songs "How Can You Mend A Broken Heart," "To Love Somebody," "Words," and many others were already woven into the world's musical fabric. When the Bee Gees tour ended, Howard and Jim joined up with Charlie

Rich, flying around in his private plane, which was appropriately named "The Silver Fox." Charlie and his crew, along with Jim and Howard, were crisscrossing America, and "Behind Closed Doors" and "The Most Beautiful Girl In The World" were burning up the music world for Charlie on both the country and pop charts at the same time "Spiders And Snakes" was climbing to the top.

Stafford was in the process of renovating an old movie star house he'd bought in North Hollywood on Cahuenga Drive right across the freeway from the Hollywood Bowl. Howard called to let us know he'd be flying into L.A. around the time we'd be getting into town, so we could all meet up at Stafford's house and begin writing songs. It occurred to me about this time that I actually had never sat down with another songwriter to bare my songwriting soul. Jim and I had discussed the rewrite of "Spiders And Snakes" by telephone a few months earlier, but somehow that was different and I wasn't really sure how the process of face-to-face songwriting was carried out. I decided it was probably best if I didn't reveal my inexperience to Gernhard and Stafford right away.

I still didn't have much news about the TV show but word came to me through Howard and Jim that its theme song was going to be "Spiders And Snakes," and that was enough to keep me chomping at the bit to get involved. As we prepared to leave the farm, Homer told us goodbye and to be careful about a hundred times, then Frances and I, along with my nephew Terry, loaded up the truck and moved to Beverly (actually, North Hollywood).

The trip from Darby, Florida, to Los Angeles, California, is just a little shy of twenty-five hundred miles. That's about forty-five hours of drive time. We made baloney sandwiches and filled our Styrofoam ice chest with Cokes so we could drive without stopping for anything except gas and pit stops. We hit I-75 near the farm and drove a little north of Lake City, Florida, then took a left onto I-10 and headed west. Did I feel then a sense that my life as a music professional was beginning with this journey? Was I excited? What do you think?

My nephew counted most of the jackrabbits crossing the road between Alabama and Arizona while Frances and I took shifts driving to meet up with a group of characters that were not at all like the gentler folk we grew up with back in Darby, Florida.

Only Made It Out to Needles (Apologies to Hoyt Axton)

Having never been west of Mississippi, we decided to at least take a look at the Grand Canyon while we were this close. We knew we were gonna reach our destination before Howard and Jim flew back into L.A., so we turned the van north then west and allowed ourselves one short side trip.

If we looked like the Beverly Hillbillies before, we now resembled the Griswolds, stopping for a few minutes at the canyon rim to take a Polaroid snapshot, then hopping back in the van and heading out to keep our schedule set up by an eccentric record producer. Having seen the Grand Canyon, it wasn't long before we were beginning to bear down on the California state line. We were now counting down the hours till we were sitting in the middle of Tinsel Town.

With the sun high in the sky, we began to see signs of a legendary place called Needles. I mentioned to Frances that the air conditioner did not seem to be staying as cool as it had been so far on the trip. A few miles down the road we started hearing the tires rubbing against the wheel wells and began smelling rubber.

"We'd better find a gas station in Needles and check on things," Frances said, and right about that time the air conditioner completely quit. We rolled the windows down and discovered that the air blowing in from outside was blowing burning hot! By now the rubber was peeling away from the tires and hunks of it were falling by the roadside. We slowed down to a crawl to try to make the final few miles to Needles without tearing anything else up. While we were creeping along, I pulled out the atlas to discover that we were heading into the Mohave Desert. We coasted into a rundown desert gas station just before we reached the town itself. It wasn't much to look at, but there were gas pumps, bathrooms, and cold drinks. "I think our air conditioner is on the fritz," I told the attendant. He said, "Hell, everybody's air conditioner is on the fritz out here, son." He checked the tires while we gulped a couple of cold root beers. "Y'all are lucky you didn't break down out yonder," said the attendant.

The front tires were missing all the tread and the back ones weren't much better. It was a unanimous decision. We needed four new tires.

Needles, I knew where I'd heard that name—that's the town in the lyrics of that song "Never Been To Spain" that Hoyt Axton wrote for Three Dog Night. Once the light bulb went off in my head I had a newfound admiration for the little hellhole we were stuck in, waiting for tires to arrive from somewhere else.

A few years later, we played some shows with Hoyt. He got a big kick out of the story of our mom driving the rubber off the wheels and us breaking down in Needles. I'm happy to say that Hoyt was a friend and a hell of a songwriter.

Camping Out in Hollywood

The new tires showed up after a few hours, the guy in the gas station bolted them on, the van was running fine, and as we left the desert behind, the air conditioner was humming like a top. My musical instruments and Gernhard's awards didn't seem any worse for wear as we rolled on westward.

Jim's house was actually very easy to find once we arrived in L.A. We just hopped off the Hollywood Freeway near the Hollywood Bowl and turned right onto Cahuenga Drive, and there it was. We knocked on the door but the house was locked up tight. There was nothing for us to do but cruise around Hollywood and be tourists for a while. We drove up and down Hollywood and Sunset Boulevards until midmorning, then we got hungry and stopped at a restaurant called The Old World on the Sunset Strip. Anthony Quinn was eating just a couple of tables away from us and Frances was all excited. I thought, *Boy, this really is Hollywood,* so after I finished my lunch I got up to go to the bathroom and cruised through The Old World to see if Steve McQueen or Raquel Welch might be hanging out in there.

When we returned to Jim's house, we were met by Gallagher. I knew the basic story on him but just hearing about Gallagher didn't do him justice. He gave us the nickel tour of the old mansion, which was really beautiful, but almost every room was being renovated. In fact, the only part of the house that wasn't being redone was the basement.

Him being a fellow Floridian, Gallagher and I had a few things in common right off, and he liked Frances as soon as she mentioned cooking something for dinner. She and Terry ran down to the grocery store while Gallagher and I got acquainted. He filled me in more on what was happening in about an hour than Gernhard had told me since I'd met him. ABC Television was producing a summer show on Jim that would take the place of *The Smothers Brothers Show* while they were on hiatus. Gallagher had left his road manager position and begun work as a comedy writer, also creating props for the show's routines and skits. "Spiders And Snakes" was the hit they had needed and they were hoping that the summer show would launch Jim into being a TV personality like Glen Campbell.

Gallagher showed us the house across the street from Stafford's that had once belonged to silent film star Rudolph Valentino. Frances got all excited again and couldn't wait to call Homer back at the farm and tell him all about her experiences her first day in Hollywood.

We organized the little basement kitchen as best we could and made a crude dining area from a folding table we found in the garage. We had it all set up in front of a big open kitchen window on the only side of the basement that was above ground. Frances wiped it down and set it with paper plates and plastic-ware she'd bought on her shopping trip. She was just about ready to serve up some hamburgers she'd made when Gallagher came swinging through the basement window and landed on his butt in the middle of the table, and the whole thing came crashing down.

Picking himself up off the floor laughing, he said only, "How the hell did that table get there?" As the script sort of read in *Cool Hand Luke*, what we had here was a failure of communication. That window, not the door, was Gallagher's routine entrance to the basement. He didn't tell us, so we didn't tell him. Who'd a thought?

Thankfully, the burgers Frances made were sitting on the stove and not the folding table when Gallagher crashed in, so we salvaged what utensils we could, consumed the burgers, and spent the rest of the evening watching Gallagher make balloon animals for my nephew, and looking over some of the props and gags that he was working on, which included a suitcase circus and a leprechaun that rode on a train around the brim of a bowler hat.

There weren't a lot of accommodations for sleeping in that house so that night we took some mattresses from the bedroom renovations upstairs and made beds for me, Frances, and Terry across the big room from Gallagher's makeshift bedroom. Before we went to bed we recounted to each other watching him swing through the basement window, then we retold it again. And again. It got funnier each time. It didn't feel the least bit odd bedding down in this strange basement in this strange new town with this strange comedian sleeping across the room with all these strange gadgets he was building. In fact, exhausted as I was from our long, hot journey, I still had time to think, once again, that after all the adventures that did not lead into a music business career, it appeared that Frances and Homer's youngest boy had actually found his way into the real music biz.

The Burglar Alarm Meets the Sledge-O-Matic and Record Promotion for Dummies

Gallagher got up early the next morning to drive to the airport to pick up Howard and Jim. Frances found a frying pan in the pantry and started some pancakes in our makeshift kitchen. We propped up the table that Gallagher had bent and warned him before he left not to come swinging in through the window. We booked Frances and Terry a flight to Florida for later the following day so she could see Howard for a while then return to the farm to check on Homer and Ginger and get back to work.

When Howard, Jim, and Gallagher got home, the mood was purely festive. The *Spiders And Snakes* album had just gone gold after selling three million singles and peaking at #3 on the national *Billboard* charts and it was also a big hit internationally. Everybody was celebrating and Howard and I were both really happy that Frances had made the long drive with me because now she was here to share in what had become our biggest success so far. Frances, however, had one more item on her agenda to cover before she flew home. Jim had performed on *The Mike Douglas Show* a couple of months earlier and during his interview with the talk show host had said that he wrote "Spiders And Snakes" without giving me any mention at all.

She waited for the right moment, then cornered Jim in the kitchen and asked him why he didn't say I'd written the song and tell the story about us rewriting it together. I didn't know she was going to ask him and I didn't hear it when she did ask him and I don't know how he answered her question but, from then on, Jim gave me credit for writing the song.

Although Jim and Gallagher fought like two nasty old women sometimes—mostly about jokes, gags, and props—they were not hard to live around and we had some really good times together at the old Hollywood mansion on Cahuenga Drive. Howard and Jim flew in and out of town almost every weekend doing shows all over the country. During the weekdays, Gallagher would usually be driving Jim to meetings with Gernhard, ABC, Mike Curb, and the Scotti Brothers, a record promotion organization that would figure heavily into Howard's and my future.

Jim and I would work on songs after dinner in the evenings, in what would become some very unusual songwriting sessions. Then we would gather with Howard and Gallagher in the front room of the old mansion. Sometimes we would invite a few of the girls from the Gernhard/Scotti Brothers office to pretty the place up. Showbiz friends and acquaintances would drop by with wine, beer, and various other potions and stimulants.

As magical as it sometimes was in La La Land, I still kept wondering what I was doing there. It wasn't that I didn't like it, but I had scarcely seen Gernhard since he had made such a fuss about me getting out there so fast, and I still hadn't met Mike Curb, about whom I had heard so much. But I managed to squelch my feelings of unease—I can say that things did not get boring around the old hacienda.

Take the time that Howard and I were working on demos while the guys were out at a meeting and the burglar alarm went off. As I said earlier, Gallagher always had some kind of prop he was working on and this new one he had was destined to become a classic. He called it "The Sledge-O-Matic." Basically it was a very large hammer, with a wooden handle that was stuck through a wooden hammerhead. If memory serves me well, I think the first prototype still had the tree bark on the hammerhead. That's the very tool Howard used on the alarm as it began to ring off the wall. We had no idea how to turn it off; we'd never had a burglar alarm back in Darby.

The enormous bell was located in the basement closet right at the entranceway to our living space. It rang so loud, Howard and I had to run through the garage and outside to escape the noise.

We had no clue what to do but we figured the police would be coming soon and would probably arrest a couple of hippie cowboys hanging out in a nice Hollywood residential area. That's when Howard got an idea: he ran back into the basement holding his ears, put on a pair of headphones from our makeshift recording studio to save his eardrums, then grabbed the big Sledge-O-Matic hammer and gave the burglar alarm a smack that could be heard all over the neighborhood.

With one mighty blow from the Sledge-O-Matic, the bell fell off the wall and went silent.

Howard walked out through the garage and onto the driveway, where I was standing. He was still wearing the headphones and carrying the Sledge-O-Matic when the police pulled up. I guess at that moment we both had stories to tell them running through our heads, about us moving to Hollywood off the farm and me writing the big hit that was on the radio and living with this crazy comedian and Jim getting his own network TV show, but actually we didn't need to do any explaining.

The police rolled down the squad car windows and said, "Everything all right here?"

We yelled out, "Oh yeah, everything's good now!" They rolled up the windows and drove off with Howard still holding the Sledge-O-Matic and wearing the headphones, and me standing next to him looking as if he had struck me instead of the burglar alarm with the ol' Sledge-O-Matic.

I was writing a lot of songs, so Howard and I had started recording demos in the crude little studio we had built in the corner of the basement. When I wasn't working on songs, I took in the sights around Hollywood. As you can imagine, some of those sights had great appeal for a boy fresh off the farm.

The Sunset Strip was emerging from the '60s, trying to hang on to the glory of that decade. The Whiskey a Go Go was still going strong, but acts like The Byrds and Johnny Rivers had given way to Iggy Pop, who crawled on a stage covered with broken glass to entertain the pre-punk audience. We saw Aretha Franklin perform at the Hollywood Bowl and caught Ricky Nelson playing at the Palomino in the San Fernando Valley. He'd recently shortened his name to Rick Nelson and was playing more country rock than the pop rock he'd raised us on during his long run on TV with his parents, Ozzie and Harriet.

I loved all the variety of my new life and was even getting used to the co-writing sessions with the audiences sitting there suggesting lines and hoping in vain for a songwriting credit. Other writers dropped in from time to time, like Dave Loggins, who had a huge hit with a song called "Please Come To Boston" in 1974. He and Jim toured a lot together. Dave ended up writing a lot of hits over the next decade and I'm really glad we got to know him. To me he was a serious songwriter, and Howard and I both have a lot of respect for his work.

Despite the perks and good times living in Tinsel Town, I never lost sight of why I was there. After meeting some of the girls at the Gernhard/Scotti Brothers office, I started hanging out over there to see if I could get into meetings with the honchos. The office was located in the Citibank

Building on Sunset Boulevard where Hollywood ended and Beverly Hills began. I'd only been to the office once before when I first showed up in town. At the time, one of the girls escorted me through the place and introduced me as the co-writer of "Spiders And Snakes." While I was there, I met the various business managers, assistants, accountants, and secretaries to Phil Gernhard and the Scotti Brothers. There were three brothers: Tony, Ben, and Fred. There were rumors, most of them coming from the office itself, about them being goodfellas, wise guys, tough guys, or whatever they called them, but Howard and I liked them and got on well with them. They were friendly and outgoing most of the time, nothing at all like Gernhard, who had by now earned the nickname "Black Bart" for his shades, dark clothes, and the way he sulked around with a gold Quaalude on a chain around his neck, smoking his little spaghetti western cigar and scowling at everybody.

I did have one tough guy moment my first visit to Ben Scotti's office. Ben was on the phone when I walked in with his secretary. She told him who I was and he asked us to give him a minute. He went back to his phone conversation without missing a beat and said very matter-of-factly to the party on the other end of the line, "If you don't play that record, I'm gonna break your fuckin' legs." Then he politely hung up the phone and said, "Hey kid, nice to meet you. I was just promoting your song to the radio."

6
As Fate Would Have It
Off to London and Thank You, Petula

DAVID: Hanging out at the office must have been the ticket because in true form, without saying good morning, how are you, Gernhard rang me and said, "Do you have a passport?"

I said no, and he said, "We'll get the girls right on it. Tony and I are producing Petula Clark in London and we want you to come along and record some of your songs on the sessions." He asked me to come to the office the next morning and go over some of the demos I'd left him and discuss travel details with his assistant.

"Okay, I'll be there," was all I said. I knew by now that he wasn't going to answer all the in-depth questions I had, and besides, he'd already said the words I wanted to hear: record some of your songs.

Turns out that Gernhard and Tony Scotti were leaving the day after our meeting to start the Petula Clark recordings. They wanted me to meet with an arranger and have him score three of my songs, "Nothin' Heavy," "Inside My Guitar," and "Baby, You're Not A Legend," then meet them in London.

I had a few more songs I really wanted to pitch to them for the session, but there was not much wiggle room around this outfit; you just had to learn to roll with them. My passport came in, my flight was booked, and I was off on my first of many trips to Merry Ol' England.

Any drugs I may have played with in my life were nothing like the shot of adrenalin burning through me as I contemplated my *international* future while deplaning in London. I hailed one of those cool little black taxi cabs I'd seen in those British films that had flooded into America along with all that British music. The taxi took me to the Cumberland Hotel at 32 Great Cumberland Place. There was no one to greet me when I arrived, but my room was ready so I checked in and called home to Darby to tell Frances and Homer that their littlest boy had made it safely to his hotel in London, England. "Spiders And Snakes" had been a smash on the British charts and Jim had just been there shooting shows for the BBC, so I felt a little connected.

I wrote a song in my hotel room that afternoon then walked around town and almost got run over crossing the street. I ate some fish and chips and drank a pint at a very nice pub. On the walk back to the hotel, I caught a really hard chill, and when I got back to my room I called the desk and asked them how to turn up the heater. In the most polite British accent I've ever heard, the desk clerk said, "Sir, it's September and we don't turn the heat on till October."

I took the lift downstairs to see if the front desk could find me some more blankets. As I passed by the lobby bar, I saw Gernhard, Tony Scotti, and Petula Clark sitting together having a drink and talking. I walked over and said hi. Tony introduced me to Petula Clark and asked if I'd had a good flight. I said, "Yeah, but I've caught a terrible chill and the heat's off in my room and I'm trying to find some blankets."

Petula Clark stood up and said, "*We* have to get you a doctor."

I didn't know what to say. I wanted to say, "I really loved your record *Downtown*, and one time I accidently played it in church with my brother instead of 'I'll Fly Away,'" but I was feeling so bad I couldn't do anything but shiver. She went to the desk and told them to send up the house doctor, then she helped me up to my room and the doctor came right away. She told the doctor to take good care of me and for him to call her if I needed anything.

The doctor looked me over and said I was fine. He said I had a case of jet lag and nerves, and ordered me a glass of whiskey and warm milk. When it came I drank it down and fell asleep under a pile of wool blankets.

My phone rang early the next morning. It was Gernhard asking if I was okay and could I be at the studio at noon with the arrangements to my songs. A couple of hours later I was at the studio running down the songs with the band. The session went fine and Gernhard and Scotti both declared that "Nothin' Heavy" was a hit.

When I got back to the hotel I had messages from the doctor and Petula Clark checking on me. I was actually doing better than fine; that night I danced the Boogaloo at Tramps with British girls whose names I never did know and with hopes of meeting one of The Beatles or Stones at the trendy club. The very next morning I was flying back to L.A. I'd spent only a couple of days in the U.K., but I liked it a lot and I knew I'd be coming back some day.

Gernhard brought the U.K. masters back to L.A. to mix them. Jim's second album was finished; I had co-written five songs on it and Howard and I sang backup on several tracks. A couple of the girls from Gernhard/Scotti's office started coming over a lot and the basement started to get a little cramped, what with Gallagher's props, my demo studio, and let's call 'em "the secretaries."

I moved into my own place on Beechwood Drive. It wasn't the greatest apartment in the world, but the demo studio had its own room that doubled for Howard's bedroom when he was in town. The most notable thing about the Beechwood apartment was that it was on the street right under the famous Hollywood sign.

Neil Diamond's Roadie and Howard's Accidental Audition

Even after I moved into my own place, I missed home a lot. When I got back to L.A., I missed London, too, although I'd only been there for a few days. Like Darby, it was a lot more quaint and friendly than the streets of Hollywood.

Howard went home to Darby more than I did because Jim played quite a bit in the South, leaving me feeling very much alone out there on the West Coast. I was just downright homesick for Darby. I missed Homer's fried chicken. I missed the Spanish moss. I missed the Gulf of Mexico. I missed the humidity. Janet and I had kept in touch since I left home, but when I talked to her, I just naturally left out the hell-raising rock and roll parts of my adventures.

I was beginning to get tired of that kind of craziness, anyway. For the first time in my life, I had money coming in from my songwriting and even if I had known how much Gernhard had sliced off, it was still more money than I had ever seen. I asked Janet to fly out to L.A. and visit me and once her parents got over their nervous breakdown over her taking a week out of high school, we worked it out.

I pretty much understood that the girls in the Gernhard/Scotti office were more attracted to my newfound royalty income than anything else. Most days they sat around there and waited for someone famous to come in, to see if they could work their way into a situation. After all, this was Hollywood, and it wasn't unusual to see David Cassidy, Frankie Valli, or a Beach Boy drop in for a meeting. During Janet's visit, we decided to get married. I felt good about having a girl from back home as opposed to the Hollywood honeys I had been hanging with who moved to L.A. from the Midwest and copped attitudes. I took a red-eye flight home and we were married at the farm by a preacher friend of ours after Janet's priest refused to marry us because she was too young. Howard made it home in time to be my best man then left right after the wedding to continue his road manager grind. I drove Janet to class every day for her last two weeks at Chamberlain High School. After her graduation, we flew back to L.A. for another crazy chapter.

Back in L.A., life was getting busy. Gernhard was getting ready to release my first single, "Nothin' Heavy," one of the tracks we cut in London during the Petula Clark sessions. I was concerned because we didn't have a complete album to follow up with if we had a hit single. I asked Gernhard about cutting more tracks with Neil Diamond's band and to my astonishment, he agreed.

I loved cutting with Neil's band. They had such great arrangement ideas for my songs and everybody put their whole heart into the sessions. At that time, the band was Dennis St. John playing drums, Alan Lindgren on keyboards, Richard Bennett was playing guitar, and Emery Gordy was the bass player, with King Ericson playing percussion.

Almost at the exact same time the sessions were going on, the planets lined up, our ducks all got in a row, and I suspect that Frances and Homer must have been praying really hard for us, because a couple of things happened next that not only set the wheels in motion but got 'em moving down the highway. Life's like that sometimes, if you're there to give it just a little push.

Howard and Jim were in Winter Haven doing a show at Cypress Gardens. Tony Scotti flew in to Florida to see the show and meet with Jim. While Howard was on stage setting up for the show, as usual he sang a song to get the sound levels. I had recently written a song called, "I'm The Only Sane Man Left Alive," and that night Howard chose to sing that song. Tony was down by the lake talking to Jim when he heard Howard's voice drifting through the sweet southern afternoon. Tony asked, "Who's that singing?" and Jim replied, "Oh, that's Howard doing sound check."

Flash back a few weeks to a recording session we were doing in Hollywood. We'd just laid down some tracks when Dennis St. John walked into the control room and said, "You know, our roadie wrote this song you should hear. It sounds like something y'all would do."

"Great, when can I hear it?" I asked. Dennis told me he'd left a copy in Gernhard's office for him to listen to but he hadn't heard back from him on it.

"I'll check it out," I said.

A couple of days later I went to Gernhard's office and asked his assistant if I could go through the pile of tapes and look for the demo Dennis had told me about. After twenty minutes of stacking and restacking tape boxes and checking labels, I found it. "Let Your Love Flow written by Larry Williams," was all the box said. Without thinking much about it, I popped it on the reel-to-reel in Gernhard's listening room.

Wow! I thought. *Cool song.* I loved the song from the minute I heard it in Gernhard's office. I looked for Gernhard but he was out of the office. I tucked the tape under my arm and left with it.

Prior to all this going down, Gernhard/Scotti and Mike Curb had made a deal with Warner Brothers Records. The new brand was called Warner/Curb but also contained the Gernhard/Scotti logo. They shipped my single "Nothin' Heavy" on the new label and before long it started to climb the pop charts but peaked at #57 in *Billboard*. I was naturally disappointed with the results of the single but not for long. For my next meeting with Gernhard, he asked Howard to come along. Tony Scotti had dropped in from his office down the hall and relayed his story about hearing Howard sing my song at Jim's sound check and how great it sounded. Gernhard asked me if we'd ever thought about singing together as a duo. We both laughed and replied that we'd been a duo or a band for years in one form or another. Tony said, then, "Well, why don't you just call yourselves The Bellamy Brothers?"

None of this surprised us, because we had been heading in that direction ever since the first time we'd played music with our father at the Rattlesnake Roundup. It did help, I believe, that the idea appeared to come from our puppeteers.

My real excitement came when I got the chance to play "Let Your Love Flow" for Howard after he and Stafford returned from a road trip. He reinforced my gut feeling that it was a song worth battling Gernhard to take it into the studio and cut.

HOWARD: If I remember, my exact reaction was, "It's fucking great!"

DAVID: Howard has a good ear, and when we both love a song, we'll battle for it. We started planning our first session as The Bellamy Brothers and immediately went to work on Gernhard to let us cut "Let Your Love Flow." Gernhard was not that hot on the song, not at first. He'd heard the demo and said he liked it but he didn't seem to *love* it.

Dennis coaxed him a little, and then Howard and I ganged up on him and he gave in.

The one problem with Howard and me recording as The Bellamy Brothers was that the people who wanted him to be a recording artist were the same people who wanted him to stay on the road as Stafford's road manager. Both roles required him to endure grueling tour schedules. He couldn't do both. He would have to choose. Events would make the choice easy.

The recording session for "Let Your Love Flow" was booked at Wally Heider's studio near Sunset and Vine in early November 1975. Of course, due to Jim's travel schedule, Howard was on the road, so it was just me, Neil's band (or The Diamondback Band, as we liked to call them in those days), Gernhard, and our engineer, Mic Leitz. I sang the scratch vocal with the band and they nailed the track with a few takes. I thought I was gonna sing the lead vocal, but Gernhard called me and said Tony wanted Howard to sing it.

HOWARD: The day I was supposed to sing, I was so sick I could hardly get out of bed. I had to snort some coke to give me the energy to get through it. Coke/jet lag/flu-fever vocal. Of course, they had recorded the original demo with Larry Williams so they were very familiar with the song. The biggest addition to the track occurred when Emory Gordy, who played bass on the session, got the idea for the intro after the track was cut, and overdubbed the now famous intro lick as an afterthought. Also, King Ericson played a rhythmic little sandpaper part between the guitar licks on the intro that people ask about to this day.

DAVID: Howard was sick as a dog from some crud he'd caught on the road, but he didn't mention it to Gernhard. This cut was clearly a shot at a hit and we weren't about to let a little thing like pneumonia get in the way of our destiny.

Nothing comes easy. Gernhard was getting stranger all the time, so we avoided telling him little things like the fact that I'd got married. He'd get very dramatic and melancholy in the studio sometimes, like he was carrying the weight of the world on his back. We had another good reason not to rattle him too hard. He carried a loaded pistol in his briefcase, along with a bottle of Quaaludes and those little mini-bottles of Jack Daniels they used to serve on airplanes. We mixed "Let Your Love Flow" with him at Sound Lab in L.A. just before Thanksgiving 1975; it took us all night. Gernhard smashed a couple of sets of headphones against the wall during the mix. He claimed to be deaf on his left side, so he'd mix a song listening to the studio monitors out of his right ear and the headphones on his left ear. In spite of the busted headphones, we finished mixing "Let Your Love Flow" at sunrise, and if we thought it sounded great after we'd recorded it, now it sounded incredible.

Chaos of Global Proportions and Party Like a Rock Star

We actually had Thanksgiving at Gernhard's house after we finished mixing "Let Your Love Flow." The dinner went so well we thought that maybe things were gonna be okay with him. About the same time, Mike Curb appeared out of hiding and became a face we could put with the name. We'd met him only once before, briefly, when he told me what a great songwriter I was after "Spiders And Snakes" went gold. Curb has always been very generous with his compliments. That should have been reason enough for me to be a little skeptical of him, but it was glorious to hear his compliments in contrast to Gernhard's dark moods and intimidating remarks.

On the whole, this was a singular bunch of characters. Tony Scotti had been an actor (he played Sharon Tate's boyfriend in *Valley Of The Dolls*). His brother, Ben, had been a defensive back in the National Football League who played for the Washington Redskins, Philadelphia Eagles, and San Francisco 49ers, and achieved national notoriety when he brawled with a much bigger teammate and sent him to the hospital. He was a rough, tough promoter but a fun guy to be around if he was on your side.

Curb was hyped as a music golden boy. I'm not sure what that meant, but people referred to him that way. We heard that he spent a lot of time playing with a slot car track he'd set up in the basement of MGM

Records just prior to taking over that label and becoming its president. Tony Scotti was married to Mike Curb's sister. Then of course there was Gernhard. The more we learned about him, the less we wanted to ask.

Whatever opinion we had of this band of in-laws and outlaws, for the moment they seemed to be very high on the new single we had just recorded, and that was enough to tie us all together for the long, strange ride.

We spent Christmas of '75 in Darby, and of course we played the mix of "Let Your Love Flow" for Homer and Frances. Of course they loved it, and Homer even gave out with his patented high-pitched "*YEEEEES!*" that he usually reserved for Bob Wills or Jimmie Rodgers, in approval of the record.

It was a special Christmas. Our parents never liked us spending money on them, but we did anyway because it was the first time we'd ever had the means to spoil them. Stuff like farm tools for Homer—and we did get Frances a new car. Janet and I went back to L.A. right after Christmas, and Howard met Stafford on the road for a New Year's Eve gig. It seemed that no matter how hard he tried, the honchos at the Gernhard/Scotti office would not let him leave his road manager job—the curse of doing something all too well.

But we are nothing if not resourceful. Howard called me from the road and said he'd thought of a plan to get him off the road and back to L.A. so we could write songs and do demos to try to get an album together. Jim was playing with Raquel Welch at the Fontainebleau Hotel in Miami Beach. The entire management company, the label, promotion staff, etc., was there for the show. It was also Raquel's birthday, so we had a party for her.

HOWARD: It was right after the party that I made my move. While I was moving a bunch of guitars in their heavy cases, I perceived some back pains so I called Jim and the doctor and moaned realistically and that was the end of my road manager career.

DAVID: He flew back to L.A. and we began recording demos on new songs. It's a good thing he faked that back injury because a couple of weeks later, the same guys who wouldn't let him off the road called to say, "We're gonna need to shoot photos and a video for Holland."

"Who's Holland?" I asked. I was a little jittery about responding to their calls since Howard had come off the road with his "back injury," and he was a little nervous because it hadn't been so long ago since Gernhard had called him just before a show in New Jersey and told him to buy a gun because he thought that "Something might be going down," whatever that meant.

Fame with No Fortune

The next call from Gernhard brought good news. He told us that the single would be coming out in Europe before the U.S. release, and we'd be making a film to send to the Netherlands, England, Germany, and Switzerland.

As usual, the details were murky, but we had learned by now to fill in the blanks and roll with them. Some of the guys in Neil's band turned us on to a tailor named Bill Witten. He made sparkly shirts for Neil Diamond, and when we went to see him we met Smokey Robinson while he was getting fitted for some new stage clothes. Witten had not yet designed what would be his most famous piece of stage clothing: a few years later, he would create Michael Jackson's iconic single sequined glove.

We got him to make us some silk cowboy shirts and "designer jeans" before the term even existed. We still weren't sure what we were doing, but we wanted to look good doing it. The photo shoot was set, and the man behind the camera was Norman Seeff, who has shot photos of everyone from Joni Mitchell and Van Morrison to Aerosmith and Steve Jobs. The shoot was a very simple setup: a neutral backdrop with Howard and me standing in front of it, except for one thing—there were two beautiful women in evening gowns with expensive accessories and high heels, fanning us with large pieces of cardboard to make our hair blow while Seeff shot pictures.

We were thinking, *Wow, ol' Norman's really a class act. Glad we got some new clothes made for the shoot.* It never dawned on us until the

Scotti Brothers and Gernhard showed up with a couple of guys from WEA Records in Holland that the two babes were there on business.

The foreign label guys came in and we had a nice meet and greet, and they expressed how much they liked "Let Your Love Flow." Norman Seeff shot more photos and the girls smiled and someone opened a bottle of champagne. Seeff got some great windblown portraits for our album cover. The girls left with the Dutch record execs after downing a couple of bottles of Dom Perignon.

A few days later, we were booked at an old Hollywood soundstage for the video shoot. Gernhard/Scotti and Warner/Curb had hired an up-and-coming film producer named Penelope Spheeris to shoot a one-camera black-and-white film short. This was several years before the term "music video" was common, but that's what we were doing. Penelope would go on to do some famous movies like the punk rock movie, *The Decline of Western Civilization*, and the movie version of *The Beverly Hillbillies*.

We didn't have any glamorous girls at the video shoot, but I believe the film must have worked some magic because within a few weeks of sending out the final edit, we got word that the record was being played heavily in parts of Europe and we needed to get there ASAP for TV and promotion.

Folks, here's where it all begins to change. *The Old Grey Whistle Stop* and *Top of the Pops* in England and TV shows across the continent had started to air the video, giving us tremendous exposure throughout the U.K. and Europe. We actually hit the charts first in Holland, which was a small market but prestigious and respected by the U.K. and Germany. It now appeared that the black and white film and the lovely ladies who fanned us at the photo shoot had done their job. Our first promo tour was like throwing Br'er Rabbit in the briar patch. First stop was Amsterdam. That beautiful city was said to feature every conceivable vice known to man, and almost all of it was legal. Not only that, but by the time we arrived, "Let Your Love Flow" was a full-blown hit in the Netherlands. The label picked us up in limousines, we ate exotic foods at great restaurants, we taped TV shows, and we did interviews with European journalists for magazines and newspapers.

Everything in this wonderful place was at our disposal. We visited the "Melk Weg," which is Dutch for Milky Way. I can only describe it as a hippie heaven complete with a kind of farmers' market for hashish, a theater that usually had some form of nude conceptual art play going on, and a bakery with mattresses so you could buy space cakes and then crash on a mattress when you got too high. Then there was the Paradiso, which also catered to the most hedonistic whims in the form of hookahs full of hash, strippers, and live bands.

HOWARD: An eye-opener for a couple of Darby boys.

DAVID: We had only been in Holland for a few days, but we were already more worldly than when we arrived. We got word while we were still there that the record was taking off in Germany. That was our next stop. The last day in Amsterdam we had off before we headed to Germany for television. The record label gave us a limo and a driver who was a historian and we rode around the entire countryside checking out windmills and canals and buying wooden shoes and Delftware to take home. When the limo took us back to the hotel that night, the driver made a detour through the red light district so we could see the ladies of the evening in the windows with their specially written menus outside their small rooms.

The limo could barely get through the narrow cobblestone streets and had to stop for bicycles and pedestrians who were window-shopping every few steps. A group of professional ladies spotted the limo and came out of their tiny places of business and began knocking on the limo windows and shouting at us to come on in. The tumult they made caused more of them to come out on the street and the pedestrians to cheer and applaud as they displayed their wares in front of the car and against the windows. We crept along at a snail's pace, causing a bizarre parade of sorts in this surreal little city of vice.

After Amsterdam, we headed to Hamburg. The single was racing up the charts in Germany. We taped TV shows, did interviews, hosted dinners, and shot photo sessions. We were starting to fall into the rhythm of the thing. We'd start the day lip-syncing "Let Your Love Flow" on a boat in the harbor for a TV network and end it in the wee hours of the morning at the world famous Reeperbahn. We've all heard the expression "party like a rock star," but if you've never crawled out of the most notorious clubs in Amsterdam at sunrise in the mid-'70s with a hit record barreling up the charts, chances are you still haven't actually partied like a rock star.

We started running into other artists from all over the world who were out on the concert and promotion trail. Dr. Hook, Bonnie Tyler, Abba, Boney M., Pussycat, Taj Mahal, even actors like Telly Savalas, all of them making the rounds in Europe in the mid-'70s as "Let Your Love Flow" was breaking. Munich was the next stop. We met Donna Summer and Bob Marley at the Munich Hilton and filmed a TV show called *Disco*, hosted by a fellow named Ilia Richter. While we were in our dressing room, the TV show host was introduced, and the young audience began to stomp their feet on the wooden bleachers and start chanting, "Heil Ilia! Heil Ilia!" Backstage in our dressing room, it sounded like they were screaming, "Heil Hitler!" Having seen one too many World War II movies, we were terrified to come out when they announced us. One of the show's producers cleared up the miscommunication and we skeptically stepped out into a studio full of screaming fans, who by now had heard "Let Your Love Flow" on both the German radio and the Armed Forces Network, which was a major radio influencer in Europe at the time.

We loved Bavaria; we took to the beer gardens like a duck takes to water, and we would return countless times over the years to perform and record in Munich. Our promotional blitzkrieg in Europe was beginning to wind down as we made a stop in Switzerland to tape a TV show in Zurich. Our first trip to Switzerland was so quick that we didn't get to see much of what was outside the TV studio. In the coming years, Switzerland would become almost a second home to us, a place to perform and to make many lifelong friends.

But for now, it was back to L.A. We had become more road wise than we had ever been and it was a good thing, too, because as we were leaving Europe we got the word that "Let Your Love Flow" was breaking big in America.

Back in L.A., we set to work trying to put together a band, and maybe we struggled a bit because we hadn't had a band for a while, but with a little too much help from Gernhard/Scotti, we would have our band. Warner Brothers had secured a spot for us opening for Loggins and Messina, who were doing their last tour together.

HOWARD: That sounds exciting, playing a big league tour, but we had one hour to play for the people and we had one hit. So we started with "Let Your Love Flow" at the beginning, then we did the reprise of "Let Your Love Flow" to close the show. In between we did all original songs— in other words, songs the audiences had never heard. Oddly enough, the show went off very well.

DAVID: The record got released in the U.S. not long after it came out in Europe, with similar results. You don't instantly grasp the impact of having a big hit record. But there were clues. We had a little radio sitting on top of our fridge in the kitchen. Right after we got back from Europe, we were eating breakfast or something, and Howard flipped that radio on, and "Let Your Love Flow" was on the radio. And when the record was over, he moved the tuning knob down the dial and "Let Your Love Flow" was on the next radio station. So we listened till the record was over and Howard moved it down the dial again and "Let Your Love Flow" was on the *third* radio station. Suddenly we were hearing it on every pop station in L.A.

HOWARD: I was taking my guitar to Art Valdez's guitar shop in Santa Monica. I'd parked my car and was walking along the sidewalk, and these kids, standing by parked car, you know, they had their windows down and the doors open, had the radio blasting and just as I walked by, the intro of "Let Your Love Flow" comes on. That made an impact because those kids, they were groovin', they were standin' there groovin', and I stopped for a moment to watch, thinkin', *This is really wild.* Shortly after that, we flew home to Darby, and I was working on an old Plymouth I had with my uncle and I turned on the radio—there it was. It was on every radio station we tuned in, or so it seemed.

DAVID: It was the largest BMI airplay record that year. It was like ecstasy for a new recording act. We should have woken up every morning in seventh heaven but, you know, there was the business, and there, in L.A., our world was in a little bit of a disarray because we had Gernhard and company puttin' the band together. We should have tried to do more of that ourselves because we'd been putting bands together all our life, but it wasn't easy to go to them and say, "Hey guys, we'll handle this." Think of it this way: they were the hard-charging control freaks and we were the polite country boys who didn't want to make waves—and anyway, we figured they knew what they were doing. And in the meantime it was like the song "Rhinestone Cowboy": *offers comin' over the phone* from all over the world! Germany can't get enough of us because we just spent eight weeks at #1. We could have *lived* in Germany and Switzerland at that point. Japan wanted us for a major tour. Later we spent half a summer in Scandinavia and played there almost every night. All of that was going on while they were trying to manage us, and we were fighting them. There was just always a tug of war going on.

I mean, we did wake up and say, "Damn, we got the #1 record in the world!" For two farm boys from Florida, we felt like we had already conquered the world. Heck, when Stafford had his hit on "Spiders and Snakes," I thought I'd conquered the world. This, now, this worldwide thing was beyond anything we could have imagined, but at the same time, we're startin' to realize, we're in a den of thieves here, neck deep in it and we can't just waller around in it forever.

The interesting thing about our record deal was, even though we were on Warner/Curb, we were kind of kept away from Warner Brothers. Gernhard and Scotti told us all they thought we needed to know. They'd call us up and say "You've got a tour with Loggins and Messina," and we'd go, "Yeah!" Like you'd expect a couple of farm boys like us to do, and the other strange thing, at that time, "Let Your Love Flow" was all over the charts, and we had not finished the album.

HOWARD: And the reason for that is that Gernhard, what he was really known for, he was a singles producer to start with. That was what they would shoot for and we were just adamant that we wanted to have a great album. It was like pulling teeth from our end. The first big battle we had with them was we wanted to put our energy into the album, and we eventually did, but if it had been a joint effort from everybody it could have been a much better project.

This was a big time for Gernhard and the Scotti Brothers. This was their record operation—with Curb and Warner Bros—and the first two singles they put out became huge, huge hits. They were "Let Your Love Flow" and the Four Seasons's "Oh What A Night." But Gernhard and the Scotti Brothers never got along. They fought the whole time and finally the Scottis split off and went to working on *Baywatch* and all that TV stuff.

DAVID: We could see that a whole lot needed getting done. But any time you tried to talk to Gernhard about anything like that, he'd just say, "Curb wants this," or "Curb wants that." By this time, we had learned that you couldn't just go into Gernhard's office and demand things. He was just crazy. He might have that .38 in his desk. We tried to put pressure on him to move the album sessions forward, and Neil Diamond's band, which was backing us on the album tracks, was a big help.

HOWARD: Neil's band really liked us because our homegrown was so good. That was our link, you know, we just became good friends; we partied together. Within three months of coming back from our first trip to Europe, with a huge amount of help from Neil's band, we finally had an album ready for release. So between finishing up the album, putting together the band, and preparing for the Loggins/Messina tour, we were dizzy-busy, and then of course there was a lot of demand at the time for us to get back to Europe because the record had become so huge there. In the summer of '76 we made it to #1 in the U.S. in *Billboard*. The German music chart reads us at #1, Wings at #2 and The Beatles at #3. Can you imagine how that must have felt! It was #1 for eight weeks! So we were doing all this stuff at one time, but there wasn't a master plan going on. I think this record took off so fast there was nobody on our team who really knew where we needed to go from there.

DAVID: Our mom and dad were riding back to the farm from town when they heard some news about their boys on the radio. The Associated Press put out a wire saying that we had been cited in Beverly Hills for not mowing our grass.

HOWARD: We had actually planted a garden in our yard and of course with us being on the road, it got up to about knee high and they came out and gave us a citation for it being a health hazard, attracting rodents. Homer and Frances are riding down the road and hear this, so they get home and check in with us about it.

A lot of people rode Frances's school bus. I still run into people today who say, "You know, I remember when 'Let Your Love Flow' came out, and Frances had this radio on the bus and when it would come on the radio, she'd turn that bus into the ditch and let us listen to 'Let Your Love Flow' before she took off down the road." She probably would sit there because the reception was good in that spot. You remember those big mobile signs that you could rent back in the '70s, they were like a billboard, with lights on them, they had tires on them and you could drag 'em? Our parents rented one and put it out on State Road 52, and it said: NO. 1 IN THE NATION LET YOUR LOVE FLOW.

DAVID: I think the record hit fast enough and big enough in Europe that we realized that we were gonna have to get it together. We still didn't figure that it would become that big a world hit, but we knew it *might*, so when we got back to L.A. we were primed to party. It wasn't that we were especially bad about doing drugs or whatever, it just seemed like we were in the right (wrong) place at the right time. We got to L.A. in the mid-'70s when pretty much every bathroom stall had somebody snortin' coke in it.

There was a single-edged razor blade in every rehearsal hall in L.A. It was a crazy world, but we were still working on music, we never quit doing that and we knew something was coming 'cause we'd had that preview in Europe. Just a few days on that promo tour there and we could tell that if this record took off everywhere like it did in Germany and Switzerland, we were gonna be busy. So we worked our tails off and put together a good enough band to go out and play for a lot of people.

HOWARD: And on that tour we had a star in his own right: Bob Thompson. He was our first roadie, and he later went on to work for Glenn Frey; he was the son of Art Carney. We called him "Norton." He wore the crinkled hat that you see those wannabe cowboys wear. Norton rode an imaginary horse named Rex. He was afraid of flying, so when we would board airplanes and we'd be coming down the jetway, he would pretend like he was boarding Rex. Flight attendants would get a big kick out of this, but then he would also get up in the middle of the flight, riding Rex down the middle of the aisle while they were trying to serve dinner. We went to a record company party in London one time, at Trader Vic's, full of really stuffy British record people, and Norton decided to ride Rex down the table, knocking over all the champagne glasses,

DAVID: Meanwhile, life was very strange in the home office. For example, Gernhard demanded that we hire this guitar player who was in Tampa. We couldn't understand why, because we already had a nine-piece band, which was way more than we wanted, but Gernhard insisted, so we hit the road with what felt like a full symphony orchestra, and right from the start, the guitar player is drinking so hard that he's more trouble than he's worth, so we decided to fire him the second day on the tour. So we go over to his room and open the door and he's got a hooker on his bed, and poker chips—*poker chips*—everywhere. We say, "Man, we got to talk to you." We didn't want to embarrass him in front of the hooker, but he said, "She can stay," so we explained that we were going to fire him and we gave him some excuses, but he just turned all emotional. "Oh no," he cried in front of the hooker and the poker chips and all. "You can't fire me, my wife's in L.A. and I've moved my kids out to the coast," but we finally ended it, we thought. Turned out that things were a bit more complicated than that. He heads back to L.A. and when he gets there he catches Gernhard with his wife. Turns out the reason Gernhard wanted him in the band was so that when he went on the road, Gernhard could go out with the guy's wife. We soon found that drama like this was going on constantly. This was all stuff that we did not really wanna deal with.

Gernhard and Scotti had brought in Stan Moress to be our manager, and Stan went to Europe with us on a couple of trips. Stan took a Playboy Bunny to Germany with us and she almost got us busted for pot.

HOWARD: The whole story was, in those days there were no smoke detectors on planes; of course, we smoked pot on planes all the time. You took a couple of joints on the flight with you and flushed them down after you used them. We were going over to do the Golden Lions Award in Dusseldorf, Germany, their equivalent of our Grammys, and Stan's girlfriend, Joanie, pipes up and says, "Y'all think I'll get in trouble if I've got some pot on me?"

DAVID: We about shit, and I could see our careers going down the tubes. So we land and, sure enough, everybody's luggage comes out except ours. We had been smoking on the plane so they knew there was pot somewhere. So all of our luggage came out on one big cart. We're all standing there watching them shake down her suitcase, and while the guy is feeling around among the contents he turns his head away and she reaches down into her suitcase and grabs the bag of pot and puts it in her purse. We took a deep breath of relief, but it wasn't over. They kept looking but they didn't find anything and they were really puzzled because they were sure we must be hiding some somewhere, so then this big dykey woman comes up and does a personal search on her. But, oddly enough, she didn't check her purse, she just checked her personally. So Joanie walked out of there with that bag of pot in her purse. Stan got in a lot of trouble with the Scottis over that.

It was a time of great promise, with some disappointment thrown in. About a year after "Let Your Love Flow" hit, we did three solid months in Europe then returned to Los Angeles. Shortly after we got back, we took our guitars into Valdez Guitars to get them fixed. Just as we pulled up at the store, we heard on the radio that Elvis had died. I don't think I'd had a lick of sleep in those three months we toured Europe, so I wondered if I was hearing right.

HOWARD: It was so wild. I watched David get "married" in a disco and not know who he got married to. German beer and schnapps'll do that to you.

DAVID: Never saw her since. I suppose I have a "wife" in Germany—somewhere.

So we got back to L.A. I called Paul Smith at International Talent and said, "Hey, we're home. Ain't it a drag Elvis died?" He says, "I was just fixin' to call you. Felton Jarvis wants to talk to you." Well, in those days, Felton Jarvis was one of those magical names, 'cause Felton Jarvis was Elvis's record producer.

I said, "Really? What about?" and Paul said, "Come by the office." The office was close by so we ran out to Paul's office and he called Felton. I get on the phone and probably said, "How you doin', sir?"

He says, "I just wanted to tell you that we were in the middle of a recording session and Elvis had to leave to do some shows. We were cuttin' your song, 'Miss Misunderstood.'" Of course, I didn't know what to say at this point. So I waited for him to go on. He says, "Elvis really loved that song, son." I didn't have to ask the big question. He knew what I was gonna ask. He said, "We cut the tracks, but we didn't do the vocal. And I don't think there's a scratch vocal on the tape. We're gonna cut the song on Carl Perkins and I just wanted to tell you how much Elvis loved that song."

And it was a long time before I ever told anybody else that story 'cause it sounds like a lie.

HOWARD: We were just in shock.

DAVID: Howard and I were singers, but we were also songwriters, and even at the end of Elvis's career, an Elvis cut on one of your songs was like finding the Holy Grail. And so Carl Perkins recorded on the track that was originally cut for Elvis. And then he cut it live at The Lone Star in New York and the live version was really good. We had recorded it on our second album. It had an ol' rockabilly beat to it. That was the summer of '77. The summer Elvis died.

HOWARD: Almost like Willie and Merle, their last project. Their producer, Buddy Cannon, called and said they were cutting "Old Hippie." We got a little stoked but we've had so much shit like that happen that we remember the old saying, "It ain't final till it's vinyl," meaning until the actual record comes out, don't count on *anything*.

Understand, we may have a good artist career ourselves but we are fans—and songwriters too—and to have a singer like Elvis or Merle cut one of our songs would have meant the world to us. To come so close and miss out hurts us as much as it would hurt any other songwriter. But you know, most songwriters I know have sad stories like that, about the song that almost got cut by this or that superstar. This is one *hell* of a business to be in.

DAVID: There was pretty much a story every day. About six months after we came back from Europe, we were getting ready to go to Japan and do the Tokyo Song Festival because the song went #1 in Japan, as well. Gernhard was kind of ramrodding that thing, and of course he was trying to sleep with our piano player at the same time. We had this girl that we had chosen to play piano for us, Big Betty, six foot tall, and he was trying to get to her. He wanted to go with us so that he could zero in on Big Betty, but before we went we had to take shots, and the shots made him so sick that he couldn't go to Japan.

Playing in Japan spawned its own indelible memories for us, especially concerning last minute backup singers. We rehearsed and got everything as good as we could. The setup and production were really bad, yet as we rehearsed, I thought we had got it down, but when we did the actual show that night—and this was live—the drummer started with a completely different feel than what the record was. Howard's up there trying to play drum parts on the guitar to keep the rhythm going, turning around and trying to show the drummer what to play, and the guy's playing something totally different. Almost as bad, they had decided to add three girl singers who were not at rehearsal that day. Well, when we hit the chorus, the girls came in with a purely Japanese riff, singing, "Ret Yaw Ruv Frow . . ." *Really loud!* On live television!

HOWARD: Of course, brothers that we were, we looked at each other and started laughing our asses off. On live television to the entire nation of Japan! We were ready to kill the orchestra leader! But we got through it. Somehow.

DAVID: That was reminiscent of another background singer story from when we were in Holland doing a show called Rock and Roll Circus.

HOWARD: Dave Edmonds, I remember was on the show, it was a big circus tent, and they had the acts lined up around the tent, and the cameras were all in the center, and they would move from one act to the next, like a circus.

DAVID: We had done rehearsals the day before, and we got there that night, went on, and started singing "Let Your Love Flow," and while we were singing I looked over toward Howard; I could see this big TV monitor and on the monitor there was this topless girl dancing between us.

HOWARD: Looking at the monitor, all *I* could see were just big bouncing boobs!

DAVID: BIG-breasted girl, and she's dancin' around and singin' along, and sure enough, they'd put her right between us, bouncing boobs and all. Not like anything we'd seen growin' up on *Lassie* or *Gunsmoke*.

I've looked for years for a video clip of that show, to see if anyone was taking any video that might have ended up on YouTube, but I never have been able to find it.

Another thing I remember, Tanya Tucker was with us, and that's when she turned eighteen. Her dad had a guard on her door, but we found a way to slip her out and took her disco dancing on her eighteenth birthday.

We were doing a delicate balance about that time between the U.S. and Europe. We had a Beach Boys tour coming up after Loggins and Messina, and we were working the U.S. really hard, trying to break this market because Europe had already broke wide open.

HOWARD: You can only imagine what kind of transition this was for us, from where we started in Darby. You know, we had moved out to L.A.

but we hadn't been there that long before we had a worldwide monster hit. The adjustment was unbelievable.

DAVID: The realization that your life has changed forever. Luckily we had a sound enough upbringing that even when we got to be our craziest, we always realized that, well, we gotta bring it back in and straighten up. We never did become addicts or anything like that, we just would have wild spurts—uh—quite a few of them was the problem! But we would always try to redeem ourselves and straighten ourselves up. You know, your sense of privilege increases when you have everything at your feet. And that's really the hard part, learning how not to abuse your privilege. Of course, I'm so damned old now that I can't even take advantage of my privilege. I think because we saw several friends fall by the wayside, we figured it out.

Another big thing that happened was when the Loggins and Messina tour ended, we were in Chicago, and there somebody stole all of our equipment. It was the first part of August and we were having a little party in the hotel that night—I just remember a lot of champagne and beer being iced down in the bathtub; we had a Ryder truck that held all the equipment; the crew would back it up by a wall and secure it as much as they could. When they went out the next day there was nothing left. They got all the guitars and the congas and amps and everything. We lost $60,000 worth of equipment in one evening, and that pretty much devastated us because at that time we didn't have hardly a cent to our names.

The theft really put us out of commission. We were able to get a few endorsements like Ovation Guitars and a few people we knew stepped up and helped us out, but not enough to get us back on our feet. We thought it was over, for a while. And we had Doobie Brothers and Beach Boys dates coming up, and we had to cancel those tours.

As our career exploded into worldwide fame, we realized that, in spite of all our early success, we were not gonna be able to work with Gernhard and Scotti and those guys, even though we were signed and our first-born was promised to them. We were not extremely hard to work with; easy going, compared to a lot of artists. But remember, we were getting virtually no money, and tours are expensive. All the money went back to them. We understand, there are fans out there so fascinated with the fame part of it that they think, well, those people made you famous, you expect everything all at once? First of all, understand that we were working very hard ourselves—in between parties—to make all this happen, and everybody needs to make a living, and if you can't make money when you're having a worldwide hit, you ask yourself, "When are we *gonna* make money?"

Gernhard had power of attorney over us, so we'd send the tour money back and we'd never see it when we got home. They'd have beach houses in Malibu and we were basically broke. At that time, we were still living on my "Spiders And Snakes" royalties. *And we were having about the biggest single of the year.* It was especially tough because we also realized that these were not the kind of people you were gonna be able to talk to about all this.

HOWARD: That's an understatement.

DAVID: If you even made a hint about something like, "Do we get any of the money that we're making?" Gernhard would say, "Ah, I gotta talk to Curb." And we'd hear nothing.

They were pretty heavy intimidators, you know, they were kinda bullies. We were really alone out there in L.A. Everybody we thought we could go to for advice was in bed with them as well. I remember there was a lawyer in Beverly Hills named Max Fink. At one of our most down periods, he loaned us five grand. He was their lawyer but we'd gotten him to do something for us, and he kind of liked us, so he handed us five grand, and that was just hope in itself.

We were always optimistic. So we went on, just, aimlessly, us hoping that somehow it would come out all right in the end. Gernhard took our cash but he gave us his credit card to eat off when we came in from the road. That's literally how we were eating at the time. In those days you couldn't use cards in grocery stores except on Sunset at the Chalet Gourmet. So we were in there eating fillet mignon and lobster, broke as hell but we could buy good food on the credit card. Eventually, he took the credit card back.

Couple of years later, we had a deal with the Golden Nugget in Vegas, with Steve Wynn, to do twelve weeks a year. We had done it several times and done real well there, and we were fixin' to go back, and our guitar player quit the night before the show was to open. By then we'd got rid of the big band Gernhard and them had put together, which was a stupid idea anyway, we had just gone along with it because we had to, but now we had a stripped down version of the band and when the guitar player quit, we couldn't do the gig, 'cause we had to have the guitar player, so we're trying to figure out what to do, and Gernhard called Howard and alluded to the thought that he was having the guitar player killed.

HOWARD: They even sent people to his house—"persuaders"—he wasn't there, but his wife, who was eight months pregnant, almost miscarried because they sent all those thugs over to their place.

7

Southbound Once Again
Back to Our Roots
in Life and Music

DAVID: In 1977 we had an album out called *Plain & Fancy*. By that time, Gernhard was hardly speaking to us except to get our money. Howard and I decided to go book with this little agency called International Talent, and when the album went gold in Scandinavia, we flew over there and did sixty shows in sixty-five days. We just blitzed it. We played a different town every night in Germany, Norway, and Sweden, and Gernhard wound up with most of that money, too. That was kind of the final nail in the coffin, because in those days, some of the money would come to us from the promoters in cash. We would try to hang on to what we could to bring back with us, but a lot of it went in the bank, and when it did, Gernhard got a hold of it; he had power of attorney, remember, so there wasn't much we could do. I remember really well when we came back from that tour because just when we got back was when Elvis died. We learned that Gernhard had bought a new beach house in Malibu, and we pretty much said, we're gonna have to get out of here, there's no way we're gonna be able live this way, making everybody else rich and staying poor ourselves, thinking maybe we should just go and hang in Europe because we knew we could play a lot there. We were just trying to figure out what to do, so we moved home in the meantime. We knew we could always go home. And we got home and we said, you know, Darby is closer to Europe than L.A. is, and it's close to Nashville—by that time, we were gonna work on our country stuff—we may as well just stay here, stay at home, at least the rent's low and we got food; we had cows we could butcher, and turnip greens and oranges to eat.

And when those big shots in L.A. found out we were planning to stay in Darby, guess what? They told us we'd never work in showbiz again.

When we moved back home, we didn't really know what we were going to do. We were just escaping, was what we were doing. We moved back to Darby in '79, right when my first son, Jesse, was born. In fact, I actually wrote "If I Said You Have A Beautiful Body" the night Jesse was born.

HOWARD: Fate taking a hand again—after they also told us that we'd never have another hit record.

DAVID: At some point Howard and I flew back to L.A. and called a meeting with Mike Curb, because Gernhard would get wacked out of his mind and every time you'd ask him a question he'd say, "It's up to Curb. Curb tells me everything to do." The wackier he would get the more he would use Curb's name. So we went directly to Curb and said, "Look, it's very hard to work with Gernhard." We were worried that we couldn't get Curb to go along with us, but it turned out not to be all that hard.

We found a couple of songs that we wanted to cut, and Curb put us with a producer named Michael Lloyd. Michael was a very nice guy. He said, "Yeah, come out and cut these tracks," but he didn't even know what a steel guitar was. He had been producing Shawn Cassidy, pop teenybopper stuff. Meanwhile, we were sensing some good possibilities on the country side. Just before we'd left L.A. for home, Mike Curb's cousin John Curb, who was a record promoter, called me and said, "You know, I heard a couple of things you guys cut, and I know I can get them played on country radio." I said, "Really, we would love that, you know we did a bunch of country stuff on the first album, with 'Let Your Love Flow,' and, basically, Mike and Gernhard didn't want nothin' to do with it."

He said, "Well, I'm workin' country stuff for Curb (the label), and I can get this played." I was, like, "Where the hell have you been?" I could *talk* to John, he was kind of a country boy like me, so we got the label to let John work the new single at country radio, and sure enough, we started getting adds pretty quick. I think the first one was a song called "Slippin' Away," our first country chart record, I believe it went into the thirties in *Billboard*. That was in '78, before we moved back home. It did well enough for them to release another one we cut, a song called "Lovin' On," and "Lovin' On" did pretty well; it went to #16 on the charts. Then we were back in Darby and I was talkin' regularly to John. By that time, Mike Curb had put us with Michael Lloyd, so we had to commute back to L.A. to make records. Working with Lloyd was a blessing in a way, because it was then and there that we acquired most of our production skills. Michael Lloyd didn't know anything about country or country bands, so he would go off every day to get allergy shots (he had about twenty cats at home), and while he was gone we'd just take the studio over and cut tracks.

We had Carlos Vega playing drums, he was a fabulous drummer, and Rick Schlosser who used to play with Van Morrison; we had all these great players, and we'd get in there and start cuttin' tracks, and it was like the most freedom we'd ever had in the studio. We did not hear from Gernhard while this was going on. We assumed that Curb had just told him, "Look, let 'em work over here, you're still gonna make the money." That was also around the time when I wrote "Beautiful Body." Dick Whitehouse had all of a sudden started running the record label on a day-to-day basis. We had gotten to know him pretty well because he was working at Curb's when we'd come by, but he started actually running the label because Mike was now lieutenant governor of California. That's when we decided to try to talk Whitehouse into letting us cut "Beautiful Body." We had played it at a Conway Twitty show in Kentucky when we were booking with him, and we got such a strong reaction to it live that we started to believe we'd lucked into another one of those "people" songs, so one night we met with Whitehouse and we poured enough vodka into him that we got him agreeable to let us cut "Beautiful Body," and that was the song that started our string of country hits. We probably cut "Beautiful Body" while Michael Lloyd was out getting his cat allergy shots. At that time, we were out there on a shoestring, man. We were staying at the old Tropicana Hotel in Santa Monica that had bullet holes in the windows. While we were living there, we cut that whole album in about four or five days. We needed to get that done as fast as we could so John Curb would have good product to promote to country radio, which was where we felt we belonged, anyway.

Groucho Marx gave us "Body." Back in L.A., we used to watch old Groucho Marx reruns. And I'd seen him use the line on his show: "If I said you had a beautiful body, would you hold it against me?" and I remember writing it down thinking, *Oh, man that would make a really good song title*, and I remembered it again the night Jesse was born and us wondering what we were gonna have to do next if we were gonna move forward in this thing they call the music business.

HOWARD: That's kind of how it went; we were reachin' rock bottom when we moved back to the farm. I was living in a tent. We did know how to put a band together, but we had to convince them to let us record "Beautiful Body." Everything you did was a battle with them. "Body" wasn't as big a hit as "Let Your Love Flow," but it was a monster hit in its own right and worldwide, as well.

DAVID: To this day, people say, "You know you had that pop hit and you had them country hits, what was you tryin' to do?" Well, we didn't really know what we were trying to do; we were tryin' to get a hit any way we could. We wanted to have hits on real good songs—that's what we liked. It didn't matter which chart. But "Body" did open up the country charts, which Gernhard and all those guys were very much against. I guess they considered country beneath them.

HOWARD: It was the way things always seemed to work. Just when it looked like we were going down, something would save us.

DAVID: People will say to us, "Why did you get into this, writing and playing music, did you do it for the money? And I'll say, "I don't think we did it for the money, but you damn sure can't do it *without* the money."

HOWARD: You gotta sustain, especially early on, 'cause we were living proof that you could have a worldwide hit and pretty much have *nothing*. They basically gave us nothing, they kept it all, and you couldn't go ask, you know it was kinda dangerous to do that. And in L.A., we felt trapped. It got to the point where we couldn't hardly go anywhere in L.A. without knowing people who knew them, and it was pretty controlling.

DAVID: When we came back home, all the people here in Darby thought we had conquered the world. I don't blame them for thinking that. We had a worldwide hit. How could they know that we had no money, really? I was living in a single-wide with my first wife, waiting for my first son to be born, and Howard was living on the land with his *fräulein*. We loved being back home. Always, the problem was you'd run into people and everybody thinks you're rich.

HOWARD: I always thought a good way to describe where we were during that period in our career was: fame with no fortune. In the end, we had no choice but to get out of L.A., or we'd just be their slaves until they'd squeezed all the money out of us that we were gonna make for them, then we'd be out on the street, broke and looking for another record deal so we could make the miracle happen again.

DAVID: When we moved back to Florida, around Christmas of 1978, we were in shock a little bit. We didn't know exactly what we were gonna do; I mean, we knew we were going to pursue things, but we didn't know how because we had burned a lot of bridges in the course of our L.A. adventure. Should we make another stand in L.A., go to Nashville, or head back to Europe? Because at that time, we were working more in Europe than anywhere else.

But it *was* great to get home. Our family was happy to be together even if everybody was dead broke. We all knew how to survive, so that part didn't really faze us. We knew *how* to be broke. We had no problem being broke. As long as we were home, being broke was well within our comfort level. But our tail was just a little bit between our legs because we'd taken our career to a level where we were on the verge of breaking everything wide open and when we realized we could no longer work with these guys, we weren't sure at that point how much power they had, whether they had power to kill our careers like they said they did.

We *did* know how to put a band together. That's what we had always done, and we'd made a big mistake to allow Gernhard and them to get into that part of our careers. They knew how to produce a hit single and promote a hit, but putting a good band together was our expertise, so when we got back to Darby, that's just what we did. To do that, we went back to our high school roots, you might say. When we were growin' up in high school and playing all the bars and rec centers down here, in the old days, there was a band called Ron and the Starfires that we really liked. There were two cousins in that band, Jesse and Carl Chambers. We found both of them. Carl played guitar and Jesse played bass. Howard found a drummer, Rodney Holt, in a local bar, and then Carl and Jesse introduced us to steel player Danny Jones. Danny would become a huge part of our sound, and almost like a brother to us.

HOWARD: He was one of the most colorful characters in our entire history. Today we still tell Danny stories because they were endless. He traveled the world with us.

DAVID: Danny had about a what, about a sixth-grade education?

HOWARD: Well, I think he had more education but you would never know it. He was one of the smartest uneducated people I've ever met.

DAVID: He had an instinctive sense of how to play steel guitar. He couldn't read any music. Everything was by ear. Producers would freak out when we took him into the studio. One of us would have to sit with him and tell him in our own musical language how to make a certain sound, and he could always pull it off.

HOWARD: He fished, and he chased women, and he played steel. And ate good food. That was all there was to Danny. He was all basic instincts. Good-looking guy; the girls loved him until they talked to him for five or ten minutes. He'd pick up a girl, and he was smart enough to know that she was smarter than him, so he'd bring her around to the rest of the band for the conversation, then he'd try to get her off by himself. He traveled the whole world and actually never knew where he was at. That's a fact.

DAVID: We'd be booking a date like in Germany and he'd have a girlfriend in California somewhere and he'd come up and say, "Howard, we goin' through L.A. on the way to Frankfurt, Germany?" Howard'd say, "Hell no, we're flyin' out of Atlanta, going to Germany," and Danny'd say, "Oh, I wanted to go by and see my girlfriend."

HOWARD: Probably my favorite story of Danny's, we played Texarkana, Texas, and the next day we were flying out to Auckland, New Zealand. We're doing this show in a honky-tonk in Texarkana and Danny hits on this girl, as always, and he didn't get anywhere because she was quite religious and he ended up just freakin' out over her, just fell in love, first sight kind of thing. She gave him a New Testament that he took on the plane with him the next day. He had it in his back pocket. So we take off, fly to L.A., then fly on to Honolulu, switch planes, take off from Honolulu; we get out about three hours and they're serving meals on the plane and the pilot declares beautiful flying weather. Danny has tapped me on the shoulder. He was sitting behind me and had this *Playboy* magazine and he had the centerfold out and he was showing me the centerfold and I turned around and agreed, "Yeah, she's hot!" And probably ten minutes after that, that plane dropped five thousand feet. I mean, atheists were praying and meals were stuck to the ceiling and I looked around to see if Danny was all right, and he had traded the *Playboy* for the New Testament that girl had given him. All I'm thinkin' is, *I sure hope this works! I don't know if he can get forgiveness that fast or not!*

DAVID: We had that band together by the summer of 1979. And we found a guy to book us on some dates. We probably should have been suspicious when we went over to meet with him at his house and he was living with six strippers. But we didn't have an awful lot of choice; we'd kind of exhausted our supply of bookers we'd worked with out in L.A. At that time even going to Nashville wasn't an option because everybody thought of us as a pop group.

This guy started booking us in clubs around the South. Wasn't hard for him to get those bookings because we'd had a worldwide hit. So we hit the road with this band we put together, which was called The Bellamy Brothers & The Dizzy Rambler Band (Carl Chambers's father's band name). The problem was, the booker couldn't get us as much work as we needed to sustain a band. We had a guarantee clause with him which he did not meet so we decided to fire him and then we did go to Nashville because that was about the time John Curb started to get us some country airplay.

At this time, we made a decision that turned our performing career around. We went to the bank and talked them into lending us the money to buy a really good sound system and an old International truck.

About the time "Lovin' On" was on the country charts, we got in contact with Jimmy Jay at United Talent, which was Conway Twitty's talent agency, a real live legitimate Nashville booking agent. I remember, we walked into his office. Conway had just finished mixing one of his new singles, and he played it for us. I think it was "Happy Birthday, Darlin'." At the time, most country bands did not have their own sound system; they usually used the sound system that was already in the hall, and Conway was no different. But he really liked our system, so we ended up doing a whole lot of shows with Conway, because we brought great sound with us and we got along with all their guys too. It was kind of a natural fit, Ronnie McDowell and us and Conway. We probably did over a hundred shows with them.

Stan Byrd, who was a promotion guy at Warner Brothers, helped us get a showcase at the Exit Inn in Nashville, and while we were unloading there our old booker served us with a $6 million lawsuit. Fortunately our lawyer, Mike Milam, was at the show and he took the service for us, and we had to fight that agent, but we had that built-in performance clause that he had never met, so nothing came of it. United Talent came to see us that night, and they liked what they saw, and what they heard, so soon we were touring with Conway, and you might say that as far as touring in the United States was concerned, that was our big break.

And the sound system was a big part of this deal. They used to give us $5,000 a night for the production and the show. We had to supply production, that is, operate our sound system, and do an hour show. But five thousand in those days was pretty good money for an up and coming country act. Keith Fowler, who would actually pay us, would give us a big ol' paper bag full of ones and fives every night. I guess it was from concession stands or something, but it was real money, and we'd pay the band and the crew and keep whatever was left, which, a lot of times was not much, because we still had to make our payments to the bank for that deluxe sound system that was helping us get all this work.

Frances was instrumental in helping us get the loan from the bank. Our parents were not rich but they had a good name in Pasco County and at that time you could go to the bank and if you knew people, and you had good credit and paid your bills, you could get loans. That's how farmers got by in those days. I think we borrowed $20,000, which was huge at the time. But we had a great sound, wherever we played. Nobody in country music had a $20,000 sound system back then. With a good P.A., lots of fireworks, our dad waitin' on our ASCAP checks at the mailbox, and two people in the office we could really trust, we were ready to go out and conquer the world.

With United Talent, suddenly we had a real booking agency representing us. We were rolling now, booking almost every weekend with Conway over the next year. By this time we were out of our management contract with Gernhard, and we could actually get to keep the money we were making. We still weren't getting rich, but we were paying the bills, and that was a very big deal.

The other timing thing that worked out for us was, once we talked Whitehouse into letting us cut "Beautiful Body," we were able to produce it and put it out immediately. And we were right in the middle of that tour with Conway and Ronnie McDowell when that song took off. While we were out with Conway, it became a monster record. And when we played "Beautiful Body" live with him at Louisville Gardens, everybody just went crazy over the song. So it worked out really well, because we were right in the middle of a series of tours where we were showcasing our new monster hit every night before eight to ten thousand people.

So we started doing all those shows with Conway and Ronnie, but after we did all those dates together we started doing a lot on our own and a lot with other acts. We went out and did a tour with The Oak Ridge Boys, and lots of shows with The Gatlins and The Kendalls. We toured with Dottie West, with Johnny Paycheck, Haggard, anybody you could imagine. This was around 1980, '81. In a way, that period after "Beautiful Body" came out was a little bit like "Let Your Love Flow," everything so busy that it was kind of hard to keep up with, only this time with a bona fide country hit under our belts. And to make it even better, we were moving on from the old regime—Gernhard and Scotti Brothers— although we still owed our firstborn to them.

When "Beautiful Body" came out, Curb sent it to Warner Bros. in England because "Let Your Love Flow" had been so big there. And Warner Bros. in England hated it because it had steel guitar on it. But there was a promotion company called Solomon & Piers in Northern Ireland that took a different attitude, because Northern Ireland is a big country music area. The company rep was in the Warners office in London and he asked them, "What have you got that's new that we might take back to Belfast to promote?" and the Warners guy goes, "Well, we got a couple of things here, the new Bellamys record but we're not gonna work it, it's a country record." The rep said, "Let me hear it," and they played it for him. He said, "That's a smash! Let me take that back with me." He took it back and they started getting it played out of Northern Ireland and it became Record of the Year for the whole U.K.: Scotland, England, Wales. It was a monster there.

HOWARD: We sold a million copies for a purely country record, which at that time was a pretty major achievement. And we judged a "Beautiful Body" contest at almost every show we were doing at the time. And don't you know that Danny was always a scout for the talent.

DAVID: And back in the home office, Frances and Lucy were becoming bigger and bigger in the scheme of things. Lucy was our next door neighbor, and she was really our best friend in the world, and best employee. She worked *with* us. She worked twenty-five years for us. She did everything. She ran fan clubs, she ran the office. Lucy was just an old country gal.

HOWARD: Honest to the core.

DAVID: She was good with figures, and she was just like a sister.

HOWARD: Everybody loved her because she had the most wicked sense of humor ever and the world's greatest laugh.

DAVID: She would come into our office and say, "Australia's on the phone for you." And it would be Austria. "Somewhere over there, I don't know them countries." When people over in foreign countries had funny names, she'd be laughin' her butt off. Me and Lucy actually retired our mother from the school bus. She was working for us and still driving the school bus, and so one afternoon I said, "Lucy, you're gonna have to get her off the bus," or she would have driven that bus probably another ten years. So Lucy called the bus people and retired Frances, and Frances came home that day and told us they had said, "Frances, you're retired next Tuesday, you're not gonna drive the bus anymore."

Frances and Lucy had that office thing down pretty good, and it would get a whole lot better. They knew where the money was coming from, and they got to be bloodhounds about sniffing out the money that hadn't come in yet. They were going to Nashville once or twice a year to take care of business. They made it their business to put up our booth at Fan Fair, the big annual country music event. Frances met a lot of people in Nashville. She became friends with everybody in the business up there. Recently we went up to Nashville to do a big Randy Travis tribute, and when we were doing a press conference, they asked us, "What's your association with Randy?" Of course we'd played lots of shows together in the old days, but the first association was Frances, because he had a booth at Fan Fair near us before he'd even had a hit record. And we were never there because we were always on the road during Fan Fair. Frances kept saying, all you guys gotta meet this young guy, he's the nicest guy and boy, he's a great singer—she'd go out to the Nashville Palace to see him sing.

It wasn't until a year or two later, after he'd had a couple of hits, that we finally ran into him on the road, and of course when we saw him on the road, he was like, "Oh, Frances is a good friend of mine." A lot of our associations with artists were people that our mom ran into.

Nobody in L.A. was really talking to us much at that point. We still didn't know quite what to do with the L.A. situation. We just knew that if we could keep a band together, we could work, and we knew that as long as we kept recording hits, and radio would play them, that meant more work. So we did that, and Frances finally got around to discussing the money situation with Gernhard. We saw the ASCAP money come in; we knew what the road money was; we set up the merchandising business, and that's when she called Gernhard up and said, "Hey, wasn't there supposed to be some money comin' in from this deal here on the publishing side?" because we had a licensing deal with Gernhard. When I wrote "Spiders And Snakes" with Stafford, I owned 70 percent of the writing on that, and Gernhard took all the publishing. But we had a licensing agreement for 50 percent, and we weren't getting paid for that, and she was determined that that was gonna change. Finally, she bugged him enough to where he started sending publishing money on a regular basis. We didn't make it a high priority, but slowly Frances wore him down.

We thought we had lawyers to track down those things that they were keeping from us, but it turned out that no one could track them down, anyway. Such was the legal system in Nashville that we found there were certain people you could not take to court in Nashville. It was impossible. We actually had lawyers send a retainer back to us because the guy we wanted to sue was their landlord.

We feel very lucky that we don't need to be owned by those guys on the West Coast anymore, and we feel sorry for the kids on their way up having to give away pieces of themselves just to get a record deal today.

If you think about it, that's exactly what we did at the beginning—gave away pieces of ourselves. We just didn't know it because they didn't tell us and we were too dumb to read the fine print.

Thank the Lord for Texas

The music we did fit like a glove in Texas. Much of Texas is cattle culture and that's how we were raised. We could work there almost every night of the week during the Urban Cowboy era.

HOWARD: Texans dance! To this day, the folks in Texas find our music danceable. It's a compliment to us that we can get people off their butts and on the dance floor. We can play a conservative theater, supposed to be a stiff crowd, and they will find a spot to dance in.

DAVID: As we mentioned, when we were working with Michael Lloyd, he literally was never there. So without talking about it with Curb, we were now producing all our own records (without getting credit for it, of course). And it was right at this time, we had a string of big country hits. We had "Beautiful Body," we had "Whistlin' Dixie," we had "Sugar Daddy," we had "Dancin' Cowboys," "Lovers Live Longer," "Do You Love As Good As You Look," "For All The Wrong Reasons," most of them #1, all of them top five. That's when we started fighting with the label over royalties. We were getting good money from ASCAP and other sources that Curb didn't control, but we were getting nothing from Curb on record sales, even though we were selling a ton of records for them.

"Whistlin' Dixie" never made it to #1, but it was a great career song. I wrote that song on an airplane. While we were working on Stafford's TV show, we used to take the redeye home when we wanted to visit. It was one of those songs that wrote itself from top to bottom. When I got home, I got my dad's old guitar out and the music flowed out just as easy as the lyrics had on the plane. It was a sentimental song for me because I was basically a farm boy living in L.A. I mean, out there I was enjoying the bright lights and we had a big hit, but there's nothing we love more than being home on the ranch, then and now, so I was definitely sentimental about it. And I thought it was a good overall picture of what I was feeling.

I think, lots of times, southern history is misunderstood. People think about one part of what the South is, when really, it's a lot of things, complex, and for me it means hot, muggy springs and summers, hard work on the farm, small towns where you all know each other and care about each other. We wound up cutting that song on an album that had a wide variety of songs.

HOWARD: There was a song called "Wet T-Shirt," which Curb wanted to release on us. It was a total novelty song, and in those days, integrity still meant something for artists. They demanded that we record it if we wanted the album released. The entire Warner/Curb label in L.A. wanted that song released, and we didn't. But the Warner Bros. promotion guy in Nashville, Stan Byrd, and ourselves, took a stance against the label, the first time we found ourselves aligned with Nashville against the home office in L.A. Stan demanded that the label release "Whistlin' Dixie." He called it a "career song," and he was totally right, even though it wasn't as big a hit as many of our other singles. The people at Curb fought us. Said it was too long for radio to wanna play it. But we didn't want to have to live with that "Wet T-Shirt" song for the rest of our career. So the label did release "Whistlin' Dixie," and the reason Chet Atkins loved us was because of "Whistlin' Dixie." The song established us as artists that didn't just put out radio-type songs. The song was historical commentary and autobiographical too.

When the Urban Cowboy trend came along, we were on the wrong label to be part of that, but they loved us in Texas, so we toured down there with Mickey Gilley and Johnny Lee, working almost every night of the week. People to this day think we're from Texas. People in Texas think we're from Texas. By now we had our own bus and we were producing our records at the ranch, though we had to come to Nashville to mix them. We didn't have a fully equipped studio; an engineer in Nashville, Johnny Rosen, owned a portable studio truck. He'd drive it down to the farm and park it in our front yard then back it up to our little studio, run some mics in, and we'd get to work. I remember one time it rained so hard we had to put plywood out to make a walkway because it was muddy and flooded. We cut "Redneck Girl," "Strong Weakness," "Reggae Cowboy," and a lot more in that funny little studio with Johnny's truck. We weren't even telling the Curb people that we were recording. We'd got to the point where we were making enough money on the road, and we had very little overhead because we were using our band to record. The biggest expense we had was Johnny's truck. We had enough money to cover that, so we knew that we could record like we wanted to. We'd bring Rosen down to record and then we'd let Bowen, who was running Warner Bros. in Nashville, know that we had an album going on, and that was pretty much the beginning of our recording down on the ranch. We were becoming self-contained, and it felt good to have that much control over our career. We were trying to get away from Curb as much as we could because they were always trying to tell us what to do, and yet they didn't seem to learn enough about who we were and what we did to have that kind of control. Gradually, one step at a time, we were able to take control of our business without getting them mad enough to pull their support out from under us, and of course, we were selling records so they didn't want to lose us. It wasn't comfortable, but it was working.

DAVID: And the hits kept coming. "Whistlin' Dixie" was a top five country hit, but the next release, "Sugar Daddy," turned out to be our third #1 hit (our second #1 on the country charts). Just shows how a hit idea can come from anywhere. I wrote that song in Knoxville. I was watching this guy working on his girlfriend's car in a parking lot. He had the hood up, and smoke was coming out of the radiator, and he turned to his girlfriend and said, "What you need is a new car." And she replied, "No, what I need's a sugar daddy." Songwriters are like dumpster divers, only instead of reaching down for useful garbage, we're always on the lookout for a memorable phrase to grab onto. I grabbed onto that phrase and hauled it back to the motel where we were staying, I think it was a Howard Johnson's, and it didn't take me long. Sometimes the song just seems to write itself.

I was writing a whole lot back then; at home, on the road, I was writing almost every day. Sometimes I write by myself, and sometimes I write with Howard. Howard is a different type of writer than I am. A lot of times, when we write together, it's not *really* sitting down and writing together. He will literally come in and say, "Hey, I got this chorus," and he'll sing it while he's pounding out the rhythm on his leg, and then look at me, and I'll know that means, "Go finish this!" It's just the way we understand each other. We wrote a song for the *Forty Years* album called "Time Rocks On," and he did that, he come in slappin' his leg and singing, "Time rocks on . . ." and I go, "Okay, I get it." He doesn't have sort of a writer's patience, but he has a lot of really creative ideas and good thoughts and good lines. And the way we read each other's minds, when we do sit down and write together, you can imagine how we finish each other's lines.

(Laughs) It happens on stage, too, and it's lucky for us that it does. There's just a telepathy I guess that happens between brothers or people who sing together for a long time, you know, you go along for ten years and you sing a song almost the same way each time, and then all of a sudden one night something just flips and for no good reason I'll change it around, like I'll sing the first part of a verse for "Beautiful Body," from the first verse, and I'll sing the second half of the first verse using words from the second verse—not something I'd ever do on purpose, it just sometimes happens for some reason, you know, mix 'em and match 'em, but if I do that, which I do every now and then, Howard will go on and make the mistake with me.

HOWARD: I just know when he's gonna fuck up!

DAVID: I have no idea why, but something tips him off that I'm gonna screw up the verse and he's right there with me to save our butts in front of thousands of people.

In 1980 we had two #1 hits, "Sugar Daddy" and "Dancin' Cowboys." We were not blind to what was going on around us in the music world. It was like the tail end of the Urban Cowboy era. We saw a whole lot of that and it must have made an impression on me.

Dancin' cowboys
Singin' horses

Gypsy music
Ringin' voices

HOWARD: Lake City, Florida, first time I ever met Tommy Cash. We were playing a very country-oriented show—not that we weren't country, but we were edgy country. David came to sound check in his Speedo, and one of the mothers of a fiddle player freaked out about David's Speedo—I guess we had made too many trips to Europe. We meet Tommy Cash right after that. Tommy comes up and says, "You write that?" and David says yes. Tommy says, "Man, that's a really heavy lyric." We knew it was kind of a ditty, just a real danceable thing with a groove, but he was dead serious. He thought it was a really heavy lyric. We never did figure that out.

DAVID: He says, "Where'd you come up with that 'Singin' horses,' man?" Maybe I was writing much deeper than I thought I was. I guess I can imagine people hearing that song and thinking, *There must be more to that song than it sounds. Maybe a hidden message. He's tryin' to tell us something!* Nope. Just a cute little dance song.

In '82 we had a big #1 hit with "Redneck Girl," which was another of those songs we do about where we come from, and I remember like yesterday what got me writing it. In that period of time, we were playing Texas a whole lot. My wife is a Texan, and I often tell her that if we had moved to Texas at that point it would have saved us the millions of dollars we spent flying back and forth between Florida and Texas. "Redneck Girl" became a really big record for us, but the interesting thing about it was, even with it going to #1, it didn't become the iconic record it became later. That I kind of attribute to the dance craze two or three years after, when the whole world started line dancing. For some reason, every dance club, every country bar the people were line dancing to "Redneck Girl." We went back into the studio and did a dance compilation with that song, "Reggae Cowboy," and a couple of other tunes that people were dancing a lot to. So it became even bigger than it had been. We had always noticed people dancing a lot to our songs and we were probably one of the earlier country groups to use percussion in addition to the usual drum kit. In fact, we had a percussionist in the band. Conga drum. Cowbell. Don't forget that we grew up around the island culture and island rhythms. They still study those dance recuts today. Amazing stuff. We always loved that, and I always liked it blended into country because it created a flow that we liked a lot. It was pretty normal for us to do that, so when people all over started dancing to the music, it wasn't like we were jumping on a craze. It was a natural fit, and all of a sudden we get these dance instructors coming to our shows telling us, "Hey, I teach classes to 'Reggae Cowboy.'" And then we'd go to Europe and England and they'd say, "Oh, we're line dancing to your songs." What you'd seen in Texas, in 1980 or '81, now, later in the decade, you'd see these people all over the place, dancing to those rhythms. We never *tried* to be a dance band. It was just a natural fit to the way we loved to play music.

So yeah, the culture here was a lot like Texas, and we related heavily to Texans. It was a family culture. They danced. They all did the two-step. And our dad grew up singin' Bob Wills and Jimmie Rodgers. We were playing there so much, and we'd see all these girls come to hear us play, and they were the epitome of the redneck girl, they'd have their name on the back of their belt. I don't know who started it down there, but it was a big thing at the time I wrote the song.

They were line dancing down there, too, but they didn't call it line dancing, it was just, dancing. Like them, we loved rhythms. All the old guys that our dad used to bring home and play with could play all those really cool rhythms and stuff, and we grew up around all those island folks, and their rhythms seeped into the music somewhat. So, "Redneck Girl" was 'cause we were immersed in that culture and had been for a long, long time. We've made a lot of friends there.

Bowen was Jimmy Bowen, record exec and producer extraordinaire, who at one time or another in the '80s ran practically every major label in Nashville and was always doing things that shook up Nashville, sometimes pleasing people and sometimes pissing them off. Bowen called me one night at the end of the Warner days and said, "There's a window of opportunity."

HOWARD: A small window.

DAVID: And Bowen said, "We're gonna go through the window,"—he was talking cryptically—I said, "What are we doin', Bowen?" and he said, "Everything's gonna be all right, you're just gonna be on a different label," and sure enough, the next day we were on Elektra, which was another label in the Warner family.

HOWARD: I was watching CNN the next morning and they had a big news flash: the country division of Warner Bros. was now going to be Elektra. Warner to Elektra sounded to me like a step down. What did I know? Of course, it would be Elektra/Curb, so we'd still have to deal with them.

DAVID: Working with Bowen was a plus for us. The one thing about Bowen was he would tell you point blank how things stood, which I really appreciated about him because there were so many people in the business who would bullshit you.

HOWARD: Lots of stories about Bowen in the industry. But Bowen was good to us. We got to be personal friends with him. Frances even helped him reunite with his son after a custody battle. On the other hand, if he didn't do something right, she'd let him know about it.

DAVID: We'd had enough of Curb, so we decided that we wanted to get thrown off the label. That was our new plan. We decided to start recording at Criteria studios in Miami. At the time, a typical country album would cost about $40,000. We figured that if we ran that bill up at Criteria, you know, down there with The Bee Gees and everybody, that they'd throw us off the label. So we go down there, start recording. One of the producers who worked with us on a couple of things was a John Cougar Mellencamp associate, and The Bee Gees band worked with us. It was comin' along pretty good and the Curb people got wind that we were down there recording and they called and we told them we were just experimenting a little bit.

HOWARD: It was 1983, around Christmas, so they didn't send anybody to check on us. I think what happened was, we were gonna put off sending the bills until we accumulated a big bill, but it was expensive to do, and finally they said, we're gonna cut off everything until you send us some product. So we finished up one song and sent it to them, and we didn't hear anything for a while. We were on the road and recording during that time, in and out all the time, and about a month or two later, we had sent them "I Need More Of You," and they must have put it out the day they got it, I guess. It was a monster on the charts in Austria, a huge, huge hit in Europe, so, needless to say, we weren't getting thrown off the label.

DAVID: They *were* pissed because we ran the bill up; I think we ran it up to around $150,000, and this was just before Bowen was changing the game when he started running up recording budgets in Nashville, so Whitehouse and them at Curb were mad at us, but "I Need More Of You" was real big in Europe, so now we had to finish up the album, which would be called *Restless*.

HOWARD: "World's Greatest Lover" was the second single on that album and it was also a big hit, so now we *knew* they had no incentive to throw us off the label.

8
Random Crazy Stories
Wheels and Spies

DAVID: Getting our own bus was a big deal. Our first bus was not a new one, but we could keep it runnin' on the road. We got the word that Conway was buying a new bus. He sold his old one to Ronnie McDowell, and Ronnie sold his old one to us, and that's how we moved up from being stuffed into a van. That's a big step up for a traveling band. Before it was Ronnie's, it was Barbara Fairchild's.

HOWARD: And it was a great bus!

DAVID: Built like a tank. For quite a while, our record labels remained confused about just what kind of an act we were. We had kicked off our career with a worldwide pop hit cut in L.A., so we had to be a pop act, and it took a bunch of country hits to make them understand what we really were. Furthermore, Curb barked like a record label but it was more like a production company that needed a major label to distribute their records, and often neither they nor their partner label would take the responsibility to support us like a label is supposed to support its act.

After a few country hits, we could identify as a Nashville country act because Warner Brothers had an office in Nashville, but if we went to Warners trying to get something done, they'd say, "Well, you're a Curb act." One time we were in L.A. and we walked into the L.A. Warner Bros. office. Curb had put an office in the basement at Warner Brothers, so we went down to Whitehouse and said, "We need a $50,000 advance; we wanna buy a bus. We need a bus real bad." Well, we knew that wouldn't fly. Curb don't give you money for nothin'. So Whitehouse marched us up to the office of Andy Wickham, the head of Warners at this time. I remember, it was the day Ronald Reagan got shot. So Andy is on the phone with our booker, Jimmy Jay, and Jimmy is trying to help us get that $50,000. I think Andy offered us $25,000.

HOWARD: I just remember Jay saying, *"Andy, do you know how much a fuckin' tour bus costs?"* So between Warner L.A. and Warner Nashville—not Curb—and thanks to Jimmy Jay, we finally got 'em to give us an advance to get that tour bus.

DAVID: We were working pretty good; lots of shows with The Oak Ridge Boys when they had just had huge hits like "Elvira" and "Bobby Sue," and tons of shows with The Gatlins and The Kendalls up in the Midwest, then we got invited on the Alabama tour, and we played countless dates with Alabama and Charlie Daniels. Those were all major tour dates and we did lots more gigs with Alabama and The Judds, as well. It was the era of the big package show, filling arenas of twelve thousand to twenty thousand, which then was a big deal. We were never prone to stage fright, but playing the major venues definitely gave us an adrenaline rush. I think that was part of the addiction—you get used to that lift, and you almost have to have it.

HOWARD: This is kind of out of the time sequence, but it's a short story so I'm gonna tell it. Speaking of packages, right after "Let Your Love Flow," we got booked with Kitty Wells and Hank Snow, and we'd only had that one hit, that big pop hit. And this was in Canada with Hank and Kitty and their long list of stone country hits, and those people up there thought we were from Mars. That felt like the longest show of our lives. We knew we were such an oddity, playing in that big old barn in eastern Canada. We'd just come off those Loggins and Messina and Beach Boys tours. And Kitty and Hank Snow were idols of ours. Our mother would sing "It Wasn't God Who Made Honky Tonk Angels" while she cooked dinner— that was her favorite song, so it was a big deal, but that crowd thought we were such a weird band because we had just come off this big pop record and there we were with all that long hair and the big mustaches playing with those great old traditional country acts—whoever came up with that package must have had a real sense of humor.

DAVID: One of the other things I wanted to mention was that between those big American package tours with The Oaks and Alabama and The Judds and Charlie Daniels, we would still be jumpin' out and doing our European stuff, a month here, a month there, we would literally be booked with Telly Savalas, and Dr. Hook, and Bonnie Tyler, and many European and Australian acts that people here have never heard of, people like Paul Young, Udo Jurgens. We played those big *Schlager* festivals in Germany and that was a totally different kind of music. It was Germany's biggest music format, their version of Americana or easy listening, kind of pop-country.

HOWARD: Us and Johnny Cash are in the Country Music Hall of Fame in Germany.

DAVID: Actually, I think we and Johnny are the *only* two American acts in their Country Music Hall of Fame, their thanks to us for all the times we performed and recorded for them. And we still come back year after year to Germany, Austria, and Switzerland. Last year we played a Schlager festival on a Swiss Mountain that had seventeen thousand people. It's a big, big format in much of Europe. We have played in and out of that format for years. We've done duets with Schlager artists.

We've done Brazilian duets. We've done duets with people from the Faroe Islands, a group of eighteen islands in the middle of nowhere between Denmark and Greenland. They love country and play our music there all the time.

And then there is the spy story.

Mike Curb's sister Carol booked us on a date in Austria. There was this lady named Helene Antonia von Damm, a former United States Ambassador to Austria who also worked as an assistant to President Reagan. She was involved with a school in Vienna, and the idea was that people from all backgrounds and religions would go to this school.

HOWARD: Jews, Muslims, Protestants, Catholics, people of all religions would go to this one school.

DAVID: It was around 1985, and this experimental school was a great success, and all these higher-ups in the United States got involved, and I guess they were primarily Republican, and they talked us into going over and playing a concert for all the people who had raised money and worked to make this experimental school work.

When we went over there, it was at the time that the White House under Nancy Reagan had just got new china—new dishes—and there was I guess a controversy over the White House spending so much money on new dishes. And the old dishes from the White House went to Austria, which was what we had dinner on. Ms. von Damm had inherited the dishes somehow at the embassy, and so they had dinner for us that night and Howard and myself—

HOWARD: We bonded with this guy who was there, we spent most of our time with him after the show. Interesting guy, kind of guy you'd like as a friend, you know.

DAVID: About three or four months after this all went down, this guy that we had bonded with, they busted him; his name was Ronald W. Pelton and he turned out to be an NSA analyst who would be caught spying for the Russians.

HOWARD: We were out of town and I was watchin' TV when the news came on and I hollered, "David! The son of a bitch we had dinner with was a *spy*!" Freaked us out, I mean he was big news.

DAVID: This goes to show you, that stuff with the Russians has always been going on.

HOWARD: Same old shit!

DAVID: As the '80s moved along, as we continued to learn how to do this thing we were doing, it seemed, at least to the untrained eye, that our career kept progressing. Most of all, we became self-sustaining, which was a good thing. But the struggle never stopped. With the record companies, it was always on a razor's edge because we never knew if they actually were on our side as one of their acts. So we kept writing songs. Kept trying to record, and then at the end of the '80s, we were working primarily with MCA and with Bowen—we really thought we were out of the Curb deal, but we weren't. And we did go to Nashville and cut a few tunes at that point, which I guess showed that with Bowen, we didn't feel we had to hide out. We cut "Old Hippie," and we cut "Kids Of The Baby Boom." We cut the *Country Rap* album. We cut *Rebels Without A Clue*. All that stuff we cut in Nashville. 'Cause Bowen talked us into lettin' Emory Gordy produce a couple of albums.

HOWARD: And we were open to Emory producing us. Emory was probably the best producer we ever had. That was around '86, when we cut the *Country Rap* album and we cut the *Howard & David* album.

DAVID: Emory was great on arrangements and he'd come up with great ideas in the studio.

HOWARD: The great harmonica player Charlie McCoy played on "Old Hippie." People don't know it but there's a bass harmonica on that record. Emory just knew a lot of tricks for coming up with a different sound. And we got along so well.

DAVID: We go way back. Remember, Emory was from Neil's band, and he played the intro to "Let Your Love Flow," and he's from Georgia, so we had a lot in common. It was pretty creative, the albums we did with Emory. He wasn't one of those label political guys; he was one of the great session players and we just got along well with him.

And we brought Richard Bennett in from California to play guitar on those sessions.

HOWARD: To bring Richard in from California was really a no-no. Bowen was against it. But Richard was a great guitar player. Very creative in the studio and finally Bowen let us bring him in, and that first session it was kind of everybody standing there sizing each other up, but after all the other guys on the session heard Richard play, it was like, "Holy shit, no wonder they wanted this guy."

DAVID: We were happy with Bowen because he was letting us do what we wanted to do in the studio. It was a mutual decision for us to use Emory as a producer because Emory was somebody from way back in the L.A. days, and he was somebody that Bowen liked a lot. He was easy to work with, and we had good success together.

Besides all the package shows of the mid-'80s, we were doing shows on our own, in theaters and fairs and clubs. And we started our merchandise business. We got T-shirts, we got bumper stickers, tags for your car, pretty much everything they were selling at the time, pictures—at that time, merchandise was a lot simpler than it is now. We come out with a song called "World's Greatest Lover," which went to #6 on the charts in 1984. Women's thong panties were gettin' real big, so we decided to get some, put "World's Greatest Lover" on them, *and they're sellin' like hotcakes.* We couldn't keep 'em in supply, so we ordered grosses of them. We had an old Stor-Mor, plastic thing that goes on top of the bus, for extra storage. We were playing up in northwest Wisconsin. We left there that night, and sure enough, the driver forgot to latch that Stor-Mor thing down, and it was packed with those panties, so we took off down the road and nobody's paying any attention. Well, this was a heyday of the CBs, if you remember, so the driver gets a call from some trucker sayin', *"Hey, looks like you got some women's panties flyin' out of that Stor-Mor, up top your bus,"* and then all of a sudden all of the other truckers come in. One guy says, "Yeah, I saw a pair of panties on a fence post a while back," and another one says, "Hey, I think I even saw a deer with some panties stuck on his antlers." So we had to pull into a truck stop and when we climbed up and looked, there was *no* panties left. We had thousands of dollars of panties strung out over the last fifty miles. But when we got home, we restocked, because they were sellin' really hot, and we sold tons of them over the next year and a half.

Dealing with the labels was usually a pain, but our one steady ally was John Curb, who always did a great job working our records with the radio stations. It's like John was in another universe, away from all the drama between us and the label. He was the best hype guy in the world. He'd call you up and holler, "Hey, I got KLLL on your song! It's *smokin'* out there!" That's how promotion guys keep up their enthusiasm. I'd much rather have my job than theirs. He'd say, "Call 'em soon as you can and talk to so-and-so. He loves you guys!" So we'd make radio calls for him. He was just really great to work with, and he's a friend to this day.

But we always fought with labels. There was never a time we didn't. We started hiring independent promotion guys to help with our records so we didn't have to depend entirely on the label promotion guys, because the labels just might pull shit on you. You'd think that you and they would be on the same side, but if they had another artist they were feeling stronger about, they might just try and get radio stations to drop your record and play the other artist instead. But there were some good independent promoters we could trust, people like Bob Saporiti and Terry Leas, and they would tell us the truth. Saporiti was special.

HOWARD: Saporiti wasn't even money motivated.

DAVID: We'd come to Nashville and try to talk to the label about all the stuff going on in Europe, they wouldn't talk to us about it. They didn't care about Europe. We had a whole career going on in India that we never even knew about. But Saporiti was hip to all the international markets, and he let us know about them.

HOWARD: Those were the good days, because there was a period when you could literally take a record up the charts with independent promotion. That period didn't last too long. The labels didn't like it because the indie guys took some of their power away.

DAVID: Saporiti claims to have saved our recording career with some sharp promotion tricks on "Redneck Girl." We were no longer on Warner Brothers even though the record came out on Warner Brothers, he recalled, and if that seems confusing, well, that's the story of our recording career with the major labels. So the record was floundering because Bowen didn't feel like working it. He had moved over from

Warner Brothers to Elektra and we weren't on Elektra yet, so, "Sorry." John Curb called Saporiti up and said, "Would you help me work this record? It's a killer record." Saporiti listened to it and he agreed that it was a killer record, plus, he had an idea for a promo that might really help the record. There's a line in the song that says, *"Redneck Girl wears her name on the back of her belt."* So John Curb and Saporiti came up with an idea for a campaign. We bought twenty-five belts and twenty-five leather belt buckles, oval shaped, which was the fad back in the Urban Cowboy days.

They went to each of the top twenty-five country stations that reported to *Billboard* magazine. The stations went to their audiences and said, "Okay, everybody write in, in twenty-five words or less, why your girlfriend is really a redneck girl." Each radio station chose a winner, and each winner would receive a belt with the girl's name on the back, carved into the leather—and then the winner in each of the twenty-five stations would go into a drawing. I think we did the drawing on the farm. They picked the winner out of the hat, so to speak, and that winner got sent to Florida to spend four or five days on the farm with us and Homer. The record wound up being a huge hit for us, and according to Saporiti—and we'd never doubt Saporiti—kinda saved our recording career.

We were sort of sling-shotting between genres depending on where we were touring. In Europe, we'd be on TV with ABBA, then we come back here and we're playing a show in Mississippi with Jerry Clower. We'd come back from Europe and come by the labels and say, "Hey, did you hear, we just went platinum in Sweden," and they're lookin' at us and, "That's nice, are you gettin' played in Missouri?" Around 1983 we booked a tour in Australia and New Zealand, and the guy who ran the Miss Universe contest was the promoter. We weren't really good at being good anyway, and when we got there we found that all the people who worked with us were Miss Universe contestants. Our drivers, our road managers, anything that you wanted done, you had Miss Universe contestants to do it.

HOWARD: I still regret not marrying one of those girls.

DAVID: And I'll never forget, we got there and the guy was petrified of us, he was scared to death of us, and we were wondering, hey, we're nice guys, wonder why he's so scared of us. And we found out that Freddy Fender had just toured with them, and this was in Freddy's heavy drinkin' days, and this guy hadn't promoted much country, so he thought that all the country artists were like Freddy. So we were jumpin' over to Australia, then back here for fifteen, twenty dates, and on to Europe, at least two hundred dates a year, and when you consider some time in between dates, it seemed like we were *always* out on the road. And our bookers in the states didn't always understand how they did things overseas, which could really mess things up. One time, United Talent booked us into Australia. We went down there and we thought we had four big dates, and then one big television show with Don Lane, who was the Johnny Carson of Australia. But after we did that TV show we found that our rookie agent had booked more Australian dates on us that conflicted with some U.S. dates coming up.

HOWARD: When we hit the airport in Brisbane, the press met us, and since it was our first time there, just a huge entourage of press. And they wanted to know, "Why are you playing those chicken-wire clubs?" They had booked us into places where you did not want to be found in Australia. For readers who do not know, the chicken wire they were talking about generally referred to protective barriers they strung up between the front of the stage and the audience to protect musicians from bottles, glasses, and other crap that the drunks and malcontents in the crowd chose to heave at the singers.

DAVID: So we called our band, which was ensconced in Sydney, and said, "Look, we've devised a plan here. We're gonna fly back real early. Meet us at the airport, and we'll fly out early back to the States before our promoter wakes up." So the next day we jump on the plane and fly to Sydney, and as we and the band are going through customs to fly home, we see that our promoter has somehow caught on to what we were doing. He was running after us, waving contracts in the air and screaming at us. It's like an old spy movie, you know, we just dart through customs and he can't follow because he don't have a ticket to go to the U.S.

What makes this story really good is that we all get on the plane, and everybody's breathing a sigh of relief, but we're not absolutely sure that we're out of the woods yet. We don't know if he's gonna call the police or what, the plane revs up, rolls down the runway, picks up speed, and sure enough, the wheels lift off of the runway, and "Let Your Love Flow" comes on the speakers through the plane's P.A.

I had a $50,000 check in my boot. And that was more than we should have been bringing through customs. And so we landed in Honolulu. Everything's perfectly normal, everybody's real nice going through there, they're lettin' the band all through, and I'm walking through, and just as I start to walk out the door, this one guy goes, "Hey, sir, just come here a second." He takes me back into this little interrogation room, and he says, "Is there anything you wanna tell me?"

And I said innocently, "About what?"

And he says, "Anything at all." And he starts to question me. Finally he gets around to it, and I know not to lie to him, because then you really get in the shitter. He says, "Do you have any money?" And I say, "Yeah, I brought a check back; I didn't have time to wire it home." So I take it out and I show it to him. And he walks out to talk to his superior, comes back, and says, "What were you all doin' down in Australia?" and I start explaining to him why we were there. And he wasn't that familiar with us. But he did know Roy Acuff. He worshipped Roy Acuff. He said, "You all ever play the Grand Ole Opry?" And we said, "Sure!" We had just played it for the first time. He said, "You know Roy Acuff?" I said "Yeah, yeah! He's a close friend of ours." By that time, I was practically claiming him as a relative.

Having traveled just about everywhere, we have stories from the most exotic places in the world. We played Saudi Arabia like in '84, before many westerners were going there, except for the oilfield workers. I think the Tandy Rice Agency was booking us at the time, and they got a call from an agency in Atlanta saying that they were looking for acts to go to Saudi Arabia, and the Bellamys were on this list of people they'd like to book, because I guess they knew some of our songs. Turns out a lot of the oilfield workers are Texans and Oklahomans. So they'd go to these foreign countries and they'd take our music with them; same thing in Norway, we'd be up there saying, "What are all those Texans doing at our show?" Turns out they were working North Sea oil.

So Tandy Rice Agency calls me and naturally I say, "How much?" because I figure, if we're gonna go to Saudi Arabia, we need to get paid good for it. They offered us a real good deal to go over there, but then they said, uh, by the way, you can't go in as musicians or entertainers. You have to go in as consultants. "You're oil consultants." Nothing illegal, it's just the way you have to do the paperwork. Turns out we were working for Aramco Oil. And they had a 747 set up for just their workers. The whole plane's first class: restaurant, bars, everything. The plane flew directly from Houston to Saudi Arabia. At the time, our band was awful rowdy—you know, bands are always rowdy. A couple of our guys drank pretty hard on the way over there, which we had warned them against. Of course, we had to go into the country toting guitars, but saying that we were oil consultants—so we got there and we had a little hitch going through customs. Our guitar player was kinda drunk, but we got him away and they loaded us in the car; we took off, but we were only a mile down the highway when these guys with automatic weapons started waving us over.

HOWARD: So we pull over and our road manager is talking to the guys with the Uzis, yes, Uzis, and soon one guy comes back and tells us we'll have to sit there for about ten minutes because, he says, the king's coming through. So we're all sitting along the side of the highway and all of a sudden we see this big, long procession of Rollses and Mercedeses coming. Hundred miles an hour, they're flying by us. We've been in Saudi Arabia about an hour and the king's already run us off the road, so what else can happen? So they put us up in this house—they have these compounds with pretty much American-like homes in them, you know, three bedroom, two bath, whatever, they get a nice big one for us and the band. And they give us an indoctrination speech, the guys from the oil companies are giving it to us, 'cause they know we're there to play music. They say, "You can't smoke any pot; if anybody offers you any type of drugs or alcohol, you have to say no. Do not have contact with women. Respect them, don't stare at 'em,"—all these things that we *can't* do. They're telling a *band* this. Okay. We understand.

DAVID: About twenty minutes after the indoctrination speech, there's a knock on our front door. We open it, and there's a girl standing there saying, "Hey guys, you wanna buy some pot?" The band is all hollering, no! NO! Get her outta here. We figure it's the first time in recorded history a band ever shut out a groupie with pot! Turns out she was just an Iranian girl, maybe working her way through college going door to door selling weed. We managed to get through the Saudi dates without getting arrested. When we were not playing, we were ardent tourists— we'd go down to see the public execution spots and all the other points of interest. Our bass player, Wally, and I got kind of bumped out of line at the bank while we were changing money by a guy carrying a machine gun. And you'd have to make way in the streets for guys leading goats— we knew we weren't in Kansas anymore.

Those are the places you remember, because they were so different from your daily lives at home. But the shows were great because all the oil workers loved it, you know, they can't believe that Aramco flew one of their country bands in to play music for them. They thought it was such a big deal. To this day when we play in the Middle East, we'll run into some grizzled oil worker saying "I was there in the '80s when you played in Daha Ran."

HOWARD: I remember back when we played Qatar; you kinda had the feeling that you were being watched. It just felt strange.

DAVID: We went to Czechoslovakia in the old days, before the wall came down, and it was like that. The Communist Party was the promoter of the show, part of a cultural exchange. We were able to get the money up front in American currency, but when we got there they wanted to film the show and shoot a TV show around it, which was an additional cost for them. So we had to negotiate that, and they could only pay us in their currency at that time, which was not worth anything outside their country. What that meant was we had to take that money and spend it the next day. So we had this extra ten thousand dollars in funny money, and we had to go shopping in Prague. We hit these antique stores, and we wanted to buy stuff you couldn't possibly get outside of the country.

I remember they had these ladies in one store looked like they were from a Lena Wertmuller or Fellini film, big nosy women who would question us, "What do you want this for?" So we ended up buying a bunch of Moser crystal. We had been to the Waterford Factory in Ireland and bought some, so we thought the Moser might be nice because it's even rarer—at that time you couldn't buy Moser outside of the Iron Curtain. So we bought all of this crystal and they boxed it and we lugged it back to West Germany, then had it shipped home. To this day I have these cabinets full of Moser crystal that we had to buy the day after this TV show.

Ray Benson (of Asleep at the Wheel) and Kathy Mattea were with us, and they had to negotiate the same deal to do the TV show there, so I think Kathy had to do some shopping as well—I'm not sure what she bought—and we get to the airport, and the airport has these kind of double staircases that go up to the top. We get to the top, and Ray, who hasn't bothered going shopping, is standing at the top of these stairs, throwing the money like some evil dictator, and all this money's floating down and people are going crazy because it's like literally raining *korunas* in the airport.

Something happens everywhere.

HOWARD: I remember one time RCA decided they wanted to break some artists overseas.

DAVID: They got real interested all of a sudden in the overseas market. The station that would be sponsoring this tour in Germany said, "Okay, we'll do this, but we want The Bellamy Brothers." We weren't on RCA, but they wanted us because we were popular over there, so they negotiated and got us to go.

HOWARD: So we're the bastard children—RCA didn't even want us on this tour. We're doing this on live TV; it was like in a stadium. They brought us on—I remember the introduction, they compared us to the tennis player Boris Becker in that we had had such a long career, and when they introduced us, the house went friggin' crazy. And all these people from Nashville who had given us so much shit through the years, they just had to sit there and eat it, cause they didn't know about our career overseas. I think that about was the best I ever felt.

DAVID: It was hard to get publicists to wrap their mind around what we were doing because most of them sort of specialized in one area or another. Warner and Curb each had their own publicity department and they didn't even acknowledge each other, and you can just imagine that sometimes stuff they needed to do fell through the cracks. So we learned to do certain things ourselves, not depend on the labels, and that really helped our career, and what we learned then helps us to this day.

HOWARD: In the early and mid '80s, we finally became an honest-to-goodness working music act, in charge of our own future, working steady, bringing home the bacon, you might say. We still had the labels to deal with, but we were in charge of our own career, doing what we set out to do. You might think that we woke up every morning smiling because things were going right, but what it really was, it all felt natural and we just moved on, writing songs, making records, playing concert dates, traveling, traveling, often too tired, and busy, to stop and smell the roses, but it was okay.

DAVID: We were where we were supposed to be, and that was fine. We had seen our parents working hard nearly every day of their lives, and it felt right that we should be doing the same, except, of course, having some good times along the way, doing what we had been put on this earth to do.

HOWARD: We had this resistance to anything that came up against us. We didn't really ever think they were gonna win. We always believed that sometime it was bound to be better. We'd say, "We won't ever do that again. We learned our lesson there." But there's always new mistakes to make.

DAVID: I think we made every friggin' mistake that it was possible to make. And we somehow survived. I don't know how. I guess one of the good things about this business is there's enough income streams, or jobs, so if one totally screws up we can kind of live on the other one. By that time we had pretty much put all of our business at home. Any money that we made went straight to our mother.

HOWARD: Now *Frances* had the checkbook, so we didn't have to worry about that.

DAVID: In addition, she had the reliable Lucy working in the office with her, and the two of them could do anything from selling a cow to booking a show in Tokyo.

In 1983 Curb changed his deal and went from Warner/Elektra over to MCA. Now that we were recording on the MCA label, with MCA promotion, and Bowen there for us, we thought that we had finally left our label troubles behind. But then we'd walk into MCA and we'd just had a #1 single and everybody there would be like, "Ee-yah, that's great! Wish you weren't on Curb." You see, it was sort of the same thing as before except instead of Warner/Curb, it would be MCA/Curb, and that pretty much hung over us all the time. Both at Warner, then at MCA, we got plenty of help from some of the promotion people. At MCA, Roger Ramsey was always our buddy, and one of the reasons we had so much strength on Texas radio was because of him. But we thought that between our attorneys and working with Bowen more, it would be better if we were away from Curb altogether. We spent forty thousand bucks in attorneys' fees to negotiate getting off of Curb, and we actually thought we were, and we did the album with Bowen, but when the record came out, all the logos on the record were the same. And so we went back to MCA and said, "Hey, what's going on here?" and they said, "Well, you're off Curb, but you see, MCA has this deal with Curb, and so we have to include it on our deal." Now, it turns out that wasn't all a lie, because MCA and Curb spent many years in a lawsuit and finally settled it years later, but some of those albums that we had then, you couldn't even find, and then later on, Curb got them all back. So they ended up with them all anyway. I know all that's confusing, not just to you reading this, but to us too.

HOWARD: You can leave but they puuulll you back in. We would try to get close enough to them to ask them what was going on. At this point, we pretty much had to talk to Whitehouse. We had no communication with Gernhard, which was not all bad.

DAVID: We didn't hear anymore from him personally, but thanks to our mother, he would pay us—we still probably didn't get what we should have gotten, because there was no way to know. As far as the record sales, we got nothing, but we figured out that we were still better off to keep cutting, because radio was playing the heck out of our records and ASCAP paid our writers' airplay royalties directly to us. And we knew that based on the popularity of our records, we could tour like crazy.

So we were better off to keep recording, even though we thought that we were not getting all the money we were owed. They would actually say to us, "Yeah, that record went to #1, but it didn't really sell that many albums; maybe we should put out another single." So we'd put out another single, even though we knew the album was selling well, because we were talking to the people at MCA and they would tell us how the album was selling. And MCA was always telling us, "Boys, you gotta get away from Curb."

That's the kind of schizophrenic relationship artists often develop with their labels: on one hand, the labels don't pay you what they owe you and that makes you mad, but on the other hand, only a label can take a couple of obscure farm boys, cut a record on them, send those records out into the world, and suddenly you're big and famous and worth something on the road. Maybe that label that's screwing you is promoting you better than the next label would. Still, it's hard to stay with a label when you know they're lyin' to you and refusing to pay what they owe you, and you have no right to check their books. Kinda takes the joy out of your career.

Getting anything done with them was like moving a mountain. Even with the awards. We're still the most nominated duo in history. We'd get nominated for everything, but we could never win because we were a Curb act and MCA, with all the voting members they had, would vote directly for their acts rather than an MCA/Curb act, so there we were—

the stepchild again. You know, Howard would rather have a root canal than go to an awards show. And I'm not much better, but I know it's good for us to go. He's like, uhhh, let's go home and feed the cows or something.

HOWARD: All these issues we had with them, it never ended. Eventually we did wind up as an MCA act. Our first album with them was *Restless*, released in 1984, the first of six albums released over the next seven years with them. That was the one where we were trying to get thrown off Curb. We still had to deal with Curb. Even when we started our own label, you might think, good, we finally don't have to deal with them anymore, but of course we did, because they owned all sorts of rights to our original recordings.

Don't get me wrong, we love what we do and after all these years we still spend most of our time on the road entertaining people because that's what we do, but it is hard—just the traveling alone is hard, and it gets harder when you know your label does not have your back.

DAVID: In order for us to make our career come together, first we had to understand that in the long run, no managers, agents, producers, publishers, or label executives could do for us what we could do for ourselves. It didn't happen overnight. We made mistakes and we still make mistakes. But those are our mistakes and we learn from them. And we even learned how to get our way at the labels. We mentioned how we got Whitehouse to let us cut "Beautiful Body," with the help of a little vodka and orange juice. And once we started working with Bowen, well, Bowen liked his weed, and we grew some fine weed, which we found could mellow him out and make him agreeable when we wanted to get something done at MCA. We'd get Bowen so stoned, he'd start tellin' you the truth about everything.

HOWARD: I think we really helped ourselves by continuing to write and record while we were fighting with the labels. By the early to middle '80s, the country material that we were recording had gotten out into the world. Prior to that, we were known mainly for "Let Your Love Flow," but now they were starting to hear new material like "Whistlin' Dixie" and "Sugar Daddy." And then we started writing with Scottish artist Frankie

Miller, hits like "I'd Lie To You For Your Love," and recording songs he wrote, such as "When I'm Away From You," and "Forget About Me." These records fit really well into the international markets. Most country artists did not have that going for them. More about Frankie later.

DAVID: And throughout the '80s we were touring massively; seemed like we were on the road all the time. We think we've performed close to eight thousand shows since "Let Your Love Flow," and toured the world so many times we actually lost count. After a while, the strife with the record company just became a regular part of the day. It was like the schedule said, "Okay, we're booking an Australian tour, and then we're coming back and doing ten shows in the western United States, and then this week we're going to Nashville to meet with lawyers and fight with Curb." That was just part of the itinerary. It was ongoing. I would call home and Mom would say, "There's a royalty statement come in today," (we'd been screaming for a royalty statement from them for a year) "but all the pertinent parts are cut out with a scissors." Stuff like this went on all the time. And it never ended. When we moved over to MCA, it changed from the standpoint that we only dealt with MCA, but all the old business we had with Curb continued to lurk in the background like a painful itch. We tried to be like a full-on MCA act. We tried to know everybody and get along with everybody at the label and keep that rolling.

And we did pretty good with them, starting with "Old Hippie," which was kind of a milestone record 'cause when that came out, radio jumped on it. Surprised me probably more than anyone. I thought it was a song I had written because I wanted to write it. I didn't think that many people would relate to it. Howard was the one who kept saying, "Oh, we gotta cut that!" and we showed it to Bowen and he said, "Hey, this is great!" That's still a song that people talk about and relate to; you get these old bikers come up to us after a show and say, "Sign this, I'm gonna take it to my buddy's grave 'cause this was his favorite song."

I think we were in a great position in that after "Beautiful Body," people expected us to stretch the boundaries of country music and we had fun writing just those kinds of songs. I remember Hoyt Axton, one of the last times I saw him, gave me a cassette with a song on it that he wrote—in fact I still have it—it's called "The IRS Killed Dottie West." He said, "I want you guys to record this, 'cause I don't think anybody else could get away with it." I guess that was kind of a compliment, and every time we go into the studio to do an album, Howard'll say, "Go get that Hoyt song. Let's see if we can do it."

9
Unmanageable
Family Business and
Homer's Last Tour

DAVID: By now, they weren't thinking of us in terms of pop or country so much, it was like, "Oh, there's a new Bellamy Brothers album." We always sort of ran the gamut on our albums anyway, 'cause we'd do like a pop song, then a kind of a country rock—we love country rock, one of my favorite music forms—then, of course, something in classic country, or something that I would call "Nashville Country," or even a reggae song or a bit of social commentary. We had developed a song style like no other country act we knew of: rhythmic, with a touch of humor, and always a lyric that our fans and many other country fans could associate with their own life.

Also, we were beginning to understand more and more that if we were going to succeed in this business over the long haul, we were gonna have to treat it like a business. I would say the first four or five years of this thing, we didn't think about business once. From the time we did "Let Your Love Flow," up to the time we did "Beautiful Body," we were ridin' pretty high, career-wise if not money-wise. We did want to know how many records we were selling. And from the time Homer pulled the first royalty check out of the mailbox, it was like, well, "Maybe they can make a living!" You certainly wanted the money that was coming to you. But around the time of "Beautiful Body" and the first couple of years of the '80s, we started thinking more for ourselves because we had come to the conclusion that we were unmanageable. It was not like we were mean people—well, we were pretty crazy but we weren't insane—we just did not fit into a management situation. A couple of times we thought, if we go and get a manager, maybe he can straighten the record company out, but nobody could do anything with the likes of Mike Curb or Jimmy Bowen. We did have a couple of managers, but not for long. There were times when we could have really used the right person, but it always fell back on us, so we decided that it was gonna be us against the world. We've lived with that piece of truth for quite some time.

As we started to work more and make more money on the road, we also started to rebuild the old home place. We bought the part of our aunt's ranch that connected to us, the part I had set on fire with a flaming arrow all those many years ago. We were leasing land too. Frances was always involved in land acquisition, to the point where we'd come home from a tour and she'd say, "Guess what I did?" And we'd say, "Lord a-mighty, what?" And she'd say, "I bought that ten acres down there that's got that little house on it. I'm gonna fix it up and sell it for a profit!" Her father was a carpenter, you know, so she wasn't happy unless she was knocking a wall out and putting in an addition.

We always operated as just kind of a family living out of the kitty. Now if we had a parent or somebody who all of a sudden just started buying Cadillacs and giving them away, it would have been a different thing, but none of our family was ever like that.

HOWARD: We might get something a little newer but, like, I drive an '05 pickup. Our bus today has got 1.5 million miles on it and it's still in great shape; all you gotta do is change an engine from time to time.

DAVID: That all goes back to our dad. He was frugal in a good way. Somebody would say something about "That ol' wreck of a bus," and he'd say, "Yeah, but a good part of it's paid for." You know, just staying away from unnecessary debt, when you had the necessary means already to get by.

We were all influential in our own way, the perfect team for the situation we were in. The other thing they did that we can't discount is, they were all really good cooks. We'd call home from heaven knows where we were touring and Frances would say, "Oh yeah, the Oak Ridge Boys are here eatin' cinnamon rolls with us."

HOWARD: And Homer's fried chicken was the best.

DAVID: Yeah, he was the expert at that.

HOWARD: And his meat loaf.

DAVID: I'd go over to the office before Christmas and tell Lucy I needed her to do something and she'd say, "I can't do that, I gotta do Frances's potato salad. She'll get me if I don't have that potato salad ready for Christmas Eve." That's pretty much the kind of office we ran, but we always got our business taken care of. When we started the record label, we would literally sit down at Frances's dining table and stuff envelopes with CDs and they'd mail them to hundreds and hundreds of radio stations.

HOWARD: You know, another visual that sticks with me is that in the middle of some high priority meeting, somebody would look out the window and all the cows would be in the yard, and no matter what we were doing at the time, everybody would get out and we'd get them cows back to their pasture, then we'd come back and continue with our meeting. At Bellamy Brothers Ranch, cows on the wrong side of the fence are first priority.

DAVID: Dad died in '87. But he had the chance to watch our career take off. He went on the road with us when we were touring with Alabama and Charlie Daniels—we did quite a few dates together with them and he got the biggest kick out of that. But Homer was very much a homebody; pretty much his whole life was at the ranch, save for those super-short summer trips we'd take to the Gulf and a few years in the Aleutian Islands defending the country during World War II.

Stories We Shouldn't Even Be Tellin'

By the middle '80s, a lot of the publishing that Gernhard controlled had started to come back to us. We formed our own publishing company, and because we wrote many of our biggest hits and we sold a lot of albums over the years, our publishing brought in some good money for us. Without management, but with a whole lot of help from the people we could trust, you might say we were making our way in the world. We were working a lot in the United States from our string of hits, and "Let Your Love Flow" had us bouncing back and forth between here and Europe. And then we started doing the big country international tours with a famous British promoter named Mervyn Conn. Conn was the perfect name for him. The one cool thing about Mervyn was he did some shows that I don't know if anybody else would have had the nerve to put together. They were big extravaganzas, and he would have Conway, and Tammy, and us, and Rita Coolidge, and Emmylou Harris, Freddy Fender, Tanya Tucker, and Jerry Lee Lewis all on the same show. And he would take that around Europe like a circus. He'd even play circus venues like the Hippodrome in Paris. It was beyond Mad Dogs and Englishmen. If anybody had had reality cameras back in those days, it would have surely been a monster TV show.

We were sitting in Heathrow Airport in London one day, waiting for a plane to Belfast, Northern Ireland, and Jerry Lee was sitting right behind us. He was talking to Elvis, having a conversation with *the late* Elvis, saying things like, "Ya know, E, you always claimed to be the king of rock and roll, but everybody knows I'm the king of rock and roll." I elbowed Howard next to me to be sure he was hearing this. He was, and there were others around us, I'm sure, heard it, too: Freddy Fender, Brenda Lee, Rita Coolidge, and some of the band and crew members of the acts on the tour. At first I thought maybe he was doing it just to mess with us all, but he continued to talk like he was having a serious conversation. "Just because you died doesn't mean you're the king of rock and roll," was one thing he said. He kept going back to who was the real king of rock and roll, over and over. He'd say, "Listen, Killer!" Everybody called him Killer because that's what he called most everybody else. And he continued to address Elvis as "E."

There was something going on with Jerry Lee. The next night at the Belfast Opera House, they carried him off the stage on a stretcher and we had to close the show.

On that tour, I think we were a necessary adjunct of Freddy Fender. He was still drinking at this point, and by this time he was a good friend of ours, so we'd take him to his room, an arm under each armpit and his feet not touching the ground.

HOWARD: One great story that Brenda Lee remembers well: We were playing Barcelona with Brenda and Jerry Lee and the rest of the entourage, but they had sent David and me on to Madrid the day before to do some TV promotion for that show, so we went on TV and did our bit, real early, and flew back that morning from Madrid to Barcelona for our live performance. The show was in this big park there, and it was just packed out. We pull in, in a limo, in back of the stage, and just as we get out of the car I start hearing bottles and broken glass flying everywhere and I'm ducking down, and hiding, you know, and wondering, *What the hell is going on?* Jerry Lee had come on and must not have liked the crowd, so he had done a real short show and left the stage early, which just pissed *everybody* off. I found out later they'd had a riot during Brenda Lee's show, before Jerry Lee. And because we had been out doing the promotion, they put us in the last slot that night to play. But this crowd was so pissed off that it was literally dangerous to be out on that stage. It was the country version of Altamont.

DAVID: So we refused to go on stage. The drum set was already in splinters 'cause they had thrown bottles at it. And James Burton, who was playing with Jerry Lee, had got his hand cut on a piece of glass. So we told Mervyn, "Look, we're not gonna go out there. This is insane," and he said, "Oh yeah, you gotta go out there and play and calm them down," and Howard said, "I'll tell you what, Mervyn, *you* go calm them down, and we'll play." So Mervyn walks out there, up to the mic, and starts speaking in English. And just as he starts to speak, a bottle whizzes by his head. He hot-foots it off the stage and declares, "That's it! Show's over!"

For all of his shortcomings, Mervyn Conn's tours were legendary. We were flying back across the English Channel and Emmylou's road manager, Phil Kaufman, affectionately known as The Road Mangler, took the microphone away from a flight attendant and started telling jokes. Then a couple of roadies took the booze cart away from the stewardess and started passing out those little bottles of liquor. Nowadays you'd surely get arrested for the things they did.

One day on this tour, we left Conway's steel player, John Hughey, and his brother, Gene, and James Burton on the tarmac in Madrid because the plane was overloaded, and everybody was going, "No, no, don't leave them!" and they were yellin' back, "*No, no, don't take us! We'd rather stay here than be on that plane when it goes down!*" They wound up catching another flight and beat us back to London. Those tours were completely wild.

Another time we played Switzerland. We had Tammy Wynette and Tanya Tucker. Jerry Lee was on that show, and a bunch more, and everybody was mad at Mervyn Conn because everybody was supposed to have business class seats and all sorts of other promised perks and nobody had any of that stuff. George Richey, Tammy's husband, decided that we're gonna get even with Mervyn when we got to Zurich. We were all in the hotel and Mervyn did not show up. So we ordered all the champagne in the entire hotel to Rita Coolidge's room and signed Mervyn Conn's name to it. Thousands of dollars. It started a war.

HOWARD: The Sofitel Hotel in Paris, they used to send bills to us in Darby for three years after we were there. It was us and Bobby Bare, and David Allen Coe's mother-in-law, they didn't have a limo for Bare and didn't have a limo for the mother-in-law, so we let 'em ride with us. We had left the hotel because once again Mervyn had run out on everyone, and we tried to stand in line and pay our bar tabs and other incidentals before we left, and they were rude—typically French—they didn't want nothin' to do with us, so we just left. We said, "It's your loss!"

DAVID: Probably owed them a grand or something. We hit the streets and you know, those little French cop car horns? We heard 'em behind us, and our driver thought maybe they were beepin' at Bare because he didn't have a seat belt on and he was spittin' tobacco in a cup. Actually they were chasin' us for the bill. So we got to the airport and the hotel manager is at the terminal sortin' out bills. They're givin' us bills and we're sayin', "Oh, that's not our name, that's Mervyn Conn, that's who you want to find." Oh, they were all confused, but they didn't have our name on them, so, they had to let us go, but eventually they thought they had it figured out, and they sent minibar bills to the farm for years. Well, hopefully they billed Mervyn Conn too.

HOWARD: With Mom monitoring the bills, David or I or both were bound to get in trouble. In 1984 we were ridin' this juggernaut called The Marlboro Tour. Promoted by Fritz Rau and Mama Concerts, it was the biggest, best, classiest tour we had ever done, with an up-to-date tour bus, the best hotels, and a genuine professionally trained road manager. We had it all. There were about ten or fifteen dates. We did all the major cities in Germany and Austria. We did Vienna, Zurich, Frankfurt, Hamburg, and the last show we did was in Berlin. And our road manager, this real flamboyant German guy, he said, "Boys, when this tour is done, I have a special place to take you, special place," and everybody's curious, of course. "It's called Mona's," is all he'll tell us. So the tour goes on, and he keeps teasing everybody about Mona's.

Finally we get to the end of the tour and everybody is waiting for this big surprise. We get to Berlin and check in, actually the day before the show, which is the worst time for you to go to a house of ill repute, which is what Mona's was. I personally had a flu bug, didn't feel well at all. So I was gonna stay in. The rest of the crew went, but just before they left, I heard a knock on my door and it was Wally, our tour manager and bass player, then and still today, and he says, "Howard, we need to borrow your credit card." Something had happened to David's. I'm not sure what it was, and at that point, I didn't know what Mona's was, what I was giving my card for.

DAVID: They found out they could get a group rate. If they put it all on Howard's card, it would be cheaper.

HOWARD: So I gave them my card and I just hung out at the hotel and the next day was show day and all I could hear from the rest of them was Mona stories, till I was sick of listening, and of course the working girls from Mona's came to hang out at the show. They were back stage, and I didn't know any of them. I still didn't feel well. Mona's turned into a three-day party. I was about the only one who wasn't married at the time. I was the only one who *should* have gone to Mona's—but didn't.

Everybody had a hell of a time, apparently, that's all I could hear about. That was the last show on the tour, and after that, we fly home and still, I heard Mona stories, and more Mona stories. It must have been three weeks or however long it took the bills to come through the office. I get a call from our mother, and she had that tone of voice she used when she was upset with you, and I heard it the minute I answered the phone. She just said, "*Howard!*" What the hell did I do now? She said, "Did you spend twenty-five hundred dollars at a place called Mona's, in Berlin, Germany?"

DAVID: Its full name was "Mona's, One Thousand And One Nights."

HOWARD: I didn't know what to say. I didn't wanna squeal on everybody. I took the blame for that whole damn thing! I took the entire blame. She was mad at me a good six months! David was married, still his first marriage, when he hadn't yet learned how to do it—marriage, that is—everybody else was married, and I knew Frances had figured out what Mona's was. I didn't want to spill the beans on them, so I just took the fall. Yeah, I did. I mean, she got over it but it took her several months before her tone of voice even came back to normal.

DAVID: She must have thought Howard was one hell of a man.

HOWARD: You know, I'd had a few escapades in my life and she just thought I'd gone on a good one this time.

10

Booking Agents We Have Known And Loved

Judy's Side of the Story

DAVID: Talking about our European tours reminds me how important booking agents are to artists. Bookers understand where your biggest audiences are. They have a feel for negotiating performance fees and the costs of the road. Good bookers don't wear you out going from Nashville to Oregon to Florida to Germany to Singapore on a two week tour. We've been lucky with agencies like United Talent and Tandy Rice out of Nashville and Jim Halsey down in Tulsa. When Halsey sold his booking agency to William Morris, James Yelich, who had worked for Halsey for years, started his own agency. He handled Alan Jackson, Merle Haggard, and us. He had a lot better comprehension of the overseas stuff than our Nashville agencies did, and sometimes we'd do twenty-five dates at a time just in Germany.

By this time we had started Bellamy Brothers Records, and the label was doing pretty good for a couple of guys who didn't know how to run a label, so we started thinking maybe we can figure out this agency thing for ourselves. So what we did, around 1992 we crossed paths with Judy Seale, who had also worked for Halsey but was now on her own, and turned her on to some of these festivals we'd been doing in Europe. She became a kind of specialist in international bookings. In Nashville I don't know anybody who could even come close to her internationally, and most of it is because she's gone there and seen it and done it; it's not just something she's heard about. She's traveled the world and been in every war zone, booking entertainment for troops. To this day, she books all our international tours. Here's how we got together, in her own words.

JUDY: When I worked for Jim Halsey, I was never an agent; I just worked for the president of the company. Artists would come to town and we'd pretty much host them. We were booking the Bellamys and they came into town for a show. They were out doing some press and other things, and I heard on the radio that the hotel where they were staying had caught on fire.

So I called them and shouted, urgently, "You have to go back to your hotel and get your stuff out of there 'cause the hotel's on fire!" That was my first conversation with The Bellamy Brothers and it sort of set the tone for my relationship with them. Everything that's kind of off the wall and strange that could happen, happens when I'm with them.

After Halsey sold his agency to William Morris, he went into management and I went with him. When Jim wanted to express his appreciation but he couldn't give you a raise, he gave you a new title. So he came in one morning and he said, "Hey, I've got a new title for you."

I said, "So I don't get a raise this year."

He said, "No, but you're gonna love this. You're gonna be Vice President of International Relations."

I said, "Jim, I've never been out of the country."

He said, "You will." And I did, and that's how I kind of started dabbling in international, and it grew and grew and grew. The Bellamy Brothers are probably *the* most requested country music artists in any country overseas. They have a history because they started in '76 with their first pop hit, "Let Your Love Flow." It was released worldwide and it was a hit in Europe, and they went back to Europe every year and built that foundation internationally and they still have that now—they still do duet records with top Swiss artists, and they did a duet with a Schlager artist, so they keep their overseas presence alive.

And they made some smart decisions to maintain their presence overseas. They kept their fees affordable, which artists today won't—if they make $300,000 a night here, they want $300,000 dollars a night in Europe, and those artists are not worth it in Europe, they just don't have the fan base. But I think probably the biggest thing was they signed with a German record label (Ralph Siegel, Jupiter Records) and they went over and recorded with that label and released product just for Europe. They did songs in their shows in Europe that I had never heard, and they're huge hits in Europe. "Crossfire" was a huge hit over there and I had never heard it till I went with them on one of their tours. They have found distribution for their music all over the world. Their fortieth album is being distributed by a German company. And now it's even being distributed in Singapore 'cause we did a concert in Singapore.

Some of the biggest problems that my international fan base promoters have when they come to Nashville is that they have trouble getting record labels to service them with product. They won't give them a free copy of an album on anybody. Even if the promoters ask for a download the labels will just say, well, download and pay for it. With the Bellamys, you just tell them you need an album and they ship it right out. These promoters are important to your business!

The Bellamys have no ego problems to get in the way of their business. They played a Schlager festival a few years ago in Switzerland. Like thirty or forty thousand people there. And then two nights later they did a two-hundred-seat intimate nightclub just to round out the weeknight.

They understand how the industry works in Europe. For one thing, there's no major country radio in Europe, which I think sometimes is a blessing. There's web-based radio and I know in Norway there was a country radio show that aired once a week on Sunday mornings at 3:00 a.m. for thirty minutes. Phil Mack has a video show all over Europe; it's the only video show with U.S. country artists on it. The only country video show in all of Europe, and it's on a pay channel. Years ago, CMT (Country Music Television) would go into the market so they could get their show there, maybe others, but those have all gone away. As opposed to the U.S. where your career is ruled by country radio.

The Bellamys don't need to have country radio support in Europe. They build their own bridges. They were the first country music artists to perform in India, Sri Lanka, just this year in Dubai, New Caledonia, and Faroe Islands, and there's not a lot of artists who have followed since then.

It's been a challenge trying to get them recognized in the U.S. for awards. It's an uphill battle. They won one year when I got them nominated for the CMA International Touring Artist Award. Their one big award; when it was about to be announced, Howard was in the toilet.

Overseas they're like Elvis! They're like Michael Jackson. They don't get an encore. They get four or five encores, people standing on their feet screaming for more. I don't think anyone here realizes what a fan base they have overseas. They're the only country artists that I can do a tour for. Other artists I can book a festival. Next weekend. I can book different artists for one night, but I can actually *tour* the Bellamys.

I don't know why we started doing this but we started playing practical jokes on each other. Back when I was at the Halsey Company, even that early in their career, they were filming a video at The Stockyards down in Fort Worth, and for some reason I hired a male stripper to dress up like a policeman, and he went in and he shut the video shoot down. He was like, "What are you doing? Where's your permit? I don't see any permits that allow you to be out on the street. You're supposed to be inside. Who's in charge?" And they point out Howard and David, and he said, "Over here, sit down, right here!" And he reaches behind him, turns on a boom-box, releases his hair, which is down to his waist, and starts dancing and stripping. And Howard's going, "Where's Judy? Where's Judy? I know she's here somewhere. Where's Judy?!"

So to retaliate, when they went to Australia, they bought a rubber snake that looked more like a real snake than a real snake looked. And they FedExed it to a guy up at the USO 'cause they knew I was going to Bosnia with him, with another group, and had him put it in my bed while we were over there. So to get back at them, I had this bust of a woman, kind of Egyptian looking, kind of green clothes with her hair braided—I don't even know where I'd got it, but I shipped it to The Nugget in Sparks, Nevada, when they were performing out there, and had the bellman put it in Howard's bed.

I didn't know Howard was sick. He had the flu. So he's on stage. They do two shows a night and he's on stage. He's sick as a dog taking all kinds of medicine, comes off the stage, he's just gonna lay down for a few minutes in his room and he said, later, he opens the door and he goes, "Oh! Oh! I'm sorry. I've walked into the wrong room and I'm backin' out. I say, that's my shit! That's my boots! That's my clothes!" So he goes, "Hey. *Hey! HEY!*" And she doesn't move! And he picked up one of his boots and threw it at her! And of course, it hit her with a *clunk*, and he realizes what's going down, at least on some level. Well, he didn't take the bust home with him, they left it there. The people at the hotel, they thought the bust was something valuable. While Howard and David are still on the road, the hotel people ship it to the boys' mother. The boys get home and there's the bust of that woman. She had made it home before they did. And Frances, she jumped all over them about leaving it there and not bringing it home.

And then we started doing milestones for birthdays. David turned fifty in Denmark. His wife, Susan, is one of my dearest friends. She calls me and says, "I wanna hire a stripper for David's birthday." I said, "Okay," and she says, "Let's go online and do it." That sounds good to me. So we go on line and she says, "Let's hire the one with the biggest boobs, because he loves big boobs!" So we found this girl and hired her online, and then she says, "Can I bring a friend with me 'cause we love the Bellamys's music," and we said, "Yeah."

It was in a big hall, a *big* hall, and the guys were on stage, and the strippers were supposed to come in and meet us, and I said, "How are we supposed to recognize her?" and Susan says, "I don't know!" Well, they walked in and everybody that was watching the show turned around and looked at them. We later found out that we had hired the most famous stripper in all of Denmark. She'd been in every publication, she had her own TV show, everything, so they walk in, we get 'em backstage, and they ask Susan, "What do you want us to do?" and Susan goes, "Whatever." And I'm thinking, *That's not a good response.*

We had their European record label there that night, presenting them with a platinum record award. So we get everybody in the back stage area, we tell the band they've got to come back there, and the band looks back and sees the two girls and they all go, *"Oh, my God!* The drummer has brought hookers backstage again and we've got the record label here!"

The stripper was doing her thing and at one point she had David lay on the floor and she crawled over the top of him, and I'm like, "Susan, aren't you pissed at all?" and she says, "He can't see a thing that close without his reading glasses!"

Howard turned sixty in Switzerland. I had to do something a little different and I tried to hire a transvestite, not realizing that in Zurich transvestites are a huge business. I mean, they get paid over $1,000 a night. I was willing to spend a couple of hundred but a thousand was a bit out of my range. So I was talking to the concierge at the hotel, asking him if he could come up with anything and he said, "Well, I actually do that at night, on my own." So we hired him to come to the restaurant and be "her," have dinner, sit on Howard's lap, hug him, and we took pictures and we whispered, "Howard, that's the concierge at our hotel," and he says, "I knew I recognized him!"

We kind of slowed down on the practical jokes as we got a little older. It gets harder to do. It takes a lot of energy. A lot of work. You know, traveling international, it's thirty-hour flights to get to places and they don't complain. Some nights we get two hours sleep before we have to fly somewhere else. I try to make their travel schedules easier for them. But they're just so good, they are, and you know, you can't always go by age, 'cause these guys run circles around some of the young ones who whine when they have to travel hard.

I have the only country music festival in all Japan, and I've had it since 1989. The Bellamys headlined it one year and we always took TNN or CMT or somebody to film. So we filmed them in the baths, the hot baths, and we turned the cameras off when they were gonna get naked and get into the water. But I paid the still photographer to take pictures of their butts and didn't tell them about it. The photographer sent me the pictures afterwards, and two years later when they were playing in Minnesota, I mailed the picture to a friend up there and he went to the show. Later he got in the autograph line and walked up to them and said, "Can you autograph this for me?" He handed them the picture of their nekked butts and their only comment was, "Boy, I sure wish she'd have done this when we were younger."

11

Career Evolution
And More Old Stories
Another International Incident and
the Bagman Producer

DAVID: Like Hank Snow, we've been everywhere. At least that's how it seems, and sometimes it gets very complicated, because of customs, history, and all the things we should have known but didn't. I don't think you can learn all that much from previous experiences. Every new disaster is just different enough from the last one that you can't recognize it coming at you.

In 1986 we toured South Africa for the first time. We were excited about this tour because we really wanted to go on safari, but there was still apartheid in South Africa at the time, and we had no idea how crazy the apartheid thing was. We just didn't know. And we weren't there to do anything wrong or mischievous. But it was *us*, so things just happened.

We had three nights scheduled in Sun City to play the first weekend, and then three nights the next weekend, so we had some days in between. We ran into a safari guy—of course—we always run into somebody. The safari guy says, "Hey, if you let me put you guys in the brochure, I'll fly you down to my safari." This was right on the border of Sabi Sabi, which means "Dangerous River," and it really is. It was right by Kruger National Park, which is about the size of the state of Georgia. So we flew down there, and they literally radioed ahead to make sure they ran the giraffes off the runway so you can land safely. You come in on this clay runway and you get into a jeep out there, and you take off down the road and you see these large herds of zebra and giraffes and it really is like a Tarzan movie. This is like the coolest thing ever, so we're really happy. We get to see a leopard, which the guy said maybe two percent of the visitors get that lucky. Leopards are nocturnal so we had to go out at night and we park under a tree, and the leopard is sitting there on the limb eating a springbok. It's so gory the hyenas are smelling it! We're out there three days, I think, like the greatest days of our lives, and when we come back to Sun City, we find out that we're in trouble, because we've broken the apartheid rule by playing Sun City, and we've still got three shows to play.

We're now on a blacklist with Sinatra, Linda Ronstadt, Paul Simon, Elton John—and because we're on this blacklist, they're gonna ban us from playing at all these European countries 'cause we've gone and broke this apartheid rule. So we come home, still not real sure what we've done. We've been in Kruger National Park smokin' the weed—it's growing everywhere out there—and lookin' at lions coming into the camp. We've been out there for three days. I mean, we could have stayed out there for six months, it was such a cool place. But we come in from the bush and we're in all this trouble, and we have to hire an attorney to write an apology letter to the ambassador of Iran, who at that time is the head of the Human Rights Committee of the U.N.

Of course, money is what they really want. We have to pay money to get out of this hole, and this is about the time that Paul Simon released *Graceland*, and he was in trouble for going there and recording with the African musicians. We had a lot of interaction with the musicians there because at the time "Crossfire" was a really big record there; it turned out we had a lot of hits there. Eventually we got out of that mess. It just cost us a fine, but for a while it looked like by the time they got finished with us, we wouldn't be able to play in Europe, we wouldn't be able to play in Australia or New Zealand, about the only place we'd be able to play might be Texas!

Well, heck, we always got in trouble for something, and maybe there was something wrong with our eyesight, because we could never see it coming. Or maybe, just maybe, we never cared enough to keep an eye out for storms and ambushes. There *is* such a thing as being *too* careful.

It's hard to be precise in the chronology of how we progressed as an act. It's always two steps forward and one step back. Or sometimes it's one step forward and two steps back. But I think it's fair to say that by '86 or '87, we were pretty well established worldwide as a touring band. We were making good records with Emory Gordy. We had our businesses in a good spot, except for the label things which, as we keep saying, never really got straightened out. The role of the record labels in our lives is so strange. I've thought about this many times. They aggravated the hell out of us. They took advantage of us every chance they could get. But they did more than anybody to give us a big-time career.

HOWARD: You know, we ran into an opportunity in late '75 to record "Let Your Love Flow." We took a shot! You've got to take a shot. You may hit. You may miss. You may hit and it still has repercussions. But without "Let Your Love Flow," there probably wouldn't have been a door open for "Beautiful Body." That's the way I've always looked at it and try not to remain bitter, even though they gave us that opportunity to go on and exposed us to the world, but wouldn't it have been nice had they done all that *and* been honest with us too?"

DAVID: As a reader you might say, "Well, you've had a great career, why can't you just get over it?" Not so easy, because for year after year after year, fighting with them took so much energy and so much emotion. We wanted to be able to concentrate on just moving our careers along and they had seen enough of us to know that if they just let us do our jobs and pay us our royalties, they'd have these two happy artists touring the world and making money for them.

I'm not saying this only happened to us. We've read a number of biographies of artists where they talk about the same kinds of things, except in some cases they are told point blank not to make a fuss or they would die. At least we never had to deal with those kinds of threats.

HOWARD: Gernhard came close!

DAVID: I think maybe if you're gonna be successful in the record business, you have to have some of those kind of guys on your side.

HOWARD: *Sort of* on your side.

DAVID: I've actually heard Gernhard called "Bagman." According to some of the guys I know from the old regime, he'd leave the office and head for a radio station with a briefcase full of cash, and the record would get added. You know, overall we've been lucky in our career. We ran smack into what you might call music business tradition, but at least we were able to speak our piece without being fitted for cement shoes, and Mom even got Gernhard to go straight with us.

HOWARD: Or at least go *straighter*.

Crazy Great Songwriters

DAVID: In the latter half of the '80s, we began to have some of the big European artists ask us to record with them. And we realized after we did one or two albums with them how much ground that covered. That was before the internet came along and it was a big deal in the countries where those records played and sold.

Also, around '86 we met Frankie Miller. Music publisher Richard Perna introduced us to Frankie after we'd recorded his song "When I'm Away From You," which was a #1 country record for us in 1983. He flew over from Scotland and we didn't know a lot about him except we really liked his writing and he had one of the greatest voices I'd ever heard. He had country and soul and everything all rolled into one.

Even by our standards, Frankie was wild. He may have been one reason we straightened up. You know, he was everybody's vision of the rock star. Frankie carried that style on every day. He drank a Nashville sushi bar out of saki one night.

HOWARD: Drank it dry. There are stories we know about him that would curl your hair, but we just can't tell 'em. Sorry.

DAVID: He had a really gigantic hit called "Darlin'." It's a European standard, not known that much in the States. Never had any other major artist releases here, but he wrote lots and lots of hits. He wrote a lot with Jeff Barry. Rod Stewart did his songs. Tom Jones did his songs. Also Johnny Cash, Lulu, Kim Carnes, Waylon Jennings, Ray Charles, Bonnie Tyler, Joe Cocker, The Eagles, Joe Walsh, Roy Orbison, Bob Seger. The list goes on and on. Rod Stewart called him the greatest soul singer the U.K. ever produced.

We hit it off with Frankie. Kindred spirits, I guess. He used to come over to our house and he'd bring paper bags full of cassette tapes that had bits and pieces of songs.

HOWARD: And song titles on pieces of paper.

DAVID: And he'd dump them all out on the couch and I'd sit there with this little cassette player and I'd put 'em on and listen to pieces. And he had this one song, it was a sort of chorus to "I'd Lie To You For Your Love," sort of unfinished, and it said, "I'm a doctor, I'm a lawyer, I'm an amateur gynecologist, and I own this bar." He had this slow version where he sounded like Otis Redding and then he had an up-tempo rock version, and Howard and I both heard it and we were like, "Man, that's a really great hook," and so, sitting on our tour bus, Howard wrote a verse, and I wrote a verse and Frankie wrote a verse, and we put them all together and they actually all worked perfectly. And then he wrote a little bridge and, I don't know, within two, three hours, we had taken the gynecologist part out of the chorus. I said, "Frankie, I don't think we're gonna get that one past radio." What did we do, put "movie star" in there?

HOWARD: Yeah, we put "movie star" in there.

DAVID: So that's kind of how that happened. Our recording of that song made it to #3 on the *Billboard* Country Charts. Frankie was friends with Jerry Lynn Williams, who was also an incredible writer. They were two of the wildest characters ever. And two of the better songwriters I've ever run across. Especially their melodies, which really worked for our vocals, you know, they had these big choruses, and they had an intensity that we just didn't hear in some of the other writers that we worked with. Jerry was actually in Fleetwood Mac for about ten days. He was going to become a member of Fleetwood Mac in one of their later incarnations, but maybe he was a little too crazy. He wrote songs for Ringo and Phil Collins.

HOWARD: A lot of hits for Eric Clapton.

DAVID: Bonnie Raitt, he wrote a couple of her hits; Jerry was another of Richard Perna's writers, come out of that Bill Hamm publishing company in Texas, Hammstein. We worked a lot with them.

HOWARD: I think readers might want to know how we choose songs. A lot of country singers today write—or at least have their name on—all the songs they cut. There are a few left, like Blake Shelton, Tim McGraw, and George Strait, who look for great songs written by other songwriters. We kind of lean toward our own because we know what we like to do, and looking for outside songs involves listening to hundreds and hundreds of them every time you want to do an album. But every so often, we'll hear a song we absolutely love, and there are a few writers we either write with or listen to from time to time, writers who write the kinds of songs we love to sing. Remember, if we cut a song we think is a hit but we don't really like it, that means we might have to sing it on our shows for the next ten years because we know our audiences wanna hear it. But even though we've written most of our hits, we know we owe our career to a great song we did not write, and if we hear another one we like that much, we'll cut it in a New York minute!

Snake, Rattle & Roll and Sued by Chimps

DAVID: Over the years, when you're an act, people call on you to do charitable work. And you want to do charitable things. Then you find out that sometimes charity is not charity at all—there's just various degrees of it, and the more you can control it, the more likely you are to know where the money actually goes.

Sometimes it's hard to decide just what you wanna do, and sometimes the idea just falls on your lap. There was this school near our home, St. Anthony's, that our kids attended and it was brought to our attention by our friend James Shaheen that we might be able to help the school by playing a concert to raise money. Over the years, we'd helped Randy Owen and Alabama raise lots of money for St. Jude's. So we had an idea to start our own jam. There had been that old rattlesnake festival down in San Antonio, not far from Darby, that went on for about fifty years, and it was one of the first places we ever played. So we decided to call our jam "Snake, Rattle & Roll," to be held on the third Saturday night every October.

We started off relatively modest. We had it at Saint Leo College close by, and it ended up in one of the cow pastures closer to the ranch. It turned into pretty much of a big redneck fest, a sort of Central Florida Woodstock. That first year, we had just had a pretty big hit with the Forester Sisters called "Too Much Is Not Enough." So we had them and a couple of local acts—did it kind of low budget to see if it would work, and we ended up having I think about eight thousand people that first year, which was pretty good for that time. We didn't do a lot of heavy promotion; we got one of the local stations to help us sponsor it, WQYK, that's always been kind of our local home country music station. We were pretty stoked after that successful first year, so we started doing it every year, and over the years we ended up having some high profile artists. George Jones came down and played it. David Lee Murphy came down and played it; Desert Rose Band, Deborah Allen, Pam Tillis, Mark Chesnutt played it, The Mavericks and Aaron Tippin played it.

Lots of stories. We had one year where it rained about eight inches during the show, and almost flooded the whole place. Then we had one year where our neighbor threw some homemade dynamite in the swamp.

It was supposed to be a one-day thing, but people started having parties around it—

HOWARD: Yeah, it led up to pre-parties and post-parties—

DAVID: It really got wild. We never had problems with the local law enforcement because they were involved. But eventually, it got totally out of hand.

HOWARD: As it got bigger and bigger, we had Walmart and Budweiser in as sponsors, and we donated to Walmart's big charity, Children's Miracle Network. But it couldn't go on forever. The last year we had it, the sheriff called our mom the day after and invited her to The Waffle House for breakfast. She went over to meet him and he said, "You know, two ranches over, there were orgies goin' on." She said, "Well, that don't happen at our jam, what they do over there I can't do nothin' about."

DAVID: There was lots of partyin' goin' on, but the neighbors didn't complain because mostly they were the ones doin' the partyin'. To this day we get comments, please bring back—oh, they beg us to bring it back. Oh, we get letters.

HOWARD: Everybody wants us to bring the jam back.

DAVID: You know, it started out small, with mostly us organizin' it, me and Howard and our mom and James Shaheen, who was our business manager and was with us for twenty years. We did a lot of good, raised a lot of money for a lot of organizations. But, oh, Lord was it a headache, especially as it went on, because the first part of it was all volunteer, but as it got bigger and more complicated—the show didn't get over till about one in the morning, our banker would open the bank at one in the morning, and we'd have to take all the cash, and there was a lot of it, and put everything in the vault. We would meet at the bank and count the money because we had designated money to go out to different charities. By the time we peaked, our crowds were in the twelve to fifteen thousand range, and that was a lot for us to handle, even with the good help we got.

HOWARD: We had George Jones, just when he fell off the wagon, and that was kind of interesting.

DAVID: Of course, we had played with him a lot in the old days so we had known about all his problems. Then there was the time we got sued by the chimpanzee farm. The chimpanzees sued us.

HOWARD: That's a true story—and the chimps won.

DAVID: The thing got real big and so, toward the end of the jams, we decided we'd bring in a promoter to help us manage it because it was too big for us to handle. We had designated certain amounts to go to different places and there was a chimp farm in New Port Richey, maybe twenty miles away, and they had requested a donation and we told them that we would designate $5,000 to go to the chimps. After the jam, we took off on a date and little did we know that when the accounting was done and they divvied up everything, the promoter had run off with the chimp's money. We didn't know that they didn't get paid, so a couple of months later we get a letter from the chimpanzees' attorney and he's trying to file a lawsuit against us because we didn't give the chimps their $5,000.

HOWARD: Anyway, they got their money.

DAVID: After ten years we decided we'd had enough aggravation and shut down the Snake, Rattle & Roll Jam, but looking back, except for the huge stress and aggravation, it was a great thing for the town, a lot of folks had a lot of fun, and we raised a lot of money for good causes, including the Manatee Hospital at Lowry Park Zoo and the Florida Panther Fund, and we're proud of what we did.

Ranch Expansion, Big Uncle Miltie, and Our Buddy Bertha

By the end of the '80s, we had accepted the fact that major labels were not our friends and would never be our friends. I think that we were beginning to realize that growing up meant doing for ourselves and not waiting for some corporation to do for us.

It just seems that the more we've learned to control our career, the happier we've been. You know, we never quit being ranchers. It's in our blood. And in the late '80s was when we started expanding our ranching operations. We leased a ranch near us and soon we had about twenty-five hundred acres, and we also had a big feed lot in Texas.

Our father passed away in '87, which of course was a major sorrow in our life—our family was so close. Our dad was a quiet man, even a little shy, but he knew what was going on around him. He knew the ASCAP check always came in the same time as the Pasco County Fair. He knew when the cows were gonna drop calves.

HOWARD: He knew a lot of things that none of us knew. He had an inner sense—people just wondered, "How does he know these things?"

DAVID: He and mom hung on to the money and they watched it, and other than Howard's credit card going toward the brothel in Berlin, they pretty much held it all down and made sure it didn't get out of our hands. So it was quite devastating when he passed away, but we put everything back together—got back on our tours and let life go on.

We were doing a whole lot of TV at that point, all over the world: Australia, South Africa, Europe, of course, all the time—tons of stuff in Europe. In the States we were doing stuff like The John Davidson Show, Dinah Shore, Merv Griffin—we did shows with Flip Wilson—Solid Gold, Midnight Special with Wolfman Jack.

HOWARD: We were with Bob Uecker when he did his first TV show.

DAVID: And he was scared shitless. And there was all sorts of interesting personalities we ran across.

HOWARD: I met Milton Berle at the urinal, and you know what the rumor was about him in Hollywood. I didn't look!

DAVID: Milton Berle pitched Howard a song at the urinal. A gospel song.

HOWARD: *A gospel song!*

DAVID: That he had written.

HOWARD: One of those old vaudeville guys and he still used that old shoe polish on his head.

DAVID: Yeah, he had that shoe polish on his head. And he was sweating and it was kind of just running down the side of his face.

HOWARD: Aw, we loved it 'cause we loved all that old stuff and I was a big Milton Berle fan.

DAVID: This was all at The Alan Thicke Show in Vancouver.

HOWARD: Charlton Heston was there. And Barbi Benton was there. I went joggin' with Barbi Benton.

DAVID: Which had to be a lot of fun.

HOWARD: I couldn't keep up with her.

We were called to do Carson when we were touring Norway. And were both literally rolled up in blankets with the flu. And we just couldn't make it. That was a drag.

DAVID: We even did some TV in New Zealand. We did stuff all over the place. Sometimes Howard and I would literally get on a plane on Friday morning, jet off to Germany, and do one of those big extravaganzas then fly back home Monday morning. I mean that was a normal weekend for us. Back then TV had a big impact on your personal appearances.

HOWARD: Because there weren't so many channels then. And if you did TV, everyone saw you. Now, you can do a show and no one you know knows about it.

DAVID: And if you did something over there like Eurovision—*Star Parade*—that was a big one! We'd go up to Sweden, Norway, TV up there. England, did a lot of shows there, musical shows, talk shows; and it got us plenty of bookings no matter where our records were on the charts.

Of course, the Mandrell Sisters had a hit TV show at the time, and when we'd appear on that show they would edit our songs. "Do You Love As Good As You Look" was too racy for them. "Beautiful Body" was too racy for them. So finally they settled on "Sugar Daddy" if we would sing, "You need a man in your arms," instead of "You need a man all night long." So we did the song—

HOWARD: And then they wanted us to do a gospel song. And they said, "You probably don't know any gospel." We told them we grew up on gospel. They probably figured guys like us with long hair wouldn't know gospel songs—that's how it was in the '80s.

DAVID: So we did a gospel song for the show. But the good part of this story is, they aired the show about two weeks after we taped it in L.A. We were in Reno, at John Ascuaga's Nugget. It's an old landmark there.

HOWARD: Every country entertainer has played there.

DAVID: Plus, they used to have stars like Red Skelton and Vic Damone and all those old crooners that sang there as well, and then toward the '80s it got to be more of a country room.

HOWARD: But the catch was you had to follow an elephant named Bertha, and then later, Bertha and Teena. They went on first. And the stage smelled like elephant shit.

DAVID: Bertha was everyone's opening act.

HOWARD: Elephant Girl rode Bertha in. We all knew her well.

DAVID: The dressing room was just off the stage. There was a little TV in the dressing room and the Barbara Mandrell show we were on was going to air that night. In fact, it had already come on. So we had one eye on the TV and with the other we were watching the elephant, 'cause you could kind of see Bertha's leg, or her butt, while you were in the dressing room. Almost everybody migrated out toward the stage 'cause we knew it was close to show time, and then they introduced us on the Barbara Mandrell show. Howard had just walked out the door.

HOWARD: Well, I got word it was show time.

DAVID: But I hung back and I was gonna watch the Barbara Mandrell show to see how it sounded, 'cause we hadn't had a chance to see how we'd done on the show.

About that time I heard the kick drum start, which was the way the drummer would kick off "Let Your Love Flow"; he'd give four beats on the kick drum, and then the intro come in. I heard the intro to "Let Your Love Flow"—oh my God, I'd better—so I took off to go to the stage, and as I did I could see that Bertha had the whole opening blocked. Just a wall of elephant.

HOWARD: I'm like, "Where in the hell is David?"

DAVID: I'm looking kinda under Bertha and I can see Howard and the band's legs on stage, and they're vamping on the beginning of "Love Flow." The only good news is that Howard starts the song with the lead vocal, so I've got a few bars to come in, but I can't get around this elephant. So I cradle my guitar in my arms and I go down on my elbows and knees.

HOWARD: I look back and David's under the elephant.

DAVID: Crawling as fast as I can to get to the mic in time, and I actually made it by the time my harmony part came.

HOWARD: Perfect timing. He got a little elephant dung on him, but at least he got there. After all those years of smelling cow poop, Bertha was a distinctly new experience.

DAVID: She just smelled like a . . . big animal.

HOWARD: Strong.

DAVID: We played the ol' Nugget for twenty years, I guess.

HOWARD: Got to know Bertha real well.

Ranch and Records, American Pie, and Gold with Gola

DAVID: And our mom and dad—I'm sure they were happy that we had careers, but they took it in stride. Our family always had kind of a blind faith. From the start, we didn't know anything about the business, and they didn't know anything about the business, so they couldn't offer advice.

HOWARD: Our father just always had a thing he would say, and only we would know what it meant. He did it at the dinner table. It was, "Watch yourself! Mind your conduct!" It was really stern, and that was it. He was a man of few words. But you knew damn well what he meant with those short, quick statements.

DAVID: And they always would say, "Look, you were raised right. Be yourself."

HOWARD: And they would tell us, "You came from tough stock."

DAVID: And they were both really tough people. They had to be. *They cleared the ranch by hand*, pretty much.

Getting back to *our* ranching, me and Howard, we didn't wake up one morning and say to each other, "Let's be cowboys again." We were always that and so it made sense. First we expanded into a bigger cow-calf operation, which Florida's kind of known for.

HOWARD: Florida still has the largest cow-calf operation in the United States. Thirty-five thousand head of mama cows, they call it. The Mormons own it.

DAVID: We expanded into a feedlot in West Texas. Then we had *lots* of cattle.

HOWARD: That was two or three years before 9/11.

DAVID: Around that time we started the record label. Everybody on Music Row was saying, "Oh, New Country, New Country," and we knew we didn't fit in to that kind of thinking, so we were sure that we were better off going independent.

HOWARD: Every country radio station's logo was "new country."

DAVID: Just before we left MCA, we went to a station for an interview—we were doing a show and they wanted us to do a radio interview, and there's this young DJ in there, and we come in and it's all about new country and I'm not sure she knew what that was supposed to mean, she was just a young assistant. And so we were talkin' and she says, "Y'all gonna be over here tonight?" and we say, "Yeah, we're gonna be on stage at nine o'clock," and blah blah blah. So we got through with the interview and she says, "Let me ask you something, do you guys know like a really good book that I can buy that'll sort of give me a history on country music?"

HOWARD: At least she was interested.

DAVID: And we realized at that point that "new country" is not gonna be really good for us.

HOWARD: We could see our demise just around the corner.

DAVID: We knew our world markets, but here in the States we realized this is not gonna work for us at all. I think the last hit we had on MCA was "I Could Be Persuaded" that we wrote with Don Schlitz—got to #7 on the *Billboard* chart. When we left MCA, that also ended our deal with Curb. We didn't really know what we were going to do in recording at that point, but we knew we had a lot of markets where we could play. And then our buddy James Yelich, who you remember came from the Jim Halsey Agency—we were sittin' one night in a sushi bar talking to James and we said, "What do you think about us starting our own label?" And he said, "Well, you're all doing everything yourselves anyway," 'cause we were hiring independent promotion guys to promote our records. "You might as well give it a try, because the worst you could do is fail."

HOWARD: You could take your own record to #1 in those days. But that didn't last too long. The big record companies got a grip on the charts and they haven't let go since.

DAVID: We ran into Don McLean of "American Pie" fame at one of those morning talk shows on Nashville TV, *Good Morning Nashville* or something. We were talking to him and mentioned that we were thinking of starting our own label. Lots of artists at that time were searching for ways to stay close to their fans. He said he'd just found a distributor down in Atlanta called Intersound. "I can't guarantee 'em but they seem pretty good," he said, and gave us a contact number. Turns out they had just opened a small office in Nashville. Within six months we had Bellamy Brothers Records goin'. We put out an album called *The Latest And The Greatest*, because we knew we had to do some of our oldies to remind everybody that there were a few hits back there. We rerecorded a few of those old catalog items, then we put about five new songs on the album and did a video on one of those songs, called "Cowboy Beat" that ended up being the CMT Video of the Year. This was in 1992.

We were off to a great start with what would become a winning formula for our future albums. Our "staff" was our mother and Lucy. Mom and Lucy would stuff envelopes and bring in some help when we needed it. They'd hire a few kids and put together an assembly line. We had our independent promotion people in Nashville, Terry Leas and Jan Wood—and Bob Saporiti, just before he went back over to Warner Bros.

When we did the video on "I Could Be Persuaded," our last MCA record, we did it down in Seaside, Florida, in the Panhandle. My wife, Susan, fell in love with a beach house there—this was before we were married—so we bought the beach house. We were kind of riding it out on the last MCA thing because at the time we thought we were gonna have to re-up with one of the majors; we didn't know we were gonna start an indy label. And so we did a pretty big-budget video. When we decided to start Bellamy Brothers Records, Terry Leas suggested that we ought to throw a party down there at the beach house to kick off our new label.

HOWARD: It was our first attempt at payola as an independent label.

DAVID: She said, "I think I can get some of the consultants to come." Consultants were, and I think still are, very important in convincing stations what records they should play.

HOWARD: To me, consultants started the demise of music for the people, because before them, the audience would call in and request new records that they wanted to hear. They had an input and a lot of the stations listened. When the audience input faded away, it changed everything.

DAVID: So we threw a big bash down there, rented some houses near ours, and lo and behold, when the single came out, the first single on Bellamy Brothers Records, we were close to top twenty in just a few weeks. Later we found it was because none of the major labels and radio stations realized we had started our own label. 'Cause we didn't make an announcement, we just released the record. To radio, it was just a new Bellamy Brothers record. And we still had, basically, the same promo people calling, so the stations had no reason to know anything had changed. So we cracked the top twenty and then all of a sudden, somebody at one of the major labels figured out, I guess, that we had gone independent. And our race up the charts came to a screeching halt. But top twenty, for an independent label, was a good start. And of course, the video went on to be the independent video of the year at CMT.

HOWARD: And then we went on to have what to me were some really great country songs: "After I Go To Hell, Can I Come On Home To You" to me was one of the best songs we've ever done. I realized radio had gone to hell—it didn't bother me when they wouldn't play certain songs through the years, but when they wouldn't play that song it just pissed me off. 'Cause we knew, this is a country hit if we ever heard one!

DAVID: Also, in that time period, we started getting a lot of video play. CMT was still playing videos by independent labels. So we started putting most of our emphasis on the videos. We did a song called "Over The Line."

HOWARD: Which CMT banned because they said it was too erotic—more label intervention. We played that video the other day and it was like the most inoffensive—.

DAVID: We had six strippers dressed in racing gear.

HOWARD: They were in *racing gear*! They were out waving flags.

DAVID: We had hot rods.

HOWARD: Too erotic, it can't succeed. By this time the word had made its way over to cable TV that an independent label just can't happen, *it can't succeed.*

DAVID: But "Cowboy Beat" and "Rip Off The Knob"—"Rip" got played like crazy. And so did another video, "Not." But then they just got to where they wouldn't touch us because, again, independents.

HOWARD: Then, after awhile YouTube came into play. We thought, well, to hell with that (cable TV). They don't control YouTube. Lord knows they've tried. So we started doing videos with *more* risqué songs around 2010. 'Cause your chances of getting views on YouTube were greater if they were a little over the top.

DAVID: When we did "Jalepenos," it was already kind of controversial 'cause we had people in Obama and Sarah Palin masks fighting over immigrant documents. And we had a guy in a Tiger Woods mask swingin' a golf club at his wife or something. We had, like, three million hits on that video.

So YouTube saved us from not being able to expose our new material.

HOWARD: We still use YouTube to get us to our big public. The only thing is, in order to get big numbers in views, you have to do something that's really off center. That's kind of our forte anyway, so it's a pretty good format for us.

DAVID: The trouble with all of it now is it's so saturated that you have to do something terribly extreme to get attention, but sometimes you'd rather do a nice, mainstream video. But when changes in the market hurt us, we don't get discouraged, we look for a new way to get our music to the public. Is it possible that someday we'll just run into a brick wall? Sure, but not until we've fought the good fight to get our music out into the world. To us, the battle has its own value. We love the music, and we love the people who love our music. Why would we ever give that up without a fight?

Funny how this business works. For so many years we wanted to get off Curb. And once we understood where we stood in the new music world with our own label, we found that Bellamy Brothers Records was a large part of our future because it was our musical contact of choice between us and our fans. The nicest thing about our label is, we have so much flexibility. We've been licensing music all over the world now for twenty years. We do a lot of business with Universal in Switzerland and Germany, and they'll call us up and want us to do a recording project with a Swiss artist, German artist, whatever, and we'll do a one-off nonexclusive project with them. We still deal with big labels, but we give them a guarantee that we're not gonna drop anything in their market on top of their project while that record is out. And it all works out really good. We recorded what we called "The Greatest Hit Sessions" with the Swiss star Gola, and Gola sang some of our hits and we sang some of his hits.

HOWARD: Turned out to be huge.

DAVID: We had one platinum album together and one gold album. And we had a live album from one of the two tours we did together that did quite well.

HOWARD: Gola's like the most different artist we've ever known. He only does a few dates a year, in Switzerland, and in his spare time he's a carpenter. Really interesting, earthy guy.

DAVID: Yeah, he says, "I wanna come over and stay with you guys and work at the ranch." And he's done so twice.

HOWARD: By that time, we had a pretty good handle on all the business it takes to run a music operation like we had. You might say that in some ways, we had grown up. We were now more likely to put our minds to work on the next tour than to spend an hour working out some stupid prank to play on each other or someone in the band.

DAVID: There's a price to be paid. Some journalist once asked us how much time we spend on the ranch and how much time on the road. I guess he imagined us living the healthy outdoor life of cowboys eatin' out of a chuck wagon and roundin' up them doggies.

HOWARD: Feels like we spend about 1 percent at home and 99 percent on the road. The older we get, the less time we spend at the ranch. I was thinking it would work the other way around. You get into that spot where, well, you're like one of the last ones left. The other night when we were over at John Rich's house—he was havin' a show there—he come on stage and give us an introduction and I turned around to see who he was talking about. He hyped us so much we thought he had to be talking about somebody else. But you get to the point where you look around and there's really not so many acts left—well, there's still a lot of the older acts alive, like yesterday we attended a Legends luncheon and were happy to see a lot of older acts there, but most of them are no longer touring.

In general, we're feeling good enough to stay on the road, but let's face it, even when you feel well at seventy, you still feel like shit.

DAVID: But I'll tell you something else, we spent about twenty years where it was pretty much a miracle that we weren't dead. I know about four or five times, *I* probably should have been dead.

HOWARD: Oh, I've rushed him to the hospital many times.

DAVID: But the most recent part of our career, we've—I know we don't always eat exactly right and everything but we've done a lot of preventative maintenance. We've done hyperbaric and stem cell—

HOWARD: We've tried it all.

DAVID: We've done everything to try to stay healthy. Are we trying to live forever? Well, no, but there are still a few record guys we'd like to bury.

Howard was pretty ill in the early '80s, and he started going to this holistic guy, Dr. Ray Wunderlich—he was such a brilliant guy.

HOWARD: We totally gave up on traditional medicine. It'll kill you!

DAVID: He wrote books on the ills of sugar forty years ago. Howard does no sugar. I do as little as possible. He doesn't do any bread. I do as little as possible. We don't drink. I don't do drugs.

HOWARD: I still do a nibble, but I don't smoke a lot of pot anymore. I do some medicinal type for aches and pains. We take CBD oil, that has the THC removed. There's no high to it. Damn it!

DAVID: It's *good* stuff. I took some this morning.

HOWARD: I take it every day.

It's a Wonder Sumpin' Ain't Killed Us

DAVID: I guess the closest I ever come to dyin' is when Howard took me to the hospital in Dade City. Well, the closest time I know.

HOWARD: A friend of ours sold us some coke.

DAVID: Well, he said it was coke. I'm not sure what that shit was. In fact, I attribute this incident to me stopping drugs pretty much—that and my first son being born. It was kind of happening at the same time. We were still pretty wild—it would have been '79, right after Jesse was born. We went over to the guy's place and snorted a couple of lines of the stuff, and I went completely blind. I mean, everything was black, it wasn't even a matter of being able to see light, or blur, or anything. Howard had done some lines also, and he wasn't feeling too good, but he wasn't blind yet.

HOWARD: I was just higher than hell, but I knew I had to get him to the doctor quickly, and somehow I got us to the emergency room—we're in our hometown, and, oddly enough, the doctor who delivered him was on duty. He says, "What have you done?"

DAVID: And I told him, and he said, "*You crazy son of a bitch!*" He says, "Come back here with me!" And I didn't know where "here" was, 'cause I couldn't see a damned thing.

HOWARD: The danger of going into an emergency room, anywhere, when you're sick, is everybody wants your autograph.

DAVID: Here's the worst thing. He (the doctor) hit me up with something that sent me spiraling, a big ol' syringe of valium or something. I woke up there a few hours later, and I was still really groggy, but I could see now, and you know how people walk by you and you're laying on a stretcher or a gurney, and this one nurse comes up to me, and I'll never forget this, because I was so glad that I was alive. She comes up and says, "My boyfriend sings out at the Red Carpet." She says, "Would you go out there and see him, and tell him if he's any good?"

I said, "Honey, you get me out of here alive, I'll tell him he's Elvis!"

HOWARD: I went into an emergency room in St. Louis one time and Chuck Berry was in the same emergency room. We both had stomach problems and I was just screwed up, and Chuck Berry was laying right over there and he was screwed up too. Wow, what a trip! I didn't go ask for his autograph, though.

DAVID: You know what's really weird? I guess you could put drug users and drinkers into little categories. We were always experimental in the world of psychedelics and psychotics. We considered those drugs to be our friends. I knew people who did heroin, but we'd never go near that. I was like terrified.

HOWARD: The mind drugs. We were always trying to expand the brain. We were always curious about the world around us. I think that's one reason why we ended up traveling so much.

DAVID: Now, except for the drug stupidity, we were a little more cautious than you might think. Some force must be with us. Like in South Africa we went and jumped over to Kruger Park, but you know what we didn't do? We didn't go up to Victoria Falls, because there was real danger there. People don't necessarily know. Like we'll tell somebody that we're going to the Middle East and they'll make a horrified face and say, "Oh, don't go to the Middle East!" You have to realize, we're not going to these places on holiday. That's how we make our living. We try to be sensible, but we don't always know what we're doing.

HOWARD: Like, Northern Ireland, back in the day! There were certain roads you didn't go down.

DAVID: When we used to tour Northern Ireland, if there was a road unmarked, you didn't dare turn down there. You'd get blown up. Howard and me and Susan were in Belfast, doing a TV show, and we had CNN on in our room, watching a scary outdoor riot. And Susan said, "That looks really familiar!" And we opened our curtains, and there it was. Whatever chaos CNN was showing on the tube was right outside our hotel window.

HOWARD: It was Hotel Europa, the most bombed hotel in the Guinness Book of Records. That's where we stayed. And you had to go through a metal detector to get through the front door.

DAVID: You know, we have a song called "We Dared The Lightning." We've always liked to test the world, go right to the edge, even to the DMZ between North and South Korea. Just for the experience. I don't know of any other reason.

DMZ, Korea. For "Demilitarized Zone." I vote for that one being the scariest. We've been in an active war zone, and I think the DMZ was scarier.

HOWARD: Yeah, they're serious.

DAVID: We played an impromptu little show in the kitchen of this building on the DMZ for the cooks and the Republic of Korea soldiers. The Americans and the ROK soldiers, which are the South Koreans, and their cooks have quarters that are never vacated. They stay there 24/7, because they're literally only from here to that wall from their counterparts, who are looking at them with guns.

HOWARD: It's a stare down, twenty-four hours a day.

DAVID: So we went in, took a couple of acoustic guitars—I think that mine had three strings on it. And we sang a few songs for the guys who never leave there. Gotta tell you, it's really, really tense. North Korea is scary. That bridge to nowhere? That's one of the scariest places I've ever seen. North Korea is my least favorite country. We also threw a barbecue for the troops in Bosnia during that war in the Balkans.

I guess we've had our share of risky things and close shaves. We've had a bus slide off a mountain in New Mexico. We've had two near crashes of airplanes. One of them occurred the day we flew into Bremen for *Der Musikladen* show. That was the day John Lennon was shot. They turned the show into a Lennon tribute, in memory of The Beatles connection to the Bremen/Hamburg area.

HOWARD: Bremen, Germany. Real cloudy.

DAVID: We were just coming down in the descent, and all of a sudden we're in a nose dive, seemed almost straight down, and none of us has a clue how close to the ground we are.

HOWARD: And I look out the window and here are these two fighter jets, they come under us and whiz right by the window and really rock our plane. Like, *Holy Shit!*

And we kept on diving!

DAVID: And the miraculous part is the pilot pulled out of it. Finally. In a 737! What a wonder that the wings didn't fall off.

HOWARD: We saw the pilot later at bag claim and he was white as chalk. But no one ever told us a thing about what caused all this to happen. And not a word about the two jets. Everyone just white as a sheet walking down into the baggage claim.

DAVID: The following day we had a meeting scheduled with the press secretary from Warner Brothers, in London, to discuss our next single. And that press secretary turned out to be Derek Taylor, the long-time Beatles's press secretary. So we wound up sitting in an office with Derek the morning after his close friend and music icon was murdered. Bless his heart, he took the meeting, but he was speechless because he'd been so close to John. He was the one who helped John and Yoko travel to Gibraltar to get married. The whole weekend turned into a surreal event, starting with a near-plane-crash, then this John Lennon tribute and sitting talking to Derek Taylor.

Oh, then we also got into a tornado on a Southwest flight, too.

HOWARD: Oh, that was last year! That was the most unbelievable domestic flight we ever had. We knew there was really bad weather in Dallas. We waited around and waited around. And they decided to take off and I'm like, "Man, it looks *bad* out there!" So we load on like sheep, we get on the plane. The plane takes off; we're probably about five thousand feet, and it starts throwing us around like we were a toy. This pilot did the opposite of what the pilot did in Germany, he kicked it straight up. It was like a rocket. Susan had both of us by her fingernails, diggin' in. I heard a bunch of "Holy shits!" It was like goin' to the moon for a while.

DAVID: The guy in the seat in front of me had a funny little hat on, and our angle was so steep that it fell off his head and landed on my lap. I had to hand it back to him when we straightened out.

HOWARD: Finally we burst through it but it seemed like one frantic forever.

Miss Universe, Lefty Frizzell, and Found in Translation

DAVID: We've had some close calls, and I don't mean to change the subject, but I think we ought to lighten up. We've had a lot of interesting introductions in our career. We had Miss World introduce us one time. A beautiful girl with an ugly IQ.

HOWARD: We have rules of the road, and after her introduction the number one rule was never let a beauty queen introduce you.

DAVID: Sometimes the people introducing you, they don't get much of a chance to be in front of crowds and they just yearn for that spot. When they finally get there, they introduce maybe an entire city, or thank everyone they know—it's like, *"Get the hook!"*

HOWARD: We recently heard the real story of the song, "Saginaw, Michigan" when Lefty Frizzell was invited by the city to go there and play the song. Bobby Bare told us the story.

The mayor of Saginaw was supposed to show up and present the key to the city to Lefty, but the mayor must have had another appointment so he sent his flunky there and they didn't get the key made so the flunky brought a gavel off the mayor's desk—Bare said it looked like a ball-peen hammer—the flunky was standing at the side of the stage with his ball-peen hammer and nobody really knew who he was. So Lefty gets introduced and kicks into "Saginaw, Michigan," and this guy with his hammer walks out onto the stage and Lefty didn't know what the guy was doing there so Lefty just left the microphone and headlocked him and run him off of the stage and threw him *into the crowd.*

DAVID: The band for some reason loves *this* story: Silkeborg, Denmark, a festival we do every couple of years. The promoter is a fine lady named Jytte. The first time we played the festival was in the mid-'90s and we had just finished recording one of our indie albums called *Sons of Beaches*, and this was one of the first times we were performing it in public. So Judy gives Jytte the job of introducing us, and maybe that was not Judy's best idea ever. We saw Jytte last year and she speaks a little better English now than she did then. She hardly spoke it at all then. So she came out on stage.

HOWARD: She's this sturdy, powerful Danish woman.

DAVID: Jytte comes out and announces, *"Ladies und gentlemen, Hovardt und Bellamy, der sons of bitches!"* There's about, twelve thousand people. Of course, now, we can't hardly sing, 'cause we're laughing so hard. Becky Hobbs, she was in the wings. She was like, falling over her piano.

HOWARD: We could hardly do the show!

Goat's Milk, TV Albums, and the Leaning Tower of Pisa

DAVID: Throughout the '90s, we regularly released albums on our Bellamy Brothers label. The major labels' stranglehold on radio and the country charts pretty much put an end to our airplay, but our good distribution kept us in what few stores were left, and our fans continued to love us, so we were happy with our record sales. Wherever we played, people came out to see us, and when they came out to see us, they bought our albums. Many of our fans want our latest and best quality recordings, and they want a piece of us they can hold in their hands. We make it a point to always have something new for them.

HOWARD: We love the process: coming up with songs, recording and mixing them in our own studio, creating videos; getting the CDs and DVDs manufactured and announcing their release is much more of a pleasure than a chore.

DAVID: We were booked to play Erfurt, Germany, I think in '89 and up till then, nobody knew the wall was gonna come down. We were there right after it came down, in Erfurt, which is in the former East Germany.

We would run into people at our shows who would smuggle our albums into East Germany and they had record listening parties—they would meet up in someone's basement and play the album in secret because it was against the law.

HOWARD: They had country music clubs, and one person would manage to get an album in the black market; they'd all secretly go to one another's home and listen. That's how they knew our music, all through East Germany and Czechoslovakia, when they were under communist rule.

DAVID: When we played the shows in Erfurt, we stayed in Berlin on the border, right where Checkpoint Charlie used to be. We played a few days later and it was really a bizarre scene because all the Russian soldiers that Russia left behind, they all would come to the show with the East Germans. They'd pretty much stopped guarding the border; they were trying to get enough money to go home.

HOWARD: We bought some of their hats and some of their medals, and gave them money to help them get back home. They were kids, like in their early twenties. I have a soldier's hat in my barn that I bought from one who was raisin' money to find his way home. Some of them never got out. Some of them stayed there and blended in.

About the time we started our label here, we ran into a friend of ours who introduced us to a producer in Munich named Ralph Siegel, and we cut an album with him, cut some new material, and an old friend of ours who's a disc jockey named Tom Jeier, he got with Ralph and they co-wrote a song called "Neon Cowboy." We recorded that and it brought us back into the German charts, one of the first singles we'd had in the main German charts in a few years. It was a big deal.

DAVID: We ended up doing four of those albums with Ralph Siegel in Munich, pretty much for the German/Austrian/Swiss—you know, the Schlager market.

Our varied recording events allowed us to experiment with the music we released for our fans. For example, we took half the songs from the *Sons of Beaches* (not Sons of Bitches) album and half the songs from a session in Munich and combined them over there for an album called *Native Americans*.

HOWARD: Ralph's father was a major publisher in Germany, with evergreen hits like the international classic "Beer Barrel Polka."

DAVID: And Ralph was a partner in a publishing company with Don Gant, one of Nashville's top publishing and producing guys in the '60s and '70s.

HOWARD: Ralph was a very wealthy, eccentric producer-record guy, so naturally we wound up working with him. He was a good guy in a lot of ways, and he paid us. It was easier to get paid by record labels in Germany and those other countries than it was to get paid in the U.S.

Ralph liked to do things just his way. We'd get in the studio, try to finish the album—we'd only have so many days to work on things, as we'd try to get back home, with so much going on in America. Ralph, he'd like to stop everything around six, seven o'clock and take us out to an elaborate dinner at these fancy joints he liked. He'd have place markers for you, and he would order for you in advance, and then we would get there and he'd find a chandelier in the restaurant from Louis XIV or something and he would try and buy it. He'd listen to the music they were playing in the restaurant and any time they played something that his father published, he'd make them turn it up.

DAVID: This was a whole different thing for us. We didn't use our band in the studio. Ralph had his musicians, his studio—we had a whole production mill going on there.

HOWARD: His mother was an opera singer. Everything we did there was kind of keyboard-oriented; it was a totally different kind of production. Those sessions were more what they would consider classic Schlager sessions. Everybody did what Ralph told them to do. Just totally different sounding, but we had a lot of success doing it.

DAVID: We did an album called *Beggars & Heroes*, and Ralph did like a *Sgt. Pepper* kind of album cover with the bar and the girls and all. You know, the Europeans are very dramatic and give a lot of attention to the cover art—in Nashville, often it's just basically take a picture of whoever the singer is and put him on the front, but Euro cover art was a whole production in itself.

222

We ended up releasing some of those tracks here, because we acquired the rights later on to also release them on our own label. But we put them out as what they were, as our European collections. A couple of those songs, like "Blue California" and "I Love You More And More And More," became line dances when some of the country fans got a hold of them and they became known here, but for the most part they're strictly for the European market. So we had all that going on in Europe while we were releasing those early albums recorded here for our own label. That, plus all the continuous touring, kept us busy and exhausted through the '90s.

HOWARD: I actually see a lot of those tunes pop up now on Facebook, you know, people that discovered them and want to share them, they're actually getting around these days. And all that music we did, you know, was a way of survival for us. In the early '90s we were still having trouble with the labels and hoping that our own record label would work, and we saw new country coming in, wondering how that would affect us, well, this European shot with Ralph was a way to keep us going while we were learning where our career at home was gonna take us next. We didn't *know*. It was, "Let's try this!" And we had quite a bit of success then; it kept our profile up anyway. And now you see all those old albums resurfacing on social media.

DAVID: When we started our own label, it gave us the opportunity to try different things. When you're trying for radio hit singles, you're kind of limited by what radio will or won't play, and once we realized that radio would not play our independent label product, we could concentrate on what we liked and what our fans would like, here and overseas. When we did those albums in Europe, we made them specifically for those markets, and we did one deal at a time, so that we would not get tied up again because for the first time in our career, record-wise, we were free. Besides the deals we did with Ralph, we were licensing everything we did from here on our label with overseas labels. We had fifteen, sixteen licensing deals around the world. We had South Africa, we had Australia, we had a Canadian deal; there was just a bunch of those all over the place, and we continue to do them like that, like, we just did a new deal in Singapore, for the *40 Years* album. Most of the deals we were licensing from here, but because we had a really big profile in Germany, Ralph had the idea for us to cut some original stuff there, and it worked really well.

Cutting those albums in Germany no doubt influenced some of the home-cut music that came later, but that was nothing new. I think that all of our music, throughout the years prior to and after and during that period, everything always influenced us. We had been influenced by the Euro sound even back when we were trying to get thrown off of Warner/Curb. When they released "More Of You" and it went big, they called us up and said, "Hey, in Austria this thing has passed Madonna and Stevie Wonder," so we were influenced by the Euro sound even then because we were there so much.

Really what our music is, is a lot of influences. Our first influence was gospel.

HOWARD: Then Jimmie Rodgers, because that's what we learned to play with our father. He used to drink moonshine and sing "T For Texas" every Christmas. He liked western swing too.

DAVID: Bob Wills and all of them,

HOWARD: He liked the old songs like "Waitin' On The Robert E. Lee," "Down Yonder," "All Around The Water Tank," and we both love Jimmie Rodgers to this day. We went from there to listening to everything, I mean, we really absorbed everything, Webb Pierce, Lefty Frizzell, all the stuff we would just hear, you know, we really lived out in the woods and just grew up on all of that old stuff, and then went to church every Sunday and sang gospel music, and then getting exposed to a lot of the island workers—and it just rubbed off from all directions. Of course all the rock and roll singers, too, Chuck Berry, Little Richard.

DAVID: During that hippie era, a lot of new music got exposed. People who weren't there then probably don't understand that everybody shared music and shared a joint and you got exposed to all kinds of music. I remember people getting turned on to bluegrass; these rich northern college kids would come down here to Saint Leo College and they would "discover" bluegrass and I'm goin', "Wow! We've had bluegrass forever! We just thought that bluegrass was old-timey music."

HOWARD: By the '90s I think we were beyond influences. It was all just music that we knew, and we'd blend it together without another thought.

DAVID: When we did our albums in the '90s, I think we used pretty much all those influences. Remember, we did an album called *Reggae Cowboy*, which has influences that go back to our childhood .

HOWARD: There's a good story on the "Reggae Cowboy" song, which we released in the early '80s. "Reggae Cowboy" was sandwiched between two #1 hits, but it only got as high as #21 on the *Billboard* country chart, and I think one reason may have been that people weren't understanding the lyrics. Some people thought we were singin' "Get into Reagan, cowboy," some thought we were sayin' "real gay cowboy," some thought "Reggie cowboy." They really didn't know what reggae was. I don't think country radio knew what reggae was. We got so many letters about it, but radio was not impressed, and the record didn't do that great. We rereleased the song later on when we started our own label, and people were a little more into reggae. We did a dance mix of it, and the clubs played the heck out of it. We did a whole album of reggae-influenced songs, including "Some Broken Hearts Never Mend," which we still play live today; we did a Bob Dylan song, "I'll Be Your Baby Tonight." We reggaed "I'll Fly Away," a really great version of that song. We could do what we wanted because radio, for the most part, wouldn't play us anyway. I mean, we never puckered up very much to start with, but once we saw we couldn't get radio play, we really went renegade, and those albums still hold up very well; *Over The Line* is a pretty strong album, and so was *Sons Of Beaches*.

DAVID: By the late '80s, we were changing too. Our dad died in '87. Our family was always so close. Our mom and dad watched out for everything on the home front, including our kids, and including the ranch, which allowed us to tour the world and bring home the bacon but also to experience all this stuff and these influences. But he passed away and our kids were getting older at that point. And he was this huge figure in our life, this old-school cowboy, a man of few words but many deeds, with all that quiet wisdom thrown in. After he died, I don't think either one of us felt as bulletproof as we had before. That was definitely a big change.

Now, those boys of ours, in a lot of ways they're like me, more than I'd like to admit. Five sons, and they're all different, but they're all alike. It's a strange thing. They're kind of a cult unto themselves. They're just a group of Bohemians. I've got one son, Cole, who's a college lit professor and a poet. He's published two books of poetry and I keep telling him he's not gonna get rich publishing poetry. And my oldest two sons, of course, Jesse and Noah, are in the music business and they do really, really great stuff, but it's always stuff I think that's a little bit out of the mainstream. They're stubborn like us, but they do what they want and it's great music. Dustin, a graduate of Central Florida University, works with us at the ranch, helping us with computers and social media and overseeing the day-to-day operations. Aaron, my youngest, is a film school graduate who works on sporting events, reality shows, and movies being done in Central Florida. All five of them play guitar and other instruments. As far as anyone knows, we're just a nice, normal family.

HOWARD: I have a daughter named Cheyenne. Her mother was my German wife, Ilona, that I was married to for twenty-three years. People think I couldn't stay married, but we lived together for a long time, though I lived in my barn the last five years of that marriage.

DAVID: He's got the only barn in the world with a bachelor pad in it.

HOWARD: Her mother's father was in the war. He was captured by Americans. And we had an uncle who just passed away at the age of ninety-six, who was captured by the Germans. I introduced my uncle to Cheyenne's grandfather and they became very good friends. The difference was that our uncle was beaten pretty bad by his captors, while Cheyenne's grandfather was brought here to a work camp and got to where he loved America.

Cheyenne lived an interesting childhood. She grew up on the ranch and she's an animal freak. She's a nutritionist. She says it's my fault because I brought her up so healthy. We used to feed her all organic foods from the ranch, all fresh eggs, vegetables and goat milk. She still lives very close to us, and she's the only one I've got that I know of.

We had an old neighbor, no names mentioned, because every rock and roller in the country would know it, he's passed on, anyway, he dealt a little pot—that's an understatement, too, and I noticed that our goat that we milked would always disappear and one day the neighbor called me and said, "Howard, please come get this damned goat; he's in my barn, eatin' my herbs." That damned goat would go over there—he was living on pot, and we were feeding the milk to our daughter, not realizing there was a reason our daughter was awfully sedate most of the time. I thought she was a real placid kid. So we raised her on stoned goat milk. We always kid Cheyenne about being raised on the good milk.

DAVID: We *had* to be successful and we had to make money because otherwise we couldn't have done what we wanted to do. Our kids didn't have to do that because we had paved a little bit of the way but, at the same time, it's still tough on them because doing what you want to and not conforming is always a hard thing to do. And the industry is tougher now; it's a rogue industry with the mainstream owned by a few big corporations.

HOWARD: Maybe even a little crooked, like the Leaning Tower of Pisa.

DAVID: Which brings us to our Leaning Tower of Pisa story. We had been touring internationally our whole career, of course, but Judy Seale was able to group all this international stuff together. You see, before, it was harder to do because somebody would say okay, we want you to go to Switzerland and do a one-off and we'd have to fly over and do one or two shows and then fly back, an awful lot of travel just for a show or two. Judy was able to organize booking opportunities into tours that made the travel more efficient and less exhausting. She also started her own company called Stars for Stripes that worked to entertain troops in the military. Between festivals we went off with her to entertain the troops, as well.

Around 1997, we went down to Aviano in northern Italy, then over to

Bosnia—and we took a film crew with us and shot some segments for a twenty-five-year DVD. The Vatican, Venice and us in the gondolas, and eventually we found ourselves in Pisa. We're filming the leaning tower and Howard and I are standing out in front of it and talking about it for the cameras when one of the crew guys says, "Let's see if we can go inside and maybe film an interview from inside, you know, that'd be different." We thought that might be cool; the Leaning Tower was world famous, an important landmark. Well, they don't sell tickets to the place, it's just the chapel and the tower, sittin' there. We found this little construction site behind it, 'cause they were doing some work there; I guess it's an ongoing thing they do to keep it leaning at a certain angle and not letting it lean any farther. So we found someone there, guy in work clothes, and asked him, is it possible to go inside, because there's doors to it, and a spiral staircase inside, and the guy said, "Oh yeah, we're fixin' to leave for the day, can you guys just lock it up when you leave, and put the key through the slot here?"

And he gives us the key to the Leaning Tower of Pisa!

We just hung out in the tower and did some shots of us walking up and down the stairs.

HOWARD: It's the funniest thing, it was just so informal, yeah, here's the key—so we did our filming and we locked up the Tower of Pisa.

DAVID: In the late '90s, between the songs we recorded for Ralph Siegel and the albums we were releasing on our own label, we were building up a good catalog of recorded music that we controlled. The Siegel albums covered what we called the GAS countries, Germany, Austria and Switzerland, but it still left the U.K., the Scandinavian countries, and others open. So we put together a Swedish collection and we put together a Norwegian collection and marketed them on television, and both became gold. TV sales—that was another byproduct of our starting our own label and doing the European albums, as well.

We were doing some shows over there, and we had this promoter out of Denmark and he knew about this record label and he said, "You know, they do television marketing and I think the people know y'all's songs so well that it's perfect for them." And he had done some other country acts from here, I think Buck Owens, maybe Bobby Bare, because Bare is still famous and popular in Norway. So we put together these packages for them, maybe fifteen songs, and they started marketing them and they became huge.

We did some TV marketing in the U.S., but not on a big scale and never really broke through the way people like Slim Whitman and Christy Lane did. I think that when we were able to hook up with companies that knew how to do TV marketing correctly, we had a lot of success.

HOWARD: Slim Whitman was the pioneer of TV marketing, and, you know, he was related to our secretary Lucy, that we mentioned earlier.

DAVID: So into the new millennium we continued to have a lot of success overseas, and our overseas business at that time continued to thrive because Judy Seale had tied those tours together. Sometimes a country act will see our touring schedule in Europe and they'll call Judy up and say, "Hey, can you put me a schedule like that together," and what she always tells them is, "I would be glad to if you had started with a hit in '76 and kept going over there." It's not as it appears, really. It's a combination of her being able to put tours together and us having been playing overseas for the last forty years.

I've told this story a few times and I think it's worth retelling here. We were in South Germany at a military base, I think it was Oberammergau, we had finished a festival in Switzerland and were down there playing this military date on a weeknight that Judy had booked for us. Howard and I were signing autographs when the show was over, and I actually saw two guys in front of us get in a fight over where we were from. The one guy was saying, "I know they're from Denmark because I grew up with them there." And the other guy was saying, "No, they're from Austria, because when I was a kid, that's where they lived." They were fighting over us being Danish or Austrian.

I didn't wanna get in the middle of it, 'cause we were actually sitting there facing an autograph line. I think Judy or my wife or somebody walked over there and said, "You know they're from Florida." And then both of them turned around to the girls, shouting, "No, No! They're not from Florida." But it's funny because we've spent so much time in a lot of these markets and it never dawned on us that people would think we were from there. A lot of Texans think we're from Texas.

HOWARD: We have to give Texas a lot of credit in this book—I believe that if it wasn't for Texas, The Bellamy Brothers would not have survived. They were our standby place to go for years, all the work we really wanted. We're even honorary Texas Rangers. And I believe they love us down there largely because they can dance to everything we play.

DAVID: But you also realize we're Kentucky Colonels!

HOWARD: Yeah and we have the keys to the city in Santa Fe, New Mexico, Interlaken, Switzerland, Guam, and other places, I'm sure.

DAVID: Yeah, it's hard to say where our second home is, but if it's anywhere, Texas would probably be it.

HOWARD: And yes, we've recorded with Willie Nelson. We have a song that David wrote called "Don't Go Running Faster Than Your Guardian Angel Can Fly." We recorded it with Willie on the *Angels & Outlaws* CD, we had Dolly and just about everybody else on the album.

12
Into The New Millennium
Snow Balls and the President's Grip

DAVID: At the turn of the century we played an event in Switzerland called The Millennium. This was when everybody was worried about Y2K and what might happen to the planes that were flying, and they decided to do the show on the streets of Interlaken, in the dead of winter, icicles hanging off all the trees.

HOWARD: They had this one Jamaican band playing reggae music outside and there were icicles hanging from the stage.

DAVID: We went over there and maybe we were a bit concerned, too, 'cause if you remember, nobody knew what was gonna happen; everybody was worried about Y2K. Judy was with us and remembers all too well what happened that week.

JUDY: Actually, the Bellamys were well prepared for Y2K. They had their basement stocked. All the food, generators, they were ready. Naturally they were skeptical about travel that weekend, but they weren't going to turn down an event like this!

DAVID: We'd booked the return tickets, too, but about four or five days later we decided to just stay in Switzerland because we figured by that time if the planes were gonna start falling out of the sky, we'd know about it. So we stayed over there and while we were marking time my wife, Susan, talked us into going sledding.

JUDY: She wanted us to go on a sled ride, with the dogs pulling the sleds, you know, but the people there said that they had already put 'em up for the year, but then one of them said, "I've got a friend who will take you and let you do a sled run down the Eiger, one of the tallest of the Alps." I don't think we thought twice about it. "Sure," we said. So when we arrive at the slope, David falls twice before we even get to where the sleds are, that's how icy it was out there. He was flat on his back twice. So we get there and I'm thinkin' it's gonna be like a little quarter of a mile track, you go down and then you go back up and you ride down again. No! It's down the Eiger! In front of the skiers, down those steep slopes with the curves and the cliffs and the ravines. So off we go and I'm like, holdin' onto my sled trying to get my balance—there's no rope for steering. There's no brakes—your brakes are your feet. You don't steer, you just go where the sled goes.

And all of a sudden I'm easing down the mountain, diggin' my feet in the snow to keep a pace I can handle. Well, some German woman comes up behind David; she's mad because he hasn't left yet and says something in German and gives him a big *push*, so he comes speedin' by me and clips my wrist, and breaks it, and he's gone! At some point Howard is flyin' down the mountain and the trail turns. And we don't know how to turn, like I said, there's no rope. He must of figured that stayin' on that sled was suicide so he just rolls off his sled, which continues on its own way, over a ledge, and lands in a tree, not Howard, thank the Lord, the sled, hangin' in a tree.

DAVID: They were little wooden sleds made of slats with just two iron runners under them. So we almost all got killed there. Way more dangerous than Y2K ever dreamed of being. The first thing that happens is Howard's sled goes off the side of the mountain and lands in the top of a pine tree. You can imagine how high we were when you have to go downhill to hit the top of a pine tree.

HOWARD: What started as a snow-covered trail turned into ice, and the sleds started going faster and faster, with no way to slow them down. The percent of grade was—well, felt like we were going straight down. I saw a curve coming and I realized that if I'm on the sled at that curve I'm headed into a deep ravine. So in my mind I said, *I gotta bail off this thing.* So I did, I bailed, and my body slid forever—I didn't go off into the ravine, at least. But the sled went airborne and landed in the top of a tree down in the ravine. I had to walk the rest of the way back. I still have a bad shoulder from that little adventure.

DAVID: So now we got a sled at the top of the tree. Judy got her wrist broke. The worst thing that happened was, we finally all make it to where we thought was the bottom of the hill—we could see the chalet from where we were, and all I could think of was, like, *There's hot chocolate over there!* But the wild deal is, you have to go across the ski slope to get to the chalet, and the skiers hate the sledders because the sleds cross the ski slopes, so, when you go across them, you got a bunch of schussing skiers jumping over your head on skis at about a hundred miles an hour. So you're going crossways, like crossing a road, and all those crazy skiers are like flying over you and cussing you in Swiss German. But we did make it, and ended up getting some hot chocolate.

JUDY: We, all of us, had bruises all the way up our bodies from trying to stop, trying to turn, trying to live. None of us had ski clothes. They had old sweat pants. I had on jeans. So the snow all went up our pants legs. We were downright packed with snow, the entire lower half of our bodies.

DAVID: And then we got on the train to go back and of course none of us had the right clothes to wear. When we first planned the trip, we hadn't known we were going sledding, remember it was a whim of my darling wife, Susan, who must have had a sudden desire to get us all killed. So we get on the train packed solid with snow.

HOWARD: I had snow packed in my pants all around my balls.

JUDY: It's warm on the train so we're all melting. We were making puddles of water and swift-running streams and all the other passengers were mad at us because they were having to sit with their feet in water—our water! When we finally get back downtown, there's this huge square in town, and guess where the dogsleds are. Right there going round and round the square, nice and safe like we should have been, instead of careening down the Eiger trying our best to be Y2K's first genuine victims!

DAVID: We finally made it back home. Y2K didn't kill anyone that we knew of. But that particular time was not my best because, you know, sometimes things just happen. Two months prior to going overseas and doing all this, I had made an appointment to have surgery on my shoulder as soon as we got back, because I had a bone spur and a torn rotator cuff, from what we call guitar shoulder, which is what you get when you play two hundred dates a year bangin' on a guitar. So a few days later I had my shoulder surgery and I looked forward to the time off that we'd scheduled so I could recuperate, two or three weeks before we'd go back to work. I'm sitting at home and I've got one of those machines that keeps cold water flowing past the operation site to ease the pain. And I've got my arm in one of those temporary slings to keep it propped up. And I get a call from Judy, and she says, "George W. Bush wants you guys to come to New Hampshire and play for him."

And I said, "Really? What's the deal?" I knew the campaign season was in swing, but what did he need us for? She said, "Well, the New Hampshire primaries are coming soon and he wants you guys to come up. They had some cancellations and they're kind of in a bind for entertainment." Now, we try hard to not be political. At heart I think that all politicians are crazy.

HOWARD: But they were paying us.

DAVID: They were paying us, and we had met George and Laura at Roy Orbison's home before they were married, and they were always fans. I said, "Well, Judy, my arm's in a sling here," but she said they only needed for us to sing five or six songs, so I called Howard, and he said, "Well, okay, let's give it a shot." So they sent a plane down, picked us up, and the next thing you know we're in New Hampshire at the New Hampshire primary with Bush running against McCain. We get up there, in heavy snow, and we go backstage, and there's one speech, one rally after another in this place. The boys get their gear set up, and I'm working out which five or six songs we're gonna play.

Somebody says Governor Bush—he was governor of Texas then—wants to see you guys, so he comes around there and the first thing he says to us was, "Boys, you sure got my nuts out of a vice." Howard looks at me and says, "I like this guy!"

So we play our five or six songs, and after the show they tell us that his dad and mom and everybody here are gonna have a little meet and greet. So we all stand, Governor Bush comes by, and one of his brothers comes by, his mom, and finally, his dad, the former president, is the last one, and when he comes through, he takes my hand, gives my arm this *presidential snap*, and almost rebreaks my shoulder.

I had tears in my eyes!

HOWARD: You could *see* the tears rollin' down. Like a flood.

DAVID: I was goin', "Nice to meet you, Mr. President," my voice quivering pathetically. It was like snapping a twig. I thought I was gonna go on my knees! *He* was in *fine* shape. I think it was when he was still jumping out of planes. Finally the meet and greet ended and I stuck my arm back in the sling and got back to the hotel and put tons and tons of ice on my arm.

Might have been painful, but it was good business. We ended up playing about eight campaign shows for George W. that year and then when he ran the second time, we played another five or six shows.

HOWARD: Turned out that he really was sort of a fan of ours. He said, "You know, I used to drink beer to 'Redneck Girl' all the time in West Texas." So for people who think he was just a guy from New England pretending to be a Texan, I gotta say, he seemed like a genuine Texan to us, *and we know a lot of Texans.*

DAVID: Yeah, we did a bunch of those shows, and the odd thing was, we weren't that political but they must have liked us, 'cause they kept bringing us back. Heck, we've played for Democrats and Republicans and of course those communists back in the days of Czechoslovakia. I don't know what that says about our music, but I don't think it says a damn thing about our politics.

HOWARD: We played for a governor's race in Florida—for both sides, but they both paid good. It was a business decision.

DAVID: To us, it feels like politics is down to "my crook or your crook," and we don't claim to be able to tell who's the bigger crook. Can you? And are you sure?

HOWARD: The only thing you can depend on a politician doing is letting you down.

DAVID: One of the things our father instilled in us is not to talk politics or religion. He was right. I mean, you have your opinions, of course, but to air them in public, the way things are these days, you're just askin' to be blasted on the social media.

Fire Alarms and War Zones

JUDY: You just can't be too careful. Things happen to us, no matter where we are, what we do—we were at a hotel just a couple of years ago—and Howard is the one, we have to do a pat-down on him, every time we get off the plane, every time we go somewhere, because he puts down his iPhone; he always leaves it somewhere. But he has an angel on his shoulders. He always gets it back. If it were our phone, we would never see it again. He'll leave it *in the seat on the plane*, and he will get it back before we go to the next flight. There was one hotel where he'd lose his keys every time, and people at the desk, when they'd see him walking toward the desk, would just automatically pull out another key and hand it to him. Cause they knew he'd lost that key again.

Things happen in their lives. I used to think things happened to me, but then I realized they only happen to me when I'm with them. Howard and David were in a hotel in Germany, and when we checked in, the guy on the front desk was really, *really* rude. And then he had someone else take us to our rooms who was really, really nice. And we found out later that these two men—the rude one and the nice one—were married. The really, really nice one was like, anything you need, just let me know. What *we* didn't know was this was one of those hotels where sometime in the evening, they close the front desk down, they lock the place up, and you're on your own all night. You can't get in touch with anybody. You couldn't even get into the lobby; they locked us out of the lobby, which hotels never do. David had walked out of his room into Howard's to do something, left his key in his room, and the door blew shut.

It was about ten o'clock at night. He's in his sweatpants. Everything he needs is in his room. So he calls me and I say, "Well, there's a phone number on the door of the hotel; I think I'll go down and call it." So I went down and called and I got the mean guy. He says, "There's nothing I can do for you! It's too far for me to come back. I'm sorry." And he hangs the phone up. So I thought, *Hmmm, okay.* So I went back to David and I said, "I'm going to my room, and I'm gonna find something, it may be a shoe, whatever. See that fire alarm up there? I'm gonna break the glass in it, because somebody will have to come then, and we'll get you in your room." I'd gone up, got the shoe, and was headed down and the nice guy showed up. I was glad, but then again, it might have been interesting to see what would have happened if I had busted the glass and tripped that alarm.

I mentioned that the road is a tough way to make a living. So to keep from wearing out one guy or another, we split some of their responsibilities. I always call David about booking dates. He's the business person. Howard does all the interviews. In my mind, Howard seems more involved with the ranch, with the cattle, with *that* business. David is more involved with the day-to-day music business and the tour dates. I know anytime it's an international tour, and it's a long trip like Sri Lanka or somewhere, they discuss it before they say, yeah, we'll do it, or not, they collaborate on that, but otherwise I deal strictly with David on the booking and Howard on the interviews.

And I think, too, it's good cop, bad cop. You do not want Howard to have to get on you. Fortunately I've never experienced that. Like the musicians, if he has to step in and calm them down, then it's gotten to a bad point. Not that David doesn't take care of that business too—it's just that you don't want to get Howard mad because he is so quiet, so if he has to get involved, it's important, and he *will* let you know how he feels.

I've never seen them argue, ever; never seen a cross word between the two of them. Even if they did it in private, you'd eventually hear about it. Somebody would tell. Somebody would talk. But I've never heard the smallest hint of any real anger between them.

But they've seen bad blood around the world. I've done tons of military tours, and the Bellamys have been on a lot of them, from Iraq and Afghanistan to Guam and Korea. We never went into Iraq that something didn't happen, always. We took ground fire; there were mortars, there were missiles. Something happened every single trip and nobody ever freaked out because you're gonna have fifteen guys in uniform on top of you taking care of you. You're gonna be the safest person there.

YouTube and Napoleon's Lighthouse

DAVID: Around 2001 we did a settlement with Curb that enabled us to make our original record deal better than it was. It still wasn't great, but it was better. In return, we had to do two projects for Curb. One of them was the duets album, and one of them was a gospel album.

HOWARD: We were able to do duets with Willie Nelson and Dolly Parton—she even wanted to shoot a video on the song we did with her. We did a song with Cliff Richard, we did one with Neil Diamond; we did "Let Your Love Flow" with Chaka Khan and "Whistlin' Dixie" with Alan Jackson.

DAVID: Little did we know that Curb had made deals with the labels that we were getting the artists from, to not release any of the songs as singles. We didn't know this, of course, until the album was done. There were a lot of really cool duets that we ended up doing together, and then we did the *Jesus Is Coming* album, which ended up getting two Dove award nominations. The song "Drug Problem" was from that album. It goes over really good live, people love the idea.

Around 2002 we were beginning to understand that even though we were still selling a lot of records to our fan base, we had to stop thinking about country radio because it was becoming more apparent all the time that they were never gonna play new music by older acts. So we started doing other stuff to make our new music available. It was around this time that we put out our Swedish Collection, which was really the same as the Norwegian collection but our distributors in Sweden wanted to market it as the Swedish collection, of course. We knew we still had a presence out there in the marketplace, but we had to come up with new ways of letting the people know we were continuing to make new music that they could take home with them.

HOWARD: Not only could we not get country radio airplay, Country Music Television wouldn't play our independent videos anymore. But we were seeing new ways of exposing and marketing our music, and we had a lot of youth around saying, "Have you thought about YouTube?" So we realized that we had another avenue and I think we mentioned before that on YouTube we've had success doing off-the-wall tunes because the weirder the video, the more chance you have of people checking it out. So we started putting out really crazy songs like "Boobs" and "Jalapenos."

DAVID: "Boobs" is a happy little ditty videoed poolside with us and some appropriately attired well-endowed lovelies. The hook is a feeling understood by healthy males all over the world:

Would you please tell your boobs

To stop lookin' at my eyes

Now you might think this is just a nasty song appealing to the worst instincts of young men and women, and the huge number of hits we've had would convince you that you're right. But if you look a little closer you'll see at least a half dozen videos from nations in Europe and Asia showing line dances choreographed especially for this song. And if you watch the videos all the way through, you'll see that the dancers are not thinking about boobs, they're thinking about getting their steps right, and having a great time doing it.

Not long before our mom got sick, she forwarded an email to me. We were in Branson, Missouri, at the time doing a six-week run at the Welk Theater. Lots of acts love that sit-down gig where you stay in one place, but we kinda like to move every night. A moving target is harder to hit, you know. She sent me an email, and wherever it came from, on the bottom of the email, it said, "Life is like a batch of jalapenos. What you say today will come back and burn your ass tomorrow." I thought, well that's really funny and it applies to so many situations in your life, particularly politics. I mean, every politician, that's all they do is eat their words. I couldn't let that pass, so I wrote that song during that long stay in Branson. We still get lots of requests for it at our shows. And by the way, that's how lots of songwriters find ideas for songs. When they read, when they watch TV, when they have conversations with friends, one part of their brain is always open for a great hit idea that they can surround and craft into a song.

There were also a lot of international outlets that kept our music alive and well, so we were never at a point where we were making records and wondering if anybody was gonna hear them. There were radio stations throughout Europe that would play us plenty.

HOWARD: And Africa to the South Pacific.

DAVID: We weren't happy about losing our U.S. airplay, especially understanding the politics that were the cause, but we tried our best not to abandon any market. And it seems to us that at the same time we were losing our airplay here, we actually were getting more and more work in Texas. It was like the less they heard us on radio, the more they'd book us to hear us live. I don't know if that's true or not but it just seemed that way.

I keep up with certain acts on the road like The Oak Ridge Boys, they're friends of ours and I kinda communicate with them through Twitter—we yell back and forth at each other. I think acts like them and us, and quite a few others, work more than we ever have. There are a lot of older fans that don't necessarily download so much, but they'll still buy tons of CDs, and the fact that they can't hear our new stuff on the radio just makes the CDs more valuable to them. That whole period, when we were losing our domestic airplay and then our video exposure, we worked the road pretty much solid. And during that time we did the "Catahoula" video, which was very successful on YouTube. We had quite a bit of video footage, so we licensed compilations of videos all over the world, and sold a lot in Europe, Australia, and South Africa.

One other thing happened during this time that you can't discount. My kids showed me that all of this old stuff that we'd been doing in Europe and all over the world for the past thirty years was now being dumped on YouTube. My son Noah would email me and say, "Look, here's a video of you guys on Musikladen in Bremen, Germany."

HOWARD: I'd see things I didn't remember we did.

DAVID: That happens to us a whole lot. In fact, our band was making fun of us the other day because they had seen a German video we did for Ralph Siegel, what was it, "Jackpot"? They were going, "What is 'Jackpot'?" It was this crazy stuff Ralph Siegel wrote that we did on German TV.

HOWARD: It was one of those things we did just to get the producer to let us do some of our other songs.

DAVID: "Jackpot" was the one he wanted us to do on television, of course. And so there's a video on it that's really bad, and there was another older deal that we found the other day called "Bound To Explode" that we did in '77 that neither one of us actually remembered.

HOWARD: Yeah, there's things that you just forget about because you actually do so much, it's just hard to remember all of them.

DAVID: I also found a video of us—for years, we'd say to each other, "Hey, remember we were in the back of that boat in Hamburg, going around the lake out there and singing 'Let Your Love Flow'?" If we watch movies or something comes on television, one of the kids will say, "Oh, this is so and so place in Japan," and look at me and I'll say, "We played it!" Pretty much any venue we've seen on television, we've played. When you've played eight thousand dates in your career, it seems like you've played everywhere. They have this thing where they'll turn on the TV and some show comes on and they'll turn to us and say, "Did you play here?" We see this video of us going round and round that lake in Hamburg, that exact place we used to talk about, so I told my kids, "See, I wasn't lying about this, we really were in the back of a boat going around Hamburg." We both looked like we were teenagers, though we were into our twenties.

HOWARD: That was the first foreign trip we ever did as The Bellamy Brothers.

DAVID: The fact that people were dumping a lot of our old stuff all over YouTube got us delving into that site, which is one of the things that probably drove us to make more content for YouTube, 'cause you realize how much of it was out there and then all of a sudden you have fans, sending you these videos *they're* finding on you, literally all over the world; you get something from Denmark, you get something from Asia and—what really haunts me is things I remember doing that we *can't* find on YouTube, like "Let Your Love Flow" in Japan—we'd love to see that. I think we were talking before about the old Dinah Shore show, and John Davidson with Flip Wilson, and Merv Griffin with Robert Blake, I'd really love to find those, we just know that somewhere, in some archive, or some dusty old studio closet, are tapes of these old shows. They're somewhere, and probably someone will throw them up on YouTube someday. Like I found a video just the other day from Zurich, Switzerland, a live video of us doing a song called "Foolin' Around," which was probably off *The Two and Only* album. Those are pieces of our life. We like to reclaim them if we can and share them with our fans. Some of them collect every clip on us that they can find, and that's really cool.

I don't think we'll ever get to the bottom of it all. In the old days, artists did lots of live shows, or radio and TV shows, that weren't recorded, so they know all that stuff is gone, but so much of what we did was recorded, either by the producer, or the channel or network, or somebody in the audience, and like we've said, we're curious, we wanna know how we did, and what the show was like, so when another old video pops up on YouTube for the first time, we want to see it.

HOWARD: I don't know, maybe we're our own best fans.

DAVID: And then there's all these things we did with other artists, some from other countries, some from here. Eduardo from Brazil, D.J. Otzi from Austria, Gola, Freddy Fender.

HOWARD: We did a duet with Freddy Fender that should have been a country hit. A song called "Stayin' In Love." Freddy came down to our studio in Florida and recorded it. His management didn't wanna release it. Big mistake on their part. Great song, he was singing great too.

DAVID: And this time period, maybe around 2004, there was a ton of other stuff going on. We went back to Australia. That might have been one of the first times since—

HOWARD: We were allowed back.

DAVID: Yeah, since we were allowed back in. We started working there again every couple of years. It's also about the time that we started to realize what we had in the India and Sri Lanka markets. We started to get so many people from there coming to our shows in Australia and the U.S., and I think that could have had something to do with YouTube, as well. People would make home videos using our music, and there was a video of this Indian couple, these dancers, and it looked kinda like a Bollywood type of video. It had the two of them dancing arm in arm—dancing across the screen, to "Let Your Love Flow," and they were dancing across India. As they danced, the Taj Mahal would show up in the background, then some big palace in Mumbai or wherever. Discoveries like these helped make us aware of how big some of these markets were for us, even though we had never received any royalties from India or Sri Lanka.

HOWARD: Social media let us know that we had fans in New Guinea and other places we'd never dreamed of, opened up new markets for live music on the other side of the world, and when they called, we flew across the seas to play for them.

DAVID: I'll tell you another good story that happened and I don't know if I could pinpoint the year, but I'm thinking that it's got to be '04, '05, or '06. We were down on the Gold Coast in Australia, did a big swing through there. We were playing the casino at Tweed Heads, next to

Coolangatta. While we were playing, this guy comes up to Judy and he says, "I really want to get the Bellamys to come out to New Caledonia." Judy is not quite sure where that is but she says we'd love to do it. He says, "Next time you come down here I wanna arrange a tour." So we get back home and we're trying to figure out where it is and it turns out, you remember the old TV show *McHale's Navy*? That whole series was actually set in New Caledonia.

HOWARD: It's three hours flight out of Sydney, kind of in the direction of Fiji.

DAVID: Naturally we're curious. We're always curious.

So about two years later we get an offer to do some more stuff in Australia and Judy says, "Well, I'm gonna see if this guy was serious about puttin' this island trip together," 'cause we still didn't know too much about it. She calls him and he still wants us to come, so we did some dates in Australia, and then flew out to New Caledonia. It was almost like being kings of the island, like "our people are waiting for you," they're meeting us at the airport wearing sarongs and bringing old albums from years ago.

HOWARD: It was like we'd discovered what no one before us had ever discovered.

DAVID: It was like *Mutiny on the Bounty*. It was just paradise. I mean, they can't do enough for you.

But we had to go meet the king.

The island is a French protectorate, but there's a native tribe there called the Kanaks. And the Kanaks have a king. So we have to go out and give the king a present, and sit down and have a drink with him and receive his blessing. Beautiful place out there. Everybody hangs things around your neck, and they bring you lychee nuts.

HOWARD: We were there on National Lychee Day.

DAVID: They take us out to this island called The Isle of Pines, which is off the main island of New Caledonia. On The Isle of Pines there's this exclusive hotel, and they fly us out there for the day and feed us and celebrate us, so, we're walking around and, remember *The Blue Lagoon*?

That's what it looks like. We're walking along the beach, and they've got lines in the water and we stop to talk with the shark fishers there, to see what they do; some guy's hollowing out a canoe, and we hear them talking among themselves in their tongue and the only thing we can understand is "*Bellamy Brothers, Bellamy Brothers.*" And then this guy runs from us, about fifty yards to, literally, a grass hut, and then he runs back, and he's holding our first album.

HOWARD: He was carving a canoe by hand, and he recognized us, now that breaks us up! All he didn't have was a bone in his nose.

DAVID: And of course, they wanna take you pig hunting . So we spend the day out there with them—really, really nice people—and after a wonderful day with them, we go back to our hotel in Nouméa, which is the capital of New Caledonia. The show is the next day and we don't know what to expect. There's one Cadillac convertible on the island, and that's the car they borrow to take us to the show in, 'cause they basically want to have a parade. And we go riding through the streets and end up at a soccer field, which is at the highest point on the island. We get out there and we see they've got it all decorated for us, onstage and backstage, but there's not a single fan there. Not one, in the whole place. We're looking at each other like, they're gonna run us out of here on a rail, after inviting us.

HOWARD: But the promoter was there, and he seemed happy.

DAVID: We asked him, "Is everything okay?" And he said, "Oh, yeah, everything's good."

HOWARD: Yeah he's all happy and he's ordering for us more drinks, more food, and we're going, "Okay, aren't we supposed to go on at 8:30?"

DAVID: "Oh no," he says, "don't worry, don't worry, everything's good."

HOWARD: So we're sitting around, just us and the band, shootin' the bull and we're all talking, getting a little bit concerned, and still nothing, I don't know, about an hour and a half?

DAVID: Way past show time. And all of a sudden, people started wandering—

HOWARD: And we're on the top of the hill, we can see people like ants, coming out of their houses, walking up the hill toward the stadium.

DAVID: We finally went on about 10:30 or 11:00 that night, and the place was packed.

HOWARD: They don't look at watches. When they leave you in the evening, they say, "I'll see you in the daytime."

DAVID: There was probably about six thousand people. Most of the island was there. I think it was one of the biggest shows they ever had. We didn't have an opening act. It was just us they came to see. We thought this was a once-in-a-lifetime thing, 'cause it's not really a market you can work all the time, but about two years later they decided to do it again. This time we were playing in a school, I think, but they had broken it down into three theater shows, and they were all packed—it was just this amazing place. They loved us there, and we still feel that way about them. I remember talking to Mom from there and I told her, I said, "If it wasn't for you and the kids being back at home, I may not come back."

HOWARD: The Kanaks are the indigenous Melanesian inhabitants of New Caledonia.

DAVID: They're pretty authentic. You know, I still have some video of us dancing with them, somewhere. The second time we went there, we filmed a video there. We filmed part of it in Australia and part of it there, because there's a lighthouse that Napoleon III built for his fiancé. It's on the Little Barrier Reef, which is the second largest in the world.

HOWARD: The music video we shot there was called "She's Awesome." So were the beaches, which were all topless.

The Angels Came on Christmas Eve, and Howard Sort of Explains His Wives

DAVID: We had come to rely on Frances in helping us grow our businesses, and as the years went by she continued to shoulder heavy responsibilities. She had a couple of mini-strokes, but she stayed strong until about three months before she died. Life in the country can be hazardous and she did her share of dangerous outdoor work. Once, when she was in her late sixties, she was on the roof of the house fixing a leak or something when she lost her footing and slipped and fell off the roof.

She would herd Brahma bulls on her golf cart. One would get out in the driveway and she would get that golf cart and drive him down the lane and run him back into wherever he had jumped out of. If she couldn't find the break in the fence where they'd got out, she'd drive them over the fence, then she'd call somebody to come fix the fence.

The last seven, eight years of her life she had a lot of pain, but she was still sharp and functioned.

HOWARD: But when she started going downhill with the mini-strokes, it was feeling like we might lose her.

DAVID: She would function pretty much, but we would find little things she would do that would be different, little signs of dementia.

She also pretty much raised all my boys, she and Susan. She had to make adjustments after I met Susan. Frances didn't like Susan when she first came along. She was not crazy about me getting a divorce because of the kids. Frances was jealous of Susan at first. She was a very possessive person. If you were her friend, she owned you. So at first it was an odd situation, but then as Frances got older, when she saw how much Susan helped the kids, she grew to love her. But she pretty much raised the boys single-handedly. When we were on the road they would call me and say, "Hey, guess where we are?" And I would say, "Where?" And she'd go, "We're in New Orleans." You know, they'd just haul ass and take a vacation, Frances and the boys.

Because we haven't talked much about this, let's put it in here. I think it was 1975 when I got married the first time, to Janet. We were married eighteen years. She was from Tampa. We had five boys: Jesse, born in 1978, Noah a year later, Cole in 1982, Dustin in '83 and Aaron in 1989. Susan hails from Fort Worth, Texas. We met in 1989 and were married in 1993, which means that at this writing we've been together for twenty-eight years. I also have a daughter named Mariah who has two children and lives in Silver City, New Mexico.

HOWARD: My married life has been a little more varied than David's and I think I'm better off without it. My first wife was right out of high school; she was named Pamela. We were married about 1965 and that lasted for seven years. In 1978 I married a *fraulein* named Ilona and we have one daughter, Cheyenne, born in 1979. Wife number three is a songwriter named Sharon Vaughn who has written some big hits—that marriage came in 2002 and lasted about a year. We wrote some good songs together. Then there was a fourth, Jennifer, from 2004 to 2012. Been divorced six years and probably gonna stay that way. All told, I was married thirty-nine years, four different women, a fact I'm not necessarily proud of.

DAVID: Mom died Christmas Eve, 2009, at the age of eighty-five. She had a couple of health issues that we had dealt with; she had a bad hip and all those strokes. Frances was very afraid of certain things. One of them was being put to sleep, so she would not have surgery. And she also didn't like to be on a boat in the ocean, so she didn't do cruises.

We were in Branson, Missouri, for one of the longest stints we ever did in one venue, when she got sick, which we could tell by talking to her on the phone. We had Lucy and a doctor watching out for her. We got home, and she kind of deteriorated from there. Her mini-strokes led to a sort of dementia. Her last three months were really difficult, which was very odd for her because her mind was always so sharp. It was terribly shocking for us. We had to, basically, start staying with her. We just rotated, me and Howard and Susan and the kids, Jesse and Noah—Dustin actually lived with her, stayed with her and took care of her a lot. She would do interesting things. One time, I guess it was about a month before she died, she had a walker because her hip was bad, and she was still trying to get up and walk some, I found her in the kitchen with her walker and I said, "What are you doing, Frances? Where are you going?" And she said, "I've got to get to town. I've got to go to the bank." I said, "Don't worry, we'll take care of the bank," and when I took hold of her walker I found that in the basket she had her car keys, a loaded pistol, and $10,000 cash. And she was just heading to the bank. That was Frances. She was slipping at that point, but she was still bound to live like she'd always lived and do what she'd always done.

Her other fear was nursing homes. We didn't know what to do because sometimes people could have Alzheimer's for years. So we actually went and interviewed some nursing homes but after she had one really bad ministroke, things began to go downhill fast from there. Her neurologist finally told us, "Just take her home and make her comfortable. Don't put her through any more tests; she's not going to recover." Three months later, she was gone. For Frances, I was glad she didn't stay that way for a long period of time, not knowing what was going on around her.

A big deal for her was that she loved for all the family to be home with her at one time. It got harder and harder to do as the family got more and more spread out and life got busier and busier. We think Frances waited until Christmas Eve because she knew that everyone would be there. We decided to do Christmas like normal. We always opened presents Christmas Eve, and she passed away right then, in her bedroom, while we were opening presents.

Lucy never was healthy, as long as I'd known her. She had one kidney, macular degeneration, name it, Lucy had it. But she was always in the best mood.

HOWARD: And never lost her sense of humor, even in her final days.

DAVID: Laughed about everything. I think she died around 2014. She worked for us for so long, and I told her, "Lucy, there's no way you're gonna retire because you know where all the skeletons are."

HOWARD: "You can't die!"

DAVID: So she kept working after Frances died, about another two years.

HOWARD: Finally her vision got so bad she couldn't see, so we got another lady who lived in our community and worked at school handling their business and stuff, and Lucy taught her what she could. Lucy lived just down the road from us; I could drive the golf cart to her house.

DAVID: Mom and Lucy made things run so smoothly here. You can't imagine how important that was, with us touring all the time.

13

Summing It Up But Still Rambling On

Our World According to Susan

DAVID: Here's how Susan got into our lives. When I married Susan, everybody said, "Oh yeah, he left his wife for this young chick," which actually wasn't true. I was never gonna get married again. I figured if I could get out of that first one, I was not gonna get back in it.

SUSAN: In 1989 one of my best friends called me up and said, "You wanna go see The Bellamy Brothers tonight?" I was working two jobs and going to college, so I said, "I'm pretty broke this week," and she said, "Well, I'm gonna charge it on my card." And I said, "Okay," and my friend that worked with me said, "Well, I wanna go too."

So the three of us went to where they were playing, Billy Bob's, maybe America's largest honky-tonk, which was in my hometown of Fort Worth. The place was sold out, but we got very good seats, right up front by the stage.

They also had places for people to sit *on* stage, even closer to the action, and we were invited to sit up there, so we did, and after the show we were gonna leave and go dancing, but fate stepped in, in the form of Wally, the bass player, who is like the third Bellamy brother. He comes running out there and slaps backstage passes on me and my friends. I had been backstage before in other places and my friends hadn't, so they were wanting to go and I was saying, "Oh, some of these people are not nice," but they insisted, so I said, "Okay." Soon we were back there, talking to some people who owned part of Billy Bob's, and all of a sudden I see David come out from somewhere, and he's standing there and he sends one of his friends over and the friend says to me, 'David Bellamy thinks he's in love with you, will you come and talk to him?'"

My friends were laughing and saying, "Come on, you need to go over there," and I said okay, which got them all excited. We walked on over to David, and he started telling us how they were leaving for Ecuador the next day to film a show for TNN, a fishing show, I think. My friends were bugging me, "Ask them to go dancing," and one of them goes over to Howard and says, "You wanna go dancing?" and Howard goes, "Heck, no, we gotta be up at six o'clock in the morning to go to the Galapagos Islands." David got my phone number and I guess I was a bit of a smarty-pants. I said, "How many black books do you have?" I thought I would never hear from him.

While he was gone, he tried several times to call me but he and Howard were in such a remote part of the world that he had problems getting through. So he called me right when he got back to Miami and I could barely believe it was him on the phone. He wanted to fly me to Vegas, but I was like, "No, I have to get to know you first." He said, "Well then, I'll come to Fort Worth." And I said, "Okay."

He took me to lunch and he wanted to go out that night, and I turned him down because we'd had a big thunderstorm and my power was out but he kept callin' and he said, "Well, you can come over here and study," and I was like, "No, I gotta go to the library to study for this test." It was really hard for me to study that night because I kept thinking back to lunch and us talkin' and it occurred to me that I really enjoyed that man's company. We had a lot of things in common, and it kind of scared me. This is not a good time in my life, I thought, I've not finished with school and I knew that he had obstacles, too, but the fact is we hit it off and we were pretty inseparable after that.

He kept calling me, and I finally flew out and met him in Vegas. They had a week's show with The Oak Ridge Boys at Bally's, and after that we just clicked. After I finished that semester at school, he told me I was either gonna have to stay in school or come see the world with him and as a twenty-one-year-old, I wanted to see the world. That's what I did. The year was 1989.

So I moved down to Florida. I thought I was a country girl in Texas and I knew how to ride horses and everything, but I soon realized that compared to them, I was a *city* girl. Darby was the *boonies* when I came here. My perception of Florida was beaches and cities, not country and cows. I thought it was beautiful but it was *out there*, and to make things worse, his mother was not thrilled to have somebody that—she told me when she first met me, "My son has jeans older than you!" And his cousin Sylvia, she wanted to make sure I wasn't Catholic—David's ex-wife was Catholic, and they wanted to make sure that I wasn't planning on having any kids to add to David's brood by his first wife. That's what I went into, and I was awful young and dumb and naïve at the time.

My first impression was, I don't know if I'm gonna stay in this or not! But I really loved David, and I loved his kids. It was kind of overwhelming. I was raised in a single mom family. I had pretty much everything I wanted, but I wasn't used to telling everybody where I was plannin' to go or what I was doing. I had a sister—year and a half younger than me, and it was just the three of us—so life with all the Bellamys was strange. I had to tell my future mother-in-law everywhere I was going and I thought that was the weirdest thing; you know, when you get married, you don't realize how different people are—their family is crazy—but then you realize your family is, too, just the crazy that *you* grew up with, that you knew.

We got married in '93. We were on the road traveling a lot. I was doing a lot of stuff, mainly helping with the kids, and helping David, like I was his personal assistant. That was definitely not what I thought I was gonna be doing the rest of my life, but I like to work and fit in and help. Then the concession guy left, and they weren't sure who they were gonna get, and I said, "Well, I'm just sitting here, let me do it." I just decided to take over the concessions. It was great 'cause I got to interact with the fans, and I enjoyed that a lot. Then I got into designing stuff for them, like T-shirts and such, which I loved to do. Working with the art directors at different companies we dealt with, telling them exactly what I want and they'd send me proofs and I would choose the colors, the cut, the design, incorporating our logo in most of it. But there were adjustments that needed to be made—I designed T-shirts for what my friends and I would wear, and well, it didn't sell as good, so David said, "You're not on the fan level, you're at Nordstrom's and a lot of them are at Walmart."

Finally I got on fan level, and now it's a little bit of both, a little my style and a little more their taste. I've been doing that forever. Then the internet came along and I talked David into getting our first web site. I told him we just had to have it. This was cutting edge stuff for the time and a lot of the country fans did not have late model computers so when they called up our website, it crashed their computers. We were fielding phone calls every day—people hollering "Your site crashed my computer!" and Lucy was having to fend off all their anger. We finally got the site working and so I can say I was the one that got our website together. I was putting up all that stuff about the family, about Frances being the matriarch, and the kids, and all of us, so people started realizing who I was, and when I was selling at the concession stand they would come up and ask me lots of questions. I became a personality in my own right, which was scary.

This one fan came up to me and he said, "Can you tell me how 'Spiders And Snakes' was written?" I proceeded to tell him, and he said, "Oh, no, that's not how it went." So he told me his version of how the song came to be, then he said, "Can you tell me, about . . ." something, and so I tell him another story, and again he said, "No, no, that's not how it was." David and Howard came in and sat down for autographs, and the guy continued feeding me the history of The Bellamy Brothers according to him. Finally I said, "Sir, you clearly know my husband way more than I do, I just sleep with the man every night!" I'm usually very nice to folks, but he wore me out!

When their mom passed away, Christmas 2009, then we didn't really have anybody here running the office. It was kind of chaotic at the time. I was pretty sick. I had come off the road then, and lots of things were happening at once, but I pulled myself together and said, "I'll just do the office." That's how I inherited the office. Now I do a little bit of both, office and road, and I still design our clothes and other merchandise, but I don't sell it anymore. I still go on the road—I pick all the good trips, the ones where fans who are our friends are most likely to be, and it's always fun to see them.

One thing I felt strongly about: I didn't have a great stepmother, and I had promised myself that if I had any stepkids, that I was going to make the best effort I could to be like a mother to them. I really got lucky with the kids. All those boys. And they were raised really good and real sweet and I have a good relationship with all of them. They'll call me sometimes ahead of calling David or their mom, and I believe they consider me part of their foundation.

When I met David and Howard, I just thought they were so down to earth. These are nice guys. They're more about the music, I would say, than all the kinds of political games that go on in Nashville. Not being in Nashville was like a double-edged sword for them. They didn't play the "Music City" games, because they didn't live there. They were two country boys who wanted to keep getting their music out into the world. That's what David lives for the entire time. He's just music driven. There's this story about him: when he was young he won a transistor radio in some contest and he would have his radio on him while he was hoeing oranges, and if he'd stand the wrong way he'd lose the signal, so he'd stand in these funny positions as he did his hoeing in order to keep the signal strong, and his dad would see him all contorted up and he'd say, "Get your ass behind you, boy!"

I was talking to John Rich the other day, and we were saying that besides The Everly Brothers, they actually are the godfathers of country duos. They don't get the recognition that some of the others get. Brooks & Dunn, Montgomery Gentry, Big & Rich, all these people came after them. When they first started out, they were considered a band, which meant when awards time came, they were up against Alabama. Then later a duo category was created. We can't forget the politics in award voting. The big labels had lots of employees who could vote. Curb never had a lot of voting employees, and when they were on Warner/Curb or MCA/Curb, Warner and MCA never really considered that the Bellamys were one of their acts. So The Bellamy Brothers have had more nominations than any other act for CMA awards or ACM awards. But without all that corporate voting to back them up, they've never won one.

But Howard and David have a huge base of true fans, all over the world. And they know what their fans like, so they give it to them, every performance. They played with Willie Nelson one time, and Willie wasn't playing any of his hits, but when he saw the way the crowds reacted to the Bellamys, Willie told them, "I'm gonna have to do all my hits now." 'Cause they play hit after hit after hit on their show, and the people love it because they sound just like their records. The other reason they have so many true fans is that they tour more than most artists do. At one time, they were the hardest working country band, and after all these years they still play more dates than most touring country acts. I think that's what keeps them going, playing all those shows every year for people who love to come out and listen to them live.

I love my life. Being on a bus with the band, it's like having a bunch of brothers. Sometimes it's great and you love it, and then sometimes you're like, "Oh, man." Trying to relate to people who have not lived that life, I always tell David it's kind of like you're a bunch of carnies— because you pull in, and you set up and you do the show, and then it's on to the next place.

I got to do tons of travel, got to meet lots of people, lots of fans. How many people they've touched with their music is very impressive.

I'm their travel agent; I book all their flights. That's my favorite part because it's always fun to try to figure out where I'm gonna connect with the bus and not make the band have to wait.

After all these years, they still love their career—they're still writing songs and they're still relevant. They still work in the studio almost every day they're home, Howard, David, and Randy. It's a shame how radio tends to throw older artists away, because The Bellamy Brothers are still singing really, *really* good.

It hasn't been the same for all of us since their mother passed. Their mother was a force to be reckoned with. She ran this place like Falcon Crest. She would do anything for her boys. She was an incredible lady. Frances was very good to me, but she was like The Mob. If she did something for you, you owed her your life. You better watch out for her. She liked men way better than women. But she and Homer had several blowups, three big famous blowups. She would tell me about them while we were working in the office.

Here is one: She said, "We were digging post holes, building fence," and they were using the car to pull the fencing tight. He was maybe telling her too much how to do it and she finally got so mad at him that she just floored the accelerator and pulled up all the fencing that they'd put down—she just pulled it all out. She kind of wore the pants in the family, David said, until Homer threw a fit. He said it took a long time for Homer to throw a fit, but when he did, everybody cleared out. The way I hear it, he was an easygoing guy who didn't like to be pushed.

And that's kind of the way Howard is. And that's part of the reason he can't hang onto women, because they always want to change him. He has these set little things about him, and he's fine with the way he is, he doesn't need to be redesigned.

He's still out there looking. I told David, if we ever have a reality show, all you have to do is follow your brother around on the dating scene, and then me and you behind him having to clean it all up. I had to move one of his girlfriends myself; me and some friends had to move her to a storage shed. Her stuff had been left in the barn for six months.

One time he'd given three women my phone number and promised them all that he would take them on this cruise that we were going on, and to get with me about flights. And I had to tell him that if he gave my number out to one more woman, he was in trouble. At one point, two or three of them had the gate code, and one of my friends said, "What you gonna do if they all come here at one time?" and I said, "I'm gonna pop me some popcorn and watch the show—the reality show."

iPad Pilots and The Fookin' Bellamy Brothers

DAVID: Between 2000 and 2010, I would say a lot of that era was the reaping the fruits of a lifetime of experience. The label had been established almost ten years when that decade began, and all of our touring had come together because we had Judy working for us on the international side and Rob Battle booking our domestic dates. When you have great bookers like them, you've got half the battle won. This was also when our cattle business was at its peak. We had three ranches in Florida and the feedlot in Texas with a capacity of about fifty thousand head. Howard and I personally had about six thousand head at the time. All of our businesses were going pretty well. We even had a store called The Neon Cowboy.

HOWARD: General store.

DAVID: Yeah, general store in Darby that we bought. Howard wanted to have his own supply of Ben and Jerry's, especially Chunky Monkey and Cherry Garcia. The store had everything from cattle feed to a vitamin selection, Ben and Jerry's to boiled peanuts, you name it, and a filling station on top of that. We had that place for about six years, and we decided to sell it because everybody we hired to run it was stealing us blind. And we were running the Snake, Rattle & Roll Jam as well, for ten years, while we were doing all our regular touring and running the record company.

We sold the feedlot in Lubbock. A dropping stock market and other business conditions put us in a difficult position, and for a while it looked like we would have to take a real bath. We ended up getting very lucky because two youngsters from the Chicago Mercantile Exchange came down and they were hungry to own a feed yard, and the timing was perfect, so we sold it to them, and just when we thought we were gonna lose a ton of money like everybody else because of 9/11, we were able to break even, and sometimes breaking even is a gift from God.

HOWARD: Yeah, we put those boys in the feedlot business. This goes back to our father warning us about getting too ambitious. And I kept thinking, *He's right; he's right.* You know, you get to that point, you got so much energy, you got a little money, so you diversify and do all this stuff, and you end up about breaking even, lucky that we didn't lose a fortune.

DAVID: Trust. That's one reason why, after our mom died, we scaled back the cattle operation down to just the old home place, and then kept the music, the touring business, and the merch business. It's actually me and Howard and Susan and Wally and Randy. Wally Dentz, our bass player, harmonica player, and road manager, has been with us thirty-four years. Randy Hiebert is our guitar player, studio engineer, and co-producer, and he's been here more than twenty-three years now. You get people that you know really well—I mean, even like our videos, our YouTube videos and stuff, Susan has been known to do the makeup and star in our videos; we shoot them at our friend Ronnie's house in Texas, and Joe, the guy who shoots those things, is the guy who shoots the cattle sales. We keep everything every close to the vest, try to keep the budgets in line, work with people we feel close to, and it works real well like that.

HOWARD: You just minimize the risk, you know?

DAVID: We were probably back to the core businesses by 2006 or '07. We still had a few things left over, but we had sold the store and feedlot and could now concentrate on the ranch, the music, and taking care of what had against all odds turned into an ever-growing worldwide following.

And we're always open to play in new places, make new friends, and you know, let the music flow. We had gotten offers to play in Sri Lanka for probably ten years and even India for quite a few years, and it had never been feasible. It's still not easy to tour there, but finally we had this one big offer from Sri Lanka and requests for three or four more dates in India, so in 2014 we decided to glue them all together into one tour. It was no small feat. I think Judy pulled most of her hair out organizing that tour. Physically it was very tough. In India, you can be on a freeway and it turns into a dirt road, but we did it and it became a big surprise because we knew there was an Indian audience there, and we even knew that it was pretty big, but until we got there we didn't realize just what we had waiting for us.

I'll never forget, Howard and I were in Bangalore; we had played some of the Indian shows and we were flying to Sri Lanka. We got on a Sri Lanka Airlines plane to go down there, and once we were on board Howard fell asleep. The pilot comes out and walks over to me and says, "I'd like for you and your brother to come up to the cockpit after we take off," and I said, "Okay, we'll come up and see you." So the plane takes off and we're sittin' there awhile and Howard wakes up and I said, "Hey, the pilot wants us to come up to the cockpit." So we go up there and he has some seats for us. We're flying over that strait between India and Sri Lanka, and the pilot is so busy talking to us about our songs and our career and stuff that he's not even flying the plane. He has an iPad duct taped to the windshield and anytime he does anything with the plane he just reaches over to the iPad, and I'm sittin' there going, *Oh my God, we got a duct tape iPad flying the plane and this guy wants to hear stories about how we cut "Beautiful Body."* I sure hope that when it's time to land this thing, he'll get his mind back on his flying. We flew all the way from Bangalore to Sri Lanka with us in the cockpit, which I'm sure is illegal—well, maybe not in that country, who knows, right? He had a copilot, of course, but the two of them were just carrying on.

HOWARD: They weren't paying any attention to their airplane. It was like people driving and texting. And all the flight attendants were there too.

DAVID: It was just really a neat trip. In Sri Lanka, they got these big orchid necklaces, kind of like Hawaiian *leis*, they put around your neck. The Indian part of the trip was the same, and during the shows they were singing so loud on certain songs that we could hardly hear the band play. It was bizarre. We had seen things like that early on, but after so many years in your career it's incredible to discover a new place that's so fresh that you get excited all over again. We immediately did a press conference in this big room in the hotel after we got there. And we started to tell this story of the pilot and us in the cockpit with his iPad. There was a guy there who was with the airlines and was kind of freakin' out. I said I felt like *we* had to fly the plane to get us there, and that we were a lot more worried about it than they seemed to be.

HOWARD: We landed once in Fiji, among the most memorable moments for me. You imagine these beautiful women from around the world. In Fiji they wear these things called sarongs, they've kind of made it into our culture now. Just as we walk into the airport from the plane, these beautiful women in sarongs, all wearing sarongs, and just bowing, and saying, "Our people are waiting for you." I'm thinking, *Where in the hell have we been?*

DAVID: Yeah, it's funny to walk into stuff like that. Some of it we just didn't know about. I remember checking into a hotel in Goa, a really beautiful kind of resort hotel in Goa. The bellhops are in the lobby and one of them has a guitar out and they're all singing:

I need more of you, darling, I need more of you
More, anything less wouldn't do

Our friend John Tracy from Bakersfield, California, was visiting friends down in Australia and he sent me a video. He was in an aboriginal bar in the outback and it looks like there's about eight people in the bar, one white guy playing the guitar and three aborigines singing, and they're singing "I Need More Of You." Can you imagine how it feels to know that songs you've written and recorded have reached all kinds of people, all over the world? You don't know them personally, but they've connected with one of your songs, and in a way it means they've connected with you. So when it comes to the way we make our living, we get a whole lot more than money out of it. A whole lot more. And I think that's one reason why I don't have a problem after all these years and all these songs, picking up my guitar in the middle of the night and starting to work transforming one more little bitty idea into a song. Because I'm still confident that if I write it good enough, I'll connect with people. I might even connect with aborigines in the Outback, or bellhops in Goa, or Melanesians in New Caledonia, as well as Swiss, Germans, Austrians, and Texans.

Knowing that when we're touring, we will find people who know us and our music. After a while you get used to it, and then it's almost like you feel at home anywhere you go.

HOWARD: People say, "Don't you sometimes worry being away from home?" Yeah, I love our ranch and our home, I love being here, but even in remote places, I don't feel like I'm in some place foreign because ya know so many people. So you become a master adapter; you adapt to anywhere you go, quickly.

We were all on a little tour bus going through Ireland and we pulled into this place to get fish and chips orders to go, and as we got back on the bus, this redheaded Irish chick comes runnin' out of the place and jumps on the bus and hollers, "It's the fookin' Bellamy Brothers!"

DAVID: She had just taken the whole order for the whole band; we were all in there, we were in there ten or fifteen minutes, and they were getting all the orders ready and we take our food and get back on the bus and suddenly it hits her and she comes flying out and onto the bus. *"It's the fookin' Bellamy Brothers!"*

We scored a #1 worldwide hit in 1976. During the 1980s, we had one #1 hit after another. By the 1990s radio had pretty much decided that we no longer appealed to their young audiences, and by 2000 we had been around for so long that most of our middle-aged fans were considered too old to buy records. And yet I've never seen us as busy as we are right now. I had to print out a new schedule this morning because there are already so many dates booked for next year. I think that this year is the busiest year we've had since I can remember.

HOWARD: We turn good offers down less than anybody out there that I know, 'cause we've still got the will to stand up in front of audiences and give them what they want.

Mr. Howard Goes to Washington and the Game Warden and Buffalo Hides

DAVID: Wally's got the broadest job description ever, from collecting the money from the promoters to signing off on a lot of the contracts. Between him and Judy and Rob, they'll go through all the details of all the production, all the hotels, all the travel, what kind of bus we'll have; do we need a sleeper bus or a day bus for a two-hour trip—just all the details that so many tours entail.

Susan and I had dinner with a Norwegian promoter recently. He said, "Did you know that Judy called me and made me walk the steps from the hotel to the train station?" He was trying to tell me how anal she was. And I said, "Well, I understand that, because a promoter would normally say the train station's right by the hotel. That could mean it would be fifty feet or it could be three miles." So she made him go out and walk the steps to the train station so we would know just how convenient the station *really* was to the hotel. That's the way Judy is, and you know, she and Wally have done a lot of that stuff over many years, and it's been good for us, because unpleasant surprises can really throw a tour off its rhythm.

I feel like the business—or rather the businesses, such as they are—like the concerts and the travel and the merchandising and all that, I feel that they all run smoother than ever, because everybody kind of knows what they're doing.

HOWARD: I think social media alone has helped organize our booking.

DAVID: Oh, there's no doubt, because people who want to book you can get a hold of you so easy now. You know, for years, people who wanted to book us thought they had to go through some office or other. They could have just called our house to book us, but they'd never do that.

HOWARD: They could have called our mom and booked us. Now they can contact us through Facebook. Sometimes we even bring gigs to our agents. Social media has opened us up to the world. Either of us can get a message that can lead us to a major date.

DAVID: Starting our own independent label was a big blessing because we can aim our music directly at our fans, who we know very well after forty years of playing our music face to face with them.

HOWARD: The meet-and-greet thing gets bigger as you go along with your career. I don't know why they wanna meet you so bad; I guess you become this thing they imagine in their minds for years, and if you've stayed alive this long, they just want to get to talk to you before you're gone.

DAVID: If we look back to our own younger years, we can remember what a big thing it would have been for us to meet Chuck Berry or Merle Haggard, and as you get older, you do realize that it's important to fans that they meet you and get you to sign an album. The fact that to us we're pretty ordinary doesn't make it less important. I think we come to symbolize memories of good times in their lives and when they get a signed recording, they feel like maybe they've captured some of those moments. We all would like to capture good moments in our lives, that's how they do it, and you know what? Good for them. We're glad to be of help, and we hope that we can keep doing it for years to come.

HOWARD: Especially if they've got some memory of a song. Songs can be so powerful. I mean, we see people every day who have some sort of connection to one of the songs. They found a love, they lost a love, they had a child, they lived their lives to your songs.

DAVID: And you know, we talk a lot about the people from different cultures around the world come to see us, but here in the United States, it seems, we book better today than when we were having all those #1 hits. The west is a really big market for us. We probably work a little less in the northeast and northwest than other areas, but when we do go, we do fine. We worked last summer in the northwest and it was phenomenal.

HOWARD: We don't work as much in the northwest because it's so damn far in the ol' bus.

You've got to put together a complete tour to make it worth all the travel But all of the U.S. is good for us. We talk about Texas so much because we could, literally, live there. There's so much work there for us. This year we're playing a lot of dates that we haven't done for a while. We're doing New Jersey, New York, Wisconsin, but we'll also work Montana, Wyoming, and Utah—Utah is a huge area for us. Lot of friends there.

HOWARD: Lot of Mormon fans. Interesting. We've always had them.

DAVID: The United States has always been a bigger market than Europe is. But I think we've got a lot more stories from events in the rest of the world because people like to hear about the unusual. We'll bump into people that we came up in the business with like The Gatlins or The Oak Ridge Boys, and they'll go, "Man, I saw where you guys were in India, or I saw where you just came back from Austria. What's that like? We'd like to tour there, too, you know." It's hard to explain to people that there wasn't really a master plan that brought us overseas so much, it's just that we had the opportunity and stuck with it.

HOWARD: The reason we have an international following is because "Let Your Love Flow" was a #1 song in fifteen countries. And you know, internationally, something that we realized years back, "Bellamy" means "beautiful friend." All the rest of the world got it. They already knew it. Our name, I think, helped. Gave a little substance to who we are to so many people in Europe and beyond.

Eventually we did an album called *Beautiful Friends*. We even thought at one time of redoing the old song "Ma Belle Ami," done by a group called The Tee Set.

These days, road dogs need passports if we're gonna go anywhere. About ten, eleven years ago, my last wife, Jenny, had just gotten her passport and I snuck around and looked at her passport picture. Well, she had never seen mine and she wanted to, and I wasn't gonna let her see it—you know how horrible they are, we just wanted to see each other's passport pictures so we could make fun of them. I was quite a bit older than her and I was gonna hide this ugly passport from her, but she snatched it and looked at it and as she looked at it, she turned to me and said, "Do you realize your passport's expired?" She was a bit of a prankster, so I just said, "Well, it's not out of date, Judy has seen it, Wally has seen it, it's been through our system," blah blah blah, and she didn't argue with me, she just handed it to me and, sure enough there it was, out of date and we were preparing to leave for Europe in two days. It was one of the most lucrative tours we'd ever booked, *all over Europe*, and I had no valid passport.

You know, it pays to know people. Our crazy friend Ronnie Campbell from Texas knew a lobbyist in DC who knew Tom Daschel, Democratic House Leader, and Steny Hoyer, the House Democratic Whip. The lobbyist called one of them, and I flew up to DC that night—you had to go in person—I stayed at the lobbyist's house that night. The next day I get up early and go to this office, and I could tell the staffers there resented me coming through there like that. I got the dirtiest looks, but they knew they had to do it. With disgust on their faces, they got me through the process in no time. The next evening, I had a flight back to Nashville, and we caught our flight out of Nashville to Europe the next day.

DAVID: There is nothing so very special about us. Yet, because of what we do, we have gotten to know an incredible number of people. Interesting people. Famous people. Useful people. That out-of-date passport could have cost us a big chunk of our income that year. It's back to knowing all those people everywhere. Our friend Ronnie Campbell, who we've known since the first night Billy Bob's opened, he used to be a bodyguard for the legendary Benny Binion, who used to own the Horseshoe Casino in Vegas. Billy Bob and his partners were all amplified Texas characters, and they were about as crazy as you could imagine. I mean, you could end a gig at night and go out to Meacham Field and take the jet up and look at the stars, run around town for awhile.

Benny Binion ran gambling joints and whorehouses in Dallas before they were illegal. According to Ronnie, Benny had to leave Dallas when they shut down those establishments. Benny told us that he left town in an old car that had a million dollars cash in the trunk. He went to Vegas even before Howard Hughes was there and started a gambling joint and a whorehouse. By the time Howard and I met him, he was running The Horseshoe. The first night we met him, we took a photo of him with a plexiglass horseshoe that had a million dollars worth of ten thousand dollar bills in it.

Ronnie Campbell knew I liked Indian artifacts. He said, "I got some buffalo hides from up in Mile City, Montana. If you guys want 'em, I could meet you at a truck stop just outside of Fort Worth." When we got there, we couldn't figure out anywhere to put 'em, so we strapped them to the top of the bus. This bus had no Stor-Mor on it. We had to just strap them up there to a couple of hooks. One of the band guys says, "So what happens if it rains?" And we're going all the way to California—it never rains out there in the summertime. I said, "This should be fine." So we take off to California. We get out there and it's probably rained more than they've had the last twenty summers. All those old buffalo hides got soggy and smelly. The hides had salt in them 'cause they had seasoned them, you know.

HOWARD: The salt took most of the paint off the top of the tour bus.

DAVID: And so we went through the whole tour out there with those buffalo hides strapped to the roof, all the way back across the country and, finally, we're in the Florida Panhandle driving the bus home, and we get pulled over by a game warden.

HOWARD: He says, "I wanna know who shot that bear that's on top of your bus."

DAVID: He seemed like the Barney Fife of game wardens, and we didn't have a way to get to the top of the bus, so it took hours to convince him that we had buffalo hides, not a bear hide, up on the roof.

HOWARD: We brought 'em all home and got 'em dried out, and they were actually nailed to my barn for about ten years. They looked good on the barn.

A Strange Songwriting Request—and the Texas Rangers

HOWARD: Most all of the videos we've done on our own label have been at different locations on Ronnie's ranch.

DAVID: The "Boobs" video, that's at his place. And the "Jalapenos" video, that's his hacienda. "Almost Jamaica" was shot there. You can find them all on YouTube.

Ronnie was Benny's right hand for a long time. That's how we got to meet Benny. Benny, at the heart of things, was just an old horse trader. But if you're a *good* ol' horse trader, you can make a lot of money. He was worth hundreds of millions of dollars.

HOWARD: And he was a good friend of Merle Haggard and Gene Autry—I mean, he hung with the real big boys—Hank Jr., they were all Benny fans. I think Haggard named one of his sons Ben, after him. He told Ronnie he wanted to meet us because he had seen the TV movie *Lonesome Dove*, and he was all upset because he lived in those days, when they did trail rides.

DAVID: He said it was all wrong about the cowboys leaving the herd and goin' into town to find whores. That did not happen, because you never leave the cattle unattended.

HOWARD: Or you wouldn't have a job.

DAVID: He said what happened was the whores would come out to the cattle drive.

HOWARD: And he said they called them "trail herd whores." That always amazed me. Well, he wanted us to write a song called "Trail Herd Whores."

DAVID: That's why he wanted to meet us.

HOWARD: Coincidentally he had just ordered this new Rolls Royce.

DAVID: It was a Rolls Royce limo.

HOWARD: He had ordered it from England and it had just showed up that day, and so Ronnie came in and told him, "I'm gonna take the new limo and drive you over and get the Bellamys. I'm sorry I didn't have time to get the windows tinted." And Benny says, "Hell, I don't want the windows tinted. I got a new Rolls Royce Limo. As much as this damn thing cost, I want them to see who's ridin' in the son of a bitch."

They took that Rolls Royce to the airport to meet us. Ronnie's drivin', Benny's in the back seat, he got all dressed up—he was in his seventies already at that point.

DAVID: Yeah, late seventies.

HOWARD: He got all dressed up to meet us and we became best of friends. I bought some bulls from his ranch in Texas, and we started tradin' cattle and horses with each other. That's how cowboys bond.

DAVID: He has a history, if you ever read up on him. They tried to convict him of murder and they asked him on the witness stand if he had ever killed anyone, and his actual reply was, "I never killed a son of a bitch that didn't deserve it." He was quite a character. He told us that he had met Pancho Villa when he was twelve years old. Somebody needs to make a movie about him.

HOWARD: We never got to meet Gene Autry, but we were up in Benny's suite having dinner with him when Gene called and we got to talk to him on the phone.

You know, back around 2012, they made us honorary Texas Rangers.

DAVID: We got a plaque, and a badge.

HOWARD: It's one of our biggest honors, to be Texas Rangers. I'll take that over a CMA Award anytime.

DAVID: Our office was down at our parents' old house. We used to bring everything home and give it to Mom, because she loved awards. She'd just hang 'em on the walls of that old office. Eventually we ran out of walls and had to start storing them in big ol' plastic tubs, but we made a special place on the wall for those Texas Ranger Plaques, and there they hang to this day.

Oh, one more thing. We never wrote "Trail Herd Whores," but we did actually write a song called "Biscuits And Whores," a line we rustled from Larry McMurtry. We never put it on an album, but we still may.

Stress, Obsession, and Holistic Medicine

We've been asked if all that travel and taking care of business is stressful. The way we got to where we are, the way we ended up being managers and producers and song publishers and everything that we are doing, the way that happened was, there seemed to be more stress in the people who were doing those jobs, which could make them nasty to deal with, and not only that, sometimes they would steal the money. So now, we kind of only deal with our family and our business. My wife said to me one time, "You don't really have a social life," and I said, "Well, my life is extremely social, but we keep it fairly narrow, because we basically deal with the family and the business, and almost all the decisions every day are about that, and they're all intertwined."

HOWARD: We've tried having managers from time to time, but we've decided we're unmanageable.

DAVID: I think stress can pop up anywhere, not just in business. I've seen people who get stress every time they go on vacation, or even just planning a vacation! People go ape shit over nothing!

HOWARD: My biggest stress is, like right now, we're in a major drought here in Florida and for ranching that's just a nightmare. Where your cattle should be grazing in deep grass, you got dusty dirt and you're having to buy more hay to get through to the rainy season, and that stresses me more than just about anything.

DAVID: Howard does not worry about what goes on in the office, or the reality show we're planning, he's worried about the drought.

HOWARD: You know, it's live animals, it's lives you're dealing with, and if you make the wrong decisions, they suffer, and that's your responsibility.

DAVID: Most of the time we're in control of our own careers. If we screw it up, we just screw it up. I mean, we've screwed a lot of stuff up. Everybody always dwells—they always say, "Oh, look, twenty-one #1 songs, and sold this many albums," and blah blah blah, but we've failed a lot of times. In between this #1 and that #1 is a song we thought would be a smash and it died in the middle of the charts and today during our shows nobody ever requests that song. Not everything you try is gonna work. And we like to be in a position where there's no one to blame but us if it doesn't work.

We like it that way. We'd much rather fail because of something we did than because of something we let someone else do. It's not that we think we know everything, but at least we've thought it out because we care about our careers. Those other guys, we watch them make these snap decisions simply because their calendar says they have to make a decision. And truth is, when we would fight with the label, it didn't stress us out because we don't mind a good fight when we believe in what we're fighting for. It was never a matter of, we're right *because* it's our opinion. Plenty of times a guy like John Curb or Bob Saporiti or Bowen would come up with an idea, and it was obviously better than what we were thinking, and when that happened, we didn't "give in," we said, "Yeah, man!" and went with the program. You know what stress is? Stress is when you're afraid to fight and you know you should. That's stress! I know artists who, if they don't have a manager, producer, label, everything in place, don't think they've got a career. So it's a very odd thing, it's just mental, really.

Funny how our priorities have changed. And I think our careers have played a big role in those changes.

HOWARD: Remember we talked about Chunky Monkey and Cherry Garcia? As of late, I've given them both up. It's an addiction I crave. But I can't live like I used to live. I tell people, you know, on live shows you're only as good as your last performance. Just because you've done a great show before, doesn't mean you're not gonna be judged by the one you're doin' tonight. Every time you perform, you gotta produce, and impress people. It never stops. So, to keep that performance level up, I think it's a good thing at our age to do our best to stay healthy because if you're not well, you're not gonna do a good show.

DAVID: We pay attention to our bodies. But some days . . .

HOWARD: Some days are shit. But that's the way it is with everybody. That's just life. We've tried everything. We've gone to Costa Rica and done stem cell. We've done a lot of out-of-the-box stuff, and we've been going to holistic doctors for thirty-five or forty years.

DAVID: We actually found an old holistic doctor. It happened when Howard got sort of halfway addicted to a prescription drug.

HOWARD: We never did rehab. We kind of took it on our own. Anything I ever did wrong, I always felt guilty for. I've always known better, and I tried to undo my wrongs.

DAVID: Earlier we mentioned Dr. Ray Wunderlich, who practiced in St. Petersburg. He was the kind of guy who would treat you but he would also teach you as you went to him. He wasn't the kind of doctor who would just string you out on whatever he could sell you. He was trying to get you to take care of yourself. So we stayed with him for a long, long time, and even though he's long gone, we still go to his clinic and Dr. Douglas Nelson and Joseph DiStefano, the guys who worked with him for many years.

HOWARD: For David and me, it's actually almost an obsession. We take gobs of vitamins and keep up with the latest and a lot of it is B.S., but you have to sort it out for yourself, 'cause everybody's got his own chemistry. I can't drink beer anymore 'cause I'm sensitive to yeast—breads, you know—so when I found that out years ago, which was a real drag, because I love beer, I just stopped doing it. And if you stop eating sugars, and other bad stuff, it's gonna help.

DAVID: We're not kidding ourselves. Travel takes a lot out of us. I have people text me, say, "You must be supermen." No, we're not supermen. You know, there's a lot of times you're suffering, it's not all joyous times, you know.

The other thing is a big thing, one of the hardest things when you're touring, is keeping your voices in good shape. I mean, we think our voices have done pretty well for our age. You can try all sorts of things but just resting your voice does an amazing job of keeping it in decent shape. For us, I don't know about everybody else, talking wears your voice down more than singing.

HOWARD: The most important thing on show days is the show. It's back to that mentality of thinking about the show, gonna to do a good show, gonna feel good, which is the main thing, you feel good, you're gonna do a good show.

DAVID: We've been lucky with our voices. We still sing all our songs in the same key as we did when we first started singing them.

HOWARD: "Love Flow" was in E-flat back in 1976, and we still sing it in E-flat.

DAVID: Our voices have stayed in pretty good shape but I think it's probably, just, using them. I mean, you can overuse them. But I think it's just, we've kept them *up* for so long. We've never gone like six months without singing. And our songs don't abuse our vocal chords. There are some singers where that just happens, over time, because the songs people want to hear from them are very demanding, maybe beyond their comfortable range. But it's really funny, I saw on PBS the other day, Tom Jones, in his sort of new incarnation. He's got a small little band, new arrangements on all of his hits. He was singing great! Just amazing. And he was wailing. I guess it just depends on how good care you take of your voice.

HOWARD: We don't have a regimen to maintain our voices. I think it depends on . . . takin' good naps.

DAVID: You may laugh at that, but that may be the best thing. Even Pavarotti and all the good opera singers would rest, or nap. Sleep is the best thing you can do for your voice.

We're kind of looking for things to talk about that people have asked us about. We've got this book to finish up and we don't want to leave out— well, here's something: we recorded "Beautiful Body" a certain way. The first two lines are

If I said you have a beautiful body
Would you hold it against me

When we originally recorded it we sang it straight, but over the years we changed the phrasing in the last half of that second line, and we began to hear complaints from people who came to see our shows. We want y'all to know, we don't change the way we sing a song to aggravate our fans. That's the last thing we wanna do. It's just, you start singing a song and you sing it the same way every show for a couple of years, I guess you sort of subconsciously try to come up with a more interesting way of doing it. When one of us slips into the new phrasing, the other one does the same, he doesn't even think about it, it just happens. I can never recall us getting into an argument over how we ought to sing a song.

HOWARD: Never happened.

DAVID: We also changed "Reggae Cowboy," stretched out one of the lines a little bit, for when we sing it live. People would say, "Hey, why did you do that?" But you know, people will do that even with sounds. We did a dance mix on "Redneck Girl," and we put the sound of a whip cracking in it. To this day, when we perform "Redneck Girl," and we come to that part, I'll see these guys in the audience throw their hands up like they're crackin' a whip 'cause they're used to it being there, but we never do it live, it's just in the dance mix.

HOWARD: When something gets imbedded in your brain from a record, it's hard to get it out. You believe it's supposed to be in there, so then when you don't hear it in the live show, you feel like the performers let you down.

DAVID: But we don't mean to. People like to hear the songs the way the record sounds. I know some artists that vary their songs a lot. But the fans, you know, they wanna hear them and sing along with them the way they remember them.

For the most part, when we do a show we try and make the songs sound like the record. Sometimes we'll do a song just a bit faster. And *sometimes*, we'll do a song just a touch slower.

HOWARD: We do "Body" slower now. It's more *mature.*

DAVID: You know, groove is such an interesting thing, finding that sweet spot. That's something we really search for in songs. When we've recorded a new song, it's weird, I'll wake up in the morning and listen to it and I'll think, *Damn, that's too slow!* and then later in the day I'll listen again and I'll think, *No, it's fine!*

HOWARD: You just question yourself, always.

DAVID: When we start recording a song, the very first thing we work on is the feel. We try and nail it down so it's got that *pocket,* meaning it feels exactly like we meant it to feel. And that may sound easy, and sometimes it is, but then, sometimes it's not. Some songs—when we write it we may hear a specific guitar lick in our head, so when we take the song into the studio, we'll explain it to Randy Hiebert, who runs the studio and also plays great guitar, "Hey Randy, can you make this sound like Mark Knopfler?" It's a way of communicating the kind of sound we want and it usually works. "Can you play like a Buckaroos lick here?" We've all heard a lot of music over the years and we can usually figure how to get our ideas across.

Sometimes if you're writing a song, you'll hear it in your head when you've got the hook or the chords, and then other times, you'll just work on the guitar parts later.

HOWARD: Like "Redneck Girl," that intro was derived the morning of the day we were recording, an out-of-the-blue kind of thing.

DAVID: Even "Love Flow," we cut that song like the demo, but the demo did not have the guitar intro that we used when we cut the master. Emory Gordy and Richard Bennett went back and played the intro, and Emory was the one who kinda came up with it, and you never know, without that intro, the record might not have been a big hit and you wouldn't be reading this book today. That's one of the things so strange about the recording business. Just the tiniest things—a four bar intro, a single chord change, change of one word or one note can be the difference between a major hit and a nothing record. I know that sounds weird, but believe me, that's true.

Sometimes the intro isn't much, like we had a song called "When I'm Away From You," which we kicked off by strumming in with acoustic guitars. And "Body" was a sort of a Latin acoustic strum, that's all it was, but that was the song that gave us our country career. The arrangement can be simple or it can be more complicated, it all depends on what the song calls for.

HOWARD: These days you try hard not to sound like something you may have heard before because musically, lyrically, sometimes you get the feeling it's all been done, or at least you're close to something that has already been done.

DAVID: Sometimes I think some of our new songs sound dated because they are not chaotic enough. The new tracks that we hear today, to me, a lot of them are chaotic.

HOWARD: Too chaotic to be melodic.

DAVID: Not that we want to remain the same. As we've said, we have a lot of different influences in our music so we're always trying new things in our songwriting and we love it when we can take our fans with us, kind of stretch them out a bit. That's one reason we still make new albums. We know that folks at our shows like to hear all the old hits, but we think if our new stuff is really good, it'll keep the shows fresh and exciting, and we love it when we play a song from our new album on the show and we get a great reaction. So what if they can't hear it on the radio? If they buy the album, then that new song they like so much sort of belongs to them.

We hardly ever do a show that somebody doesn't come up and say, "You know this is my first Bellamy Brothers concert and I just love you guys." People in their twenties, thirties, forties saying, "I've never been to one of your concerts and this is like the coolest thing." My kids sit around and talk about, "Well, I think this is our audience," and I tell them, "Look, everybody's your audience. If you can move that son of a bitch, he's your audience."

HOWARD: What's funny is that some of our audiences are completely different from others. We can draw crowds from deep in the woods—deep as it goes. And then we'll draw crowds of city slickers. And boy, when they meet up, I've seen the slickers sit back in awe at how the deep woods people can *get down*.

DAVID: I think back to a time when we played the Franklin Theater—I think even the theater people were surprised at how redneck most of their audience was that day. Franklin has gotten to be just a big suburb of Nashville and that's why the theater folks were so shocked, 'cause all those people who came to our show were from the hollers.

HOWARD: Sometimes people ask us why we don't talk much during our shows.

DAVID: Not that they complain.

HOWARD: More like they just wonder.

DAVID: Depends on the style of the artists. I remember seeing Neil

Diamond, he could sit in front of an audience and describe a light bulb in the theater and it would sound really interesting. It was very dramatic and it would be cool listening to Neil talk about the light bulb. Other artists ramble on and on about things and I'm going, "Man, play the damn song."

HOWARD: I think it depends on how engaging the artist is.

DAVID: But I think in our case we are better at delivering the songs than we are at public speaking. Not that we don't talk.

HOWARD: Well, for one thing, we've never written anything out to say on the show. Never rehearsed it, everything's off the cuff. If you're gonna talk, you'd better have something to say that people wanna hear.

DAVID: Usually we do about a ninety-minute show. That's a pretty long show, but even with ninety minutes, we can't get all of the hits in and play a couple of new ones, so we don't want to waste any of that time with useless talk that we don't do all that well anyway. The thing that happens to us, inevitably, is someone comes up to us afterwards and says, "Man, you left out my favorite song," which we performed the night before, of course, and this night we swapped it out because somebody else the night before said we didn't do their favorite. So really, us not talking to the audience during the show came about from trying to get as many songs in the show as we could so we can keep our audience happy. It isn't really that we don't *want* to talk to everybody, we're just trying to pack that concert with music and please as many as we can who spent their time and their money to see us.

HOWARD: I think shows have gotten a little too long. Especially as I get older, I'm sitting there watching a show and I say, "Damn! Is this thing ever gonna end?"

Grandpa's Tough Love and Sweet Reflection

HOWARD: I think we owe our mother's dad, Johnny Cooper, a debt of gratitude for steering us away from one of life's nastier habits. Looking out the kitchen window, he saw us out in the yard picking his cigarette butts up and trying to smoke them. You know in those days they had those ol'—they called 'em safety matches but I don't know why cause you could strike 'em anywhere. So we got a handful of them ol' safety matches and we would strike 'em on our jeans, like we seen them do in the westerns. And we found those ol' butts, you know they're half wet, so we're never quite gettin' them to the smokin' stage, and I heard Grandpa Cooper call us around the back porch and we went around there and he had rolled up two cigarettes full of Prince Albert tobacco—he rolled his own, it's what killed him, was lung cancer. He said, "I see you boys been wantin' to smoke!" We sat down with him and he made us smoke those hand-rolled cigarettes. *Right down to a short butt!* We turned every imaginable shade of green.

I think to this day that's the reason neither one of us smokes—cigarettes, anyway.

DAVID: The music business is not the same for us as it used to be. We no longer turn on the car radio and get the thrill of knowing that our song is being played ten times a day on two thousand radio stations around the country. But we know that these songs of ours are played all over the world. We know because we see all the millions of hits on YouTube, clicking on our songs, from people all over the world, and we know because these days wherever we play from Texas and California to Singapore, Australia and New Caledonia, we get lots of requests for our YouTube songs. Thanks to forty years of playing overseas, we have a worldwide audience that knows how to find our newest music.

Do we miss the good old days of #1 hit records and appearances on all the major award TV shows? Not really. Much of our worldwide audience today has been with us a long time. They're not going to drop us for the next big thing that comes along. We've sung and talked to so many of them over forty years that we feel like we know them, and we feel we have an obligation to give them the best music we can. That does not mean we give them the same music as we did forty years ago. I think we can agree that "Jalapenos" does not sound like "Let Your Love Flow."

And yet in a lot of ways, it reflects the same spirit as "Let Your Love Flow." Like most of our other songs, these two songs reflect our world. Howard and I are mostly cheerful souls—glad to be alive—I think after reading this book, you may understand *why.*

14
Living To Tell About It

In Conclusion, a Very Short Summary—
Every Victory Has Its Price

DAVID: Howard and I think most of you read this book because you are fans of our music and you wanted to know more about us and our careers.

But we also understand that people are fascinated with fame and success. There is something shocking about the idea that one day you can be the guy on the street who nobody looks at twice, then a record happens and just a little later the guy that didn't rate a second glance is admired, courted, loved, hated, known, and owned by millions and, amazingly enough, respected by a similarly famous group of peers. In short, almost everybody dreams of fame and success as an antidote to their fear of being unloved.

Howard and I went into music because we had to make a living doing something, and what better than to make a living doing something you love to do. I don't want you to get the idea that because he and I are brothers we feel exactly the same way about life. Early on you saw how my attitude was—music is the only thing I'm good at. From my teenage years on, I don't think I can remember a time when I thought about doing anything else. I was *bound* to spend my life playing music and singing it for people who would pay me to do it.

Howard was a completely different animal. Like me, he was born into music because of our dad, our wonderful, amazing, cowboy dad who loved music but lived cattle and horses. Just out of high school, Howard became a cattle buyer and was great at it. Living the cattle buyer's life almost killed him.

When I blundered into my early days of professional music, Howard was there, spending time with the band, helping out when he could, even donating money to the cause, but he never said, "Hey, David, lemme in on this." He was still a cattle buyer, and if he wanted to be anything else, he didn't say so. When he quit the cattle business, he thought about becoming a veterinarian and a few other things, but then I fell into my first hit as a songwriter, and when fate tapped Howard to be Jim Stafford's road manager, that seemed fine with him.

I do not understand the role that the Lord plays in our careers. I don't believe any human being truly understands the ways of the Lord. But I can understand why so many country stars believe that the Lord played a part in their success. Because there is a moment in your career when a whole lot of things come together and the result is a musical moment so fine, or so real, or so appropriate, that millions of people want to share that musical moment. And suddenly it all begins.

Think of all the things that had to come together for us. First, in this remote piece of rural Florida, two boys spend so much time singing together that their sound is natural as the wind. Second, one of them, me, is determined not to have to do real work for a living; he'd rather spend his life banging his head against a wall, bucking the odds, believing that if he kept at it, something good would happen. So he finds a guy with a half-built studio looking for egg crates to nail on his walls, and it's me that knows exactly where to get them. That's my entry into the world of recorded music. I'm learning how to work on sessions, writing songs, and even writing commercial jingles to pay for my use of the studio to record my demos.

Now comes a big moment. There is a guy in nearby St. Petersburg who is actually having success producing records. *St. Petersburg!* All over America are small cities like St. Petersburg that do not have a single individual with the connections to get you into the record business. But St. Pete has a guy, and through no great skill of my own, I am about to meet him. But there is a price to be paid. This guy is eccentric, probably dangerous, somewhat nasty, and extremely dishonest, but in the world of popular recorded music, he just happens to be the real deal. Talk about dumb luck! Had he been a complete con man with absolutely no connection to the music business, I might well have followed him down the black hole that leads to nowhere. After all, what did I know about the music business?

So because I somehow stumbled into Phil Gernhard, Howard and I would have a music career. We would fail to see a lot of money that would belong to us, but then, every victory has its price! For Phil Gernhard, the price of his many victories was that one day in 2008, alone in his Brentwood, Tennessee, home, he chose to end his career by taking his own life.

Think about my first hit as a songwriter, "Spiders and Snakes." I would have never written that song if a chicken snake hadn't chosen Howard as a bedmate and crawled into a sleeping bag with him. The song was important for three reasons: First, it made the music publishing business seem real to me. Second, it made me seem like a real songwriter to Gernhard. And third, since Gernhard wasn't throwing any money our way, "Spiders And Snakes" pretty much kept Howard and me going during those early days in L.A. Howard and I owe a lot to that chicken snake. Someday maybe we'll build a monument to it.

So now I have a producer/manager, who also happens to be connected to a record company. At this point, I'm a solo act. Howard is still a road manager. But one day song promoter Tony Scotti hears Howard singing during a sound check before a Jim Stafford show, and he suggests we become a duo. Score one for Tony. Now all we need is a hit song. It's *hard* to write or find a hit song, I mean a *real* hit song so great that it will launch a career like it was shot out of a cannon. There are plenty of what they call radio hits, songs that will take up a little radio time and make the writer a few bucks but won't sell records and won't sell tickets and in the long run won't matter. You can listen to song after song after song, and write song after song after song, year after year after year, and not come up with a hit song as great as Larry Williams's "Let Your Love Flow." But somehow it came to us, and it was written by Neil Diamond's roadie!

Did we know we had found a song so incredible that it would sell millions of singles and albums, and make people all over the world come out to see two raw country boys sing it live? Of course we didn't. *Nobody* ever knows they have a song *that* great.

"Let Your Love Flow" was almost sung by me, and there is no guarantee that if I had sung the lead the song would have caught on like it did. On the record, Howard sang the lead, and if there was ever a great match between song and singer, "Let Your Love Flow" and Howard was such a match. Howard, my brother, you have my undying gratitude for the job you did that day, sick as a dog and tough as nails, to stand up to that mic, and push the air through those wonderful pipes of yours to form the sounds:

There's a reason, for the sunshinin' sky
And there's a reason, why I'm feelin' so high

The song is a masterpiece. Larry Williams got some great paydays out of that song, but it launched our career. And it took the skills of a lot of people to make that record happen. Let's take Emory Gordy, one of the best-liked and most respected musicians in the recording histories of both Los Angeles and Nashville. He may have been playing bass on that session, but he is the one who came up with the killer guitar lick that kicked off our recording of "Let Your Love Flow," what we call a signature lick. We've all known a record we loved so much that every time we heard the intro play on the radio we'd feel the adrenalin flow through our veins, and the endorphins start to dance around our brain—that's what Emory's intro did for "Let Your Love Flow." And all the other musicians came up with perfect parts to make a world of listeners smile, tap their toes, sing along, do all those things to be a part of a sound they love. As I sit here, today, I can't help but smile at the thought that we had a part in making the summer of 1976 special for anybody who had a radio and a bit of outdoor space under the sun.

I see a video recording of a European TV show featuring two young guys, one with a flowing mustache, one without a single whisker on his face, wearing western shirts, strumming Ovation guitars, swaying to the music, lip-syncing to the track, one occasionally tossing the other a smile as they pretend to sing. "Who are those kids?" I ask myself, but I know, because here we are, still out there, now both whiskered, still singing that song, with the same joy, in the same key, for at least two new generations since that magical summer of '76.

I believe that hit-making artists are almost never prepared for their career once their first hit hits the airwaves. They may know how to perform onstage. Their singing and playing may be near-perfect, but the business, oh the business! We weren't the first, the last, or the rarest of birds to find that the people who owned us allowed us all the fame we could get but none of the fortune. Believe me, when you know how hard it is to launch your career, then see it launched, you need to make money out of it, because all the things you have to do to keep your career going suck you dry, and you know it's not going to last forever, and how are you gonna live when the (short) career is over and the money is in other pockets? So like the tough farm kids we were, we fought with the people who owned us, and fought and fought, and got nowhere, and yet while they were stealing our money, we were writing our songs and making records and finally making some money on the road, and three years after "Let Your Love Flow," we struck paydirt again, and this time it was *our* paydirt, a song I wrote from an idea *I* stole from a famous, funny old New York Jew named Julius Henry (Groucho) Marx. We used to watch Groucho on his TV show *You Bet Your Life*, and more than once he asked a female guest, "If I said you had a beautiful body, would you hold it against me?" The thought stuck with me and eventually turned into what must have been a good song because that's the song that established our career as country artists, a #1 country hit in 1979 that gave us a license to write and record songs that said more than "I Love You, Darling."

Some of you may wonder if songwriters are legally permitted to snatch spoken lines out of the air and make them our own. I assure you we can and do. In country, especially, we will find a spoken line where we can, and if it makes us raise our eyebrows, we will turn it into a song.

"Beautiful Body" ushered in the '80s for us, and the '80s were our decade for hit making, one big song after the other. I'm not going to say that we spent much time discussing what we would do when the hits ran out; we were just happy to live our story. Every new hit made us new fans, and we appreciated every one of them, whether they lived in Europe, Asia, Africa, America, or Texas. There is something wonderful about being able to create a product that gives pleasure and meaning to others, and the fact that they pay you for it just lets you know that it adds value to their lives. In 1991 we left some of the aggravation of dealing with record companies behind us by starting our own label. We no longer launch singles for radio airplay. The industry has changed. I think it costs a million dollars to promote a radio hit record these days. But we still tour the world, and wherever we go, we find big audiences who want to hear us, meet us, and buy our albums and other unique products we select for them. We love that they still care. We have a relationship, us and our fans, and they know that we will hold up our end of the bargain as long as we can. We are still card-carrying members of the music entertainment world, and we are grateful and happy for the privilege.

And how do we feel about the record people from our early days who took what they could and gave us nothing in return? Well, actually, they did give us something, something we could not give ourselves. Like our daddy, who put a brand on cattle to let the folks of Pasco County know who cared for and valued those cattle, Phil Gernhard, Mike Curb, John Curb, Dick Whitehouse, and the others at the Curb organization helped us establish The Bellamy Brothers brand that gave us value in the world of music. So we figure it's a wash. We made them a lot of money, and in return we got a recording career that set us up to play our music all over the world. We reckon that's a pretty fair exchange.

HOWARD: Most of the time.

DAVID: We wrote this book because we believe that after all these years, you might want to know how it all happened, in our own thoughts and words (and Michael's). Thank you for letting us share our music with you. We hope to see you soon.

We have three more bits of information for you: a Bellamy Brothers discography, as complete as our research could make it; a selective list of forty-three foreign shows; plus a selective list of shows we performed overseas for American troops. It kind of awes us that we've recorded so much music in our career. Many of these albums and singles are available directly from us. You can contact us through our web site BellamyBrothers.com, and for those hard-to-get European items, try Amazon and eBay. Thank you for loving our music. We love you.

Howard and David Bellamy

The brothers around 1957.

Our Dad, Homer Bellamy, with the guitar he taught us our first chords on.

Howard goes electric, early '60s.

David playing Davy Crocket with Grandpa's 12-gauge.

Homer on his horse, Mack.

The Bellamy kids' first day of school in 1956.

With our mother, Frances, and sister, Ginger, in our dungarees sporting haircuts given by our mom.

Playing music with our dad, early 1960s.

*Our parents rented this sign and placed it on State Road 52
near our ranch to let everyone know the big news.*

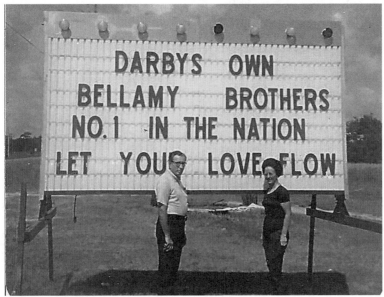

Cutting calves with our dad; not a glamorous job but it taught us to work together.

Our first Gold and Platinum from U.K. and Scandanavia in 1976.

With Commissioner Sylvia Young, dedicating our road.

Howard, doing a little farming. (Photo: David Bellamy)

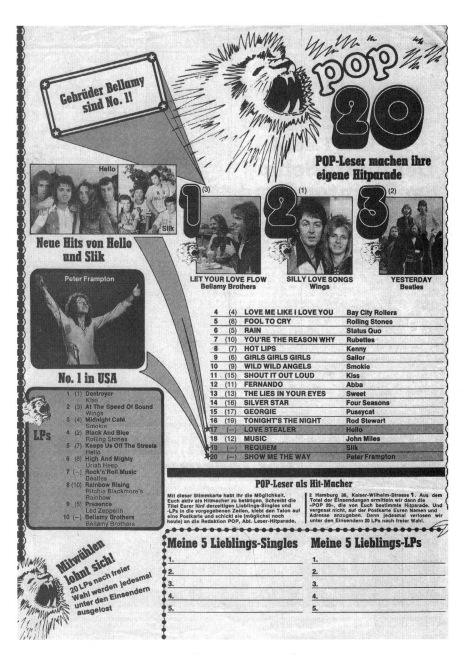

POP 20

POP-Leser machen ihre eigene Hitparade

Gebrüder Bellamy sind No. 1!

Neue Hits von Hello und Slik

Hello

Silk

Peter Frampton

No. 1 in USA

LPs

1. (1) Destroyer
   Kiss
2. (3) At The Speed Of Sound
   Wings
3. (4) Midnight Café
   Smokie
4. (2) Black And Blue
   Rolling Stones
5. (7) Keeps Us Off The Streets
   Hello
6. (6) High And Mighty
   Uriah Heep
7. (−) Rock'n'Roll Music
   Beatles
8. (10) Rainbow Rising
   Ritchie Blackmore's Rainbow
9. (5) Presence
   Led Zeppelin
10. (−) Bellamy Brothers
    Bellamy Brothers

(3) **1** **LET YOUR LOVE FLOW** Bellamy Brothers
(1) **2** **SILLY LOVE SONGS** Wings
(2) **3** **YESTERDAY** Beatles

4	(4)	LOVE ME LIKE I LOVE YOU	Bay City Rollers
5	(8)	FOOL TO CRY	Rolling Stones
6	(5)	RAIN	Status Quo
7	(10)	YOU'RE THE REASON WHY	Rubettes
8	(7)	HOT LIPS	Kenny
9	(6)	GIRLS GIRLS GIRLS	Sailor
10	(9)	WILD WILD ANGELS	Smokie
11	(15)	SHOUT IT OUT LOUD	Kiss
12	(11)	FERNANDO	Abba
13	(13)	THE LIES IN YOUR EYES	Sweet
14	(16)	SILVER STAR	Four Seasons
15	(17)	GEORGIE	Pussycat
16	(19)	TONIGHT'S THE NIGHT	Rod Stewart
17	(−)	LOVE STEALER	Hello
18	(12)	MUSIC	John Miles
19	(−)	REQUIEM	Slik
20	(−)	SHOW ME THE WAY	Peter Frampton

POP-Leser als Hit-Macher

Mit dieser Stimmkarte habt ihr die Möglichkeit, Euch aktiv als Hitmacher zu betätigen. Schreibt die Titel Eurer fünf derzeitigen Lieblings-Singles und -LPs in die vorgegebenen Zeilen, klebt den Talon auf eine Postkarte und schickt sie (möglichst noch heute) an die Redaktion POP, Abt. Leser-Hitparade,

2 Hamburg 36, Kaiser-Wilhelm-Strasse 1. Aus dem Total der Einsendungen ermitteln wir dann die «POP 20», die von Euch bestimmte Hitparade. Und vergesst nicht, auf der Postkarte Euren Namen und Adresse anzugeben. Denn jedesmal verlosen wir unter den Einsendern 20 LPs nach freier Wahl.

Mitwählen lohnt sich!
20 LPs nach freier Wahl werden jedesmal unter den Einsendern ausgelost

Meine 5 Lieblings-Singles

1.
2.
3.
4.
5.

Meine 5 Lieblings-LPs

1.
2.
3.
4.
5.

#1 on German Charts, Wings #2, Beatles #3, 1976.

*Country rock poster from Europe featuring Bellamys with Emmy Lou Harris,
Linda Ronstadt, Jackson Browne, The Eagles, Souther-Hillman-Furay Band,
Jonathan Edwards, and Gram Parsons, 1977.*

全米No.1に輝く「愛はそよかぜ」で
はなばなしくデビューを飾つた超大型新人

ベラミー・ブラザーズのすべて

SIDE Ⅰ	SIDE Ⅱ
★①サテンのシーツ	★①愛はそよかぜ
★②ナッシン・ヘヴィ	★②リヴィン・イン・ザ・ウエスト
③レイニー・ウィンディー・シャイン	③セイン・マン
★④レット・ファンタジー・リヴ	★④インサイド・オブ・ギター
★⑤ハイウェイ2-18	★⑤ヘル・キャット

★……推薦

〈来日記念盤／P-10186〉

Going #1 in Japan.

'76年はアメリカン・ロック史にとって記念すべき年になりそうだ。超強力新人、ベラミー・ブラザーズが現われたのだから!!
'76年はベラミー・ブラザーズにとって記念すべき年になりそうだ。東京音楽祭に全米No.1ビッグ・ヒット、「愛はそよかぜ」をひっさげて、初の来日を果たすとは!!

★来日記念アルバム「愛はそよかぜ」(P-10186)は6/25発売です。

296

Our early days in Las Vegas, 1977.

Dannie Jones (rest in peace).

Sharing a basement with roommate (prop comic extraordinaire) Gallagher, around 1974.

With record producer Emory Gordy recording "Old Hippie" at Emerald Studios Nashville. Also pictured, Richard Bennett (guitar), Billy Joe Walker (guitar), Reggie Young (guitar), John Jarvis (keyboards), and Matt Betton (drums).

In the studio mixing "Redneck Girl" with record producer Jimmy Bowen in Nashville.

Filming our first episode of Hee Haw.

In the studio with record producer Ralph Siegel in Munich Germany where we recorded four albums for the European market in the early to mid 1990s.

Newspaper ad for Conway Twitty tour that lasted most of 1979–80.

Touring with our good friends The Oak Ridge Boys in the early 1980s.

More great friends and touring partners, Larry, Rudy, and Steve,
better known as Larry Gatlin and The Gatlin Brothers.

Backstage at Billy Bob's Texas with The Genius, Ray Charles.

Touring with two of our favorites (performers and people), Tammy Wynette and Waylon Jennings.

Susan Bond Bellamy (left) with David and Howard in Mykonos, Greece, with the Bellamys' international agent and good friend, Judy Seale (right).

Recording a duet, "Sugar Daddy," with the great George Jones (2004).

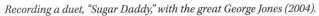

Recording "Beautiful Body" with Dolly Parton at Sound Stage Studios in Nashville in 2004. Also pictured, our friend and recording engineer, Mike Bradley.

The Bellamys and Susan in Albuquerque, New Mexico, shooting a video with our dear friend Freddy Fender.

Recording a radio show with Willie Nelson in Denver, Colorado.
(Photo: Susan Bond Bellamy)

Presenting an award to George Lindsey for "Goober Day."

Photoshoot in Kumamoto, Japan. (Photo: Country Weekly*)*

*Visiting with Little Jimmy Dickens backstage prior to our Grand Ole Opry
performance with The Bacon Brothers. (Photo: Susan Bond Bellamy)*

When we met Phil Collins at the Grammys, he said, "Sorry, I forgot my hat."
(Photo: Susan Bond Bellamy)

With Beach Boys Mike Love and Bruce Johnston in Tampa, Florida,
at the Cattlemens Convention. (Photo: Susan Bond Bellamy)

At the Crystal Palace in Bakersfield, California, with one of our heroes, Buck Owens, shooting our video for "(Don't Put Me In) The Ex Files." (Photo: Susan Bond Bellamy)

A hug from Charlie Daniels on his bus after a show in Canada. (Photo: Susan Bond Bellamy)

Recording a duet and shooting a video with David's sons Jesse and Noah for 2018 release.

Hanging with Blake Shelton on our tour bus after he crashed our show one night in a Louisiana honky tonk. (Photo: Susan Bond Bellamy)

Attending the Dove Awards after being nominated twice with our guitar player/co-producer/ engineer, Randy Hiebert, for our country/gospel album, Jesus Is Coming. *(Photo: Susan Bond Bellamy)*

On stage in The Everglades with fellow Floridian and good buddy John Anderson. (Photo: Susan Bond Bellamy)

Recording and touring with Swiss rock star Gola was an unlikely pairing that resulted in a platinum album and sold-out tours in Europe. (Photo: Sandro Diener)

T. G. Sheppard has been a great friend for many, many years.

Rob Battle, super booking agent, U.S./Canada shows. (Photo: Susan Bond Bellamy)

Onstage in Texas. (Photo: Greg Roach)

Visiting the DMZ on the border of North and South Korea in the late 1990s. (Photo: Susan Bond Bellamy)

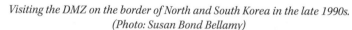

De izquierda a derecha, Brenda Lee, Freddy Fender, Rita Coolidge, Tammy Wynette, Bellamy Brothers y Jimmy C. Newman, artistas que actuarán en el Festival Country

On tour in Spain with Brenda Lee, Freddy Fender, Rita Coolidge, Tammy Wynette, and Jimmy C. Newman in the mid 1980s.

Receiving an award in Interlaken, Switzerland, from our friends Iris Huggler and Lorenz Krebs, promoters of the largest trucker festival in Europe. (Photo: Judy Seale)

One of the best touring bands on the planet, left to right, Tim Thomas (sound engineer), Randy Hiebert (guitar), Galen Butler (keyboards), Rocky Marvel (drums), Wally Dentz (bass guitar), and Jim Heep (steel guitar), Europe 2017. (Photo: Sandro Diener)

Howard, Michael Kosser, and David, collaborators for this project, at work in Darby, Florida. (Photo: Susan Bond Bellamy)

THE BELLAMY BROTHERS ALBUMS CHART HISTORY

With thanks to Sam Lowe for maintaining this info over the years.

ALBUM TITLE	YEAR RELEASED	NATIONAL ALBUM CHART/COUNTRY	PEAK POSITION
Bellamy Brothers/LYLF	1976	US Pop Billboard	69
		Canadian Pop	75
		United Kingdom Pop	21
		Danish Pop	2
		Germany Pop	30
		Sweden Pop	1
		Norway Pop	2
		Denmark Pop	3
		UK Sales Certification	Silver
		RIAA Sales Certification	Gold
Plain & Fancy	1977	Denmark Pop	5
		Sweden Pop	33
		Norway Pop	5
Beautiful Friends	1978	Denmark Pop	21
		Norway Pop	21
The Two And Only	1979	US Country Billboard	9
		Canadian Country	12
		Netherlands Pop	48
		Norway Pop	35
		Denmark Pop	35
You Can Get Crazy	1980	US Country Billboard	9
		Denmark Pop	31
		Norway Pop	31
Sons Of The Sun	1980	US Country Billboard	18
When We Were Boys	1982	US Country Billboard	15

Strong Weakness	1982	US Country Billboard	17
Restless	1984	US Country Billboard	22
Howard & David	1985	US Country Billboard	10
	2013	US Country Billboard (year-end)	45
Country Rap	1986	US Country Billboard	21
Crazy From The Heart	1987	US Country Billboard	50
Rebels Without A Clue	1988	US Country Billboard	45
Reality Check	1990	US Country Billboard	71
Rollin' Thunder	1991		
Beggars & Heroes	1992		
Nobody's Perfect	1994		
Rip Off The Knob	1994		
Take Me Home	1994		
Heartbreak Overload (Start)	1995		
Sons Of Beaches	1995		
Native America (Jupiter)	1995		
One Way Love (Intersound)	1996		
Dancin'	1996		
Tropical Christmas	1996		
Forever (Jupiter)	1996		
Over The Line	1997		
Reggae Cowboys	1998		
Lonely Planet	1999		
Life Goes By (Jupiter)	2000		
Redneck Girls Forever (Curb)	2002		

Collaborations:

Angels & Outlaws	2005		
Family Ties w/Jesse & Noah	2007		
Greatest Hits Sessions w/Gola	2010	Swiss Pop	1
BB&G Platinum w/Gola	2011	Swiss Pop	29
Simply The Best w/DJ Otzi	2012	Swiss Pop	31
		Austria Pop	3
		Denmark Pop	30
		Germany Pop	38
Bellamy Brothers & Friends	2013	Swiss Pop	5
Mermaid Cowgirl w/Gola	2014	Swiss Pop	6

Live Albums:

Live At Gilley's (Atlantic Records)	1999
Live At Gilley's (Elap Music)	1999
Live At Gilley's (Connoisseur)	2000

Christmas /Gospel Albums:

Tropical Christmas (Intersound)	1996
Tropical Christmas (Start)	1997
Merry Christmas And A Happy New Year (Jupiter)	1996
Merry Christmas And A Happy New Year (BMG Ariola)	1998
The Reason For The Season (Curb)	2002
Jesus Is Coming (Curb)	2007
Pray For Me (BBR)	2012

Compilation Albums:

Ihre Grossen Hits (WB)	1978		
Dancin' Cowboys:			
Our Favorite Songs (WB)	1980		
Greatest Hits (WBR/Curb)	1982	US Country Billboard	9
		RIAA Sales Certification	Gold
Best (Curb)	1984	Austria Pop	2
Greatest Hits (MCA/Curb)	1985	US Country Billboard	33
		RIAA Sales Certification	Platinum
	1993	Austria Pop	39
Greatest Hits 2 (MCA/Curb)	1986	US Country Billboard	27
Greatest Hits 3 (MCA/Curb)	1989	US Country Billboard	50
		US Country Billboard	10
Neon Cowboy (Jupiter)	1991	Germany Pop	48
The Very Best Of (Sony)	1991		
The Latest And The Greatest (BBR)	1992	US Country Billboard	68
Best Of (Curb)	1992		
Gold Greatest Hits (Curb)	1993		
Best Of The Best (Warner)	1993		
Gold And More (Curb)	1994		
Diamond Star Collection (Arcade)	1994		
Let Your Love Flow (Curb)	1994		
Best Of Original (Curb)	1994		
20 Years Of Hits Box Set (BBR)	1994		
The Best Of (Eurotrend)	1994		
Let Your Love Flow (Rondo)	1994		
The Best Of (Eurotrend)	1994		
Greatest Hits (Curb)	1995		
Greatest Hits (Bellaphon)	1995		
20 Greatest Hits (Intermusic)	1995		
Best Of The Best (CMC)	1995		
Best Of The Best (BBR/Start)	1995	Norway Pop	7

Crazy From The Heart/Rebels Without A Clue (Start)	1995			
Reality Check/Rollin' Thunder (Start)	1995			
Bellamy Brothers 2-CD Collection (Cornerstone)	1995			
The Very Best Of (Arcade)	1996			
At Their Best (EMI/Capitol)	1997			
The Very Best Of (CMC)	1997			
Let Your Love Flow (Platinum)	1998			
Let Your Love Flow (Start)	1998			
Greatest Hits (Brilliant)	1999			
The Ultimate Collection 1976–2000 (Massive)	2000			
Millennium Collection 2-CD (Selected Sound)	2000			
Let Your Love Flow (Laserlight)	2000			
Best Of (Trucker)	2000			
Best Of The Best 2 (Jump)	2000			
Our Danish Collection (Start)	2000	Denmark Pop	6	
25-Year Collection 2-CD (Delta)	2001			
Our Norwegian Hits (EMI)	2001	Norway Pop	5	
		Norwegian Sales Certification	Double Platinum	
Our Swedish Collection (EMI)	2001	Sweden Pop	4	
Nur Das Beste – Die Schonsten Songs 1991–2000 (BMG Ariola)	2002			
Brazos Logistics (BBR)	2003			
The Very Best Of (Landmark)	2003			
By Request (Start)	2003			
Dancin' Cowboys (Start)	2006			
Our Best Country Songs	2006	Denmark Pop	6	
Uforglemmelige Klassikere	2006	Norway Pop	19	
The Lost Tracks (BBR)	2006			

Number One Hits (Curb)	2008		
Old/New Country (Start)	2008		
Let Your Love Flow & Other Number One Hits (Curb)	2008		
Greatest Hits 3 Deluxe (BBR)	2010		
The Anthology Volume 1 (Unv)	2010	Norway Pop	1
		Swiss Pop	6
		Sweden Pop	19
		Swedish Sales Certification	Double Platinum
The Anthology Volume 2 (Unv)	2011	Swiss Pop	75
Greatest Hits Volume 1 (BBR)	2011		
Ultimate Collection Box Set (RD)	2012		
14 Great Hits (Sony)	2013		
Greatest Hits (BBR)	2015		
40 Years: The Album (BBR)	2015	Swiss Pop	47

DVDs:

Greatest Video Hits: The Ultimate Collection From 1976–2000 (Massive)	2000
25-Year Collection: Around The World (BBR)	2001
25-Year Collection: Around The World (Select)	2001
Our Best Country Songs (Harlekin)	2006
Country Legends Live Mini Concert (Timeless)	2007
The Anthology Volume 1 (BBR)	2009
The Anthology Volume 2 (BBR)	2010
Greatest Hits Sessions w/Gola (Univeral)	2010
BB&G Platinum w/Gola (Universal)	2011
Simply The Best w/DJ Otzi (Universal)	2012

We believe that we have played approximately eight thousand shows in the forty-plus years that we have toured as The Bellamy Brothers. Most of those dates have been domestic. In fact, it's hard for us to imagine a corner of the United States where we haven't performed.

We have also sung at hundreds of foreign venues, many of them repeatedly. Below is a selected list of forty-three events we have played around the world. As you can imagine, the stories we've told in this book only scratch the surface. Hard work? I'd say so, but then, we wouldn't still be doing it if we didn't love it. Thanks for coming to see us. Y'all make it all great.

David and Howard Bellamy

SELECTED FOREIGN SHOWS SINCE 1994

1.   Country Gold Festival – Aspecta – Mt. Aso – Kumamoto, Japan

2.   Trucker and Country Festival – Interlaken, Switzerland

3.   Norsk Country Treff Festival – Breim, Norway

4.   Americana Festival – Nottingham, U.K.

5.   Emerald Country Music Spectacular – Queensland, Australia

6.   New Caledonia – Not sure of the name of the big venue we played there

7.   Schupfart Country Music Festival – Schupfart, Switzerland

8.   Schutzenhaus Albisguetli – Zurich, Switzerland

9.   SCC Country Music Festival – Silkeborg, Denmark

10.   Furuvik Country Music Festival – Furuvik, Sweden

11.   Ostee Festival – Keil, Germany

12.   Floralia Festival – Oostehut, Netherlands

13.   North Wales Music Festival – North Wales, U.K.

14.   Naturbuehne Greifensteine – Ehrenfriedersdorf, Germany

15.   Country Fest Bauska – Riga, Latvia

16.   Lofoten Festival – Leknes, Norway

17.   Country Music Festival – Thorshavn, Faroe Islands

18.   Lida Festival – Stockholm, Sweden

19.   Theatre Savoy – Helsinki, Finland

20.   Rosfjord Stans Hotel Beach Party – Lyngdal, Norway

21.   Hallenstadion – Zurich, Switzerland

22.   Dallhalla – Rattvik, Sweden

23.   Bayern Oldies Festival – Regensberg, Germany

24.   Botn Festival – Sandnessjoen, Norway (but we didn't get paid!)

25.   International Trucker & Country Festival – Hannover, Germany

26.   Geiselwind Trucker Festival – Geiselwind, Germany

27.   Seljord Classic Festival – Seljord, Norway

28.   Willingdon Catholic Gmkhana – Mumbai, India

29.   Camai Ground, Miramar – Goa, India

30.   Sugathadasa Indoor Stadium – Colombo, Sri Lanka

31.   R. SA Oldie Nacht, Waldbuhne – Schwarzenberg in Sachsen, Germany

32.   Aloisius Country Festival, Vilstaler Steinbrau – Pocking, Elchendorf, Germany

33.   Qatar National Convention Center – Doha, Qatar

34.   Royal Caribbean *Rhapsody of the Seas* – Australia and New Caledonia

35.   Million Fish Festival – Sjovegan, Norway

36.   Flumserberg Schlager Festival – Flumserberg, Switzerland

37.   BR-RADL Tour – Wemding, Germany

38.   Rock and Blues Cruise – Italy, Greece and Croatia

39.   Emirates Golf Course – Dubai, UAE

40.   Kallang Theatre – Singapore

41.   Armagh Country Festival – Armagh, Ireland

42.   Independence Stadium - Windhoek, Nambia

43.   Cape Town Stadium - Cape Town, South Africa

PERFORMING FOR THE TROOPS

BOSNIA   7/4/99   Tuzla, Bosnia   Eagle Base
             7/5/99   Sarajavo, Bosnia   NATO Base

GUAM   10/11/99   Naha, Guam   Anderson AFB

KOSOVO   9/25/00   Kosovo   Camp Bondsteel
             9/26/00   Kosovo   Camp Monteith

KOREA   12/23/04   Taegu, Korea   Camp Walker
             12/24/04   Dongducheon, Korea   Camp Casey
             12/25/04   Dongducheon, Korea   Camp Stanley
             12/27/04   Chuncheon, Korea   Camp Page
             12/28/04   Seoul, Korea   Yongson Garrison
             12/29/04   Seoul, Korea   DMZ
             12/30/04   Uijonbu, Korea   Camp Red Cloud
             12/31/04   Pyeongtaek, Korea   Camp Humphreys

About Michael Kosser

Let Your Love Flow: The Life and Times of The Bellamy Brothers is Michael Kosser's twentieth published book, including seven novels about Native Americans published by St. Martin's Press during the '90s and thirteen nonfiction books about the music business. His volume titled *How Nashville Became Music City, U.S.A.* has become must reading for authors and journalists seeking to understand the country music recording industry.

As a songwriter, he has garnered more than one hundred cuts, including recordings by George Jones, Charlie Rich, Conway Twitty, Ray Price, Tammy Wynette, Barbara Mandrell, The Kendalls, Jim and Jesse, Marty Robbins, Bill Anderson, Freddie Hart, Stonewall Jackson, T. G. Sheppard, Skeeter Davis, Louise Mandrell, Tommy Overstreet, Blake Shelton, Josh Gracin, and Colt Ford. His hit songs have earned him a number of ASCAP and BMI awards.

Kosser was a long time senior editor and columnist for *American Songwriter Magazine.* He has written extensively for Nashville news media and various national music publications. He and his wife, Gina, live in Nashville, Tennessee.

"I've never had a better time working on a book than I've had with Howard and David," he says. "And when you read it, you'll know why. There's fun and truth on every page. These guys have LIVED!"